PALGRAVE MACMIL
CRITICAL STUDIES IN GENDER, SEXU

Highlighting the work taking place at the cros
studies, gender studies, cultural studies, and pe.   ... ɔtuuɪes, this series
offers a platform for scholars pushing the boundaries of gender and sexuality studies substantively, theoretically, and stylistically. The authors draw on
insights from diverse scholarship and research in popular culture, ethnography, history, cinema, religion, performance, new media studies, and techno-
science studies to render visible the complex manner in which gender and
sexuality intersect and can, at times, create tensions and fissures between one
another. Encouraging breadth in terms of both scope and theme, the series
editors seek works that explore the multifaceted domain of gender and sexuality in a manner that challenges the taken-for-granted. On one hand, the
series foregrounds the pleasure, pain, politics, and aesthetics at the nexus of
sexual practice and gendered expression. On the other, it explores new sites
for the expression of gender and sexuality, the new geographies of intimacy
being constituted at both the local and global scales.

Series Editors:

PATRICIA T. CLOUGH is Professor of Sociology and Women's Studies
at Queens College and The Graduate Center, CUNY. Clough is on the edi-
torial boards of *Women's Studies Quarterly*, *Body and Society*, *Subjectivity*,
Cultural Studies/Critical Method, *Qualitative Inquiry*, and *Women and
Performance*. Clough is the coeditor of *Beyond Biopolitics: Essays in the
Governance of Life and Death* (with Craig Willse, 2011); author of *The
Affective Turn: Theorizing the Social* (with Jean Halley, 2007); *Autoaffection:
Unconscious Thought in the Age of Teletechnology* (2000); *The End(s)of
Ethnography: From Realism to Social Criticism* (1998); *Feminist Thought:
Desire, Power and Academic Discourse* (1994); *The End(s) of Ethnography:
From Realism to Social Criticism* (1992).

R. DANIELLE EGAN is Professor and Chair of the Gender and Sexuality
Studies Program at St. Lawrence University. Egan is the author of *Dancing
for Dollars and Paying for Love: The Relationships between Exotic Dancers
and their Regulars* (2006) and coauthor of *Theorizing the Sexual Child in
Modernity* (with Gail Hawkes, 2010), both with Palgrave Macmillan. She is
also the coeditor of *Flesh for Fantasy: Producing and Consuming Exotic
Dance* (with Katherine Frank and Merri Lisa Johnson, 2006). She is on the
editorial board of *Sexuality and Culture*.

Titles:

*Magnus Hirschfeld and the Quest for Sexual Freedom: A History of the First
International Sexual Freedom Movement*
Elena Mancini

Queer Voices: Vocality, the Uncanny, and Popular Music
Freya Jarman-Ivens

On the Literary Nonfiction of Nancy Mairs: A Critical Anthology
Edited by Merri Lisa Johnson and Susannah B. Mintz

Antarctica as Cultural Critique: The Gendered Politics of Scientific Exploration and Climate Change
Elena Glasberg

The Parallel Lives of Women and Cows: Meat Markets
Jean O'Malley Halley

Positioning Gender and Race in (Post)colonial Plantation Space: Connecting Ireland and the Caribbean
Eve Walsh Stoddard

A Critical Inquiry into Queer Utopias
Edited by Angela Jones

Young People and Pornography: Negotiating Pornification
Monique Mulholland

Juliet Mitchell and the Lateral Axis: Twenty-First-Century Psychoanalysis and Feminism
Edited by Robbie Duschinsky and Susan Walker

The Aesthetics of Cute in Contemporary Japanese Art
Yoke-Sum Wong [forthcoming]

Juliet Mitchell and the Lateral Axis

Twenty-First-Century Psychoanalysis and Feminism

Edited by

Robbie Duschinsky and
Susan Walker

palgrave
macmillan

JULIET MITCHELL AND THE LATERAL AXIS
Copyright © Robbie Duschinsky and Susan Walker, 2015.
Softcover reprint of the hardcover 1st edition 2015 978-1-137-38117-0

All rights reserved.

First published in 2015 by
PALGRAVE MACMILLAN®
in the United States—a division of St. Martin's Press LLC,
175 Fifth Avenue, New York, NY 10010.

Where this book is distributed in the UK, Europe and the rest of the world,
this is by Palgrave Macmillan, a division of Macmillan Publishers Limited,
registered in England, company number 785998, of Houndmills,
Basingstoke, Hampshire RG21 6XS.

Palgrave Macmillan is the global academic imprint of the above companies
and has companies and representatives throughout the world.

Palgrave® and Macmillan® are registered trademarks in the United States,
the United Kingdom, Europe and other countries.

ISBN 978-1-349-47958-0   ISBN 978-1-137-36779-2 (eBook)
DOI 10.1057/9781137367792

Library of Congress Cataloging-in-Publication Data

Juliet Mitchell and the lateral axis : twenty first century psychoanalysis
and feminism / edited by Robbie Duschinsky and Susan Walker.
    pages cm
    Includes bibliographical references and index.

    1. Brothers and sisters—Psychological aspects. 2. Psychoanalysis and
feminism. 3. Women and psychoanalysis. 4. Mitchell, Juliet, 1940–
I. Duschinsky, Robbie, 1986–

BF723.S43J85 2015
150.19′5—dc23   2014035155

A catalogue record of the book is available from the British Library.

Design by Newgen Knowledge Works (P) Ltd., Chennai, India.

First edition: March 2015

10 9 8 7 6 5 4 3 2 1

Contents

Introduction

Robbie Duschinsky and Susan Walker

Juliet Mitchell is widely acknowledged as a groundbreaking theorist and psychoanalyst. Mitchell's work has been influential, and there are many testimonials to its influence. Grosz (1990, 19) has described her ideas as a "moment of radical rupture" and as having inspired a generation of researchers. And Lament (2013, 12) writes that "Mitchell's far-ranging sleuthing among numerous domains—psychoanalysis, anthropology, sociology, psychology, literature, and her own personal reflections deserves our applause and high praise." Mitchell's role is also significant as a contributor to and commentator on the developments in Western thought since the 1960s. In particular, as Flax (1992, 179) observes, "Mitchell has been an influential contributor to the development of feminist theory. She has entered into and affected some of the most important intellectual and political debates stimulated by the re-emergence of women's movements."

However, there has yet to be any book dedicated to Mitchell's ideas. Perhaps part of the reason for this absence is, as Connell (2012) has noted, that Mitchell's work has "the energy and passion of the liberation movement without the showing-off." Another volume could have been written as a retrospective on the debates impacted by Mitchell's work. However, we were inspired by the acuity of her insights for tackling contemporary concerns. Changes in society have, curiously, made many of her reflections on equality, violence, collective movements, subjectivity, sexuality, and power *more* rather than less relevant over time, as these issues have developed and become core parts of public and academic debates. Reading Mitchell now, engaging with her ideas, offers access to distinctive and highly valuable ideas that contribute directly to these debates. For example, we live in a society in which women must walk a tightrope of assumptions in performing an identity perceived as assertive but not aggressive, successful but not square, sexy but not a slut; Mitchell's work offers resources for making sense of how sexuality, which had been touted as the site of freedom, has itself become a fundamental site of oppression in an ostensibly equal society.

Mitchell is a socialist, a feminist, and a psychoanalyst, and has combined these three positions in her theorizing. Her career spans five decades from the 1960s to the present day. In the 1960s, "*The Longest Revolution*" pioneered the conjunction of feminism with Marxist thought, laying the ground for socialist feminism in Britain. In the 1970s, *Psychoanalysis and Feminism* opened the way for feminist usage of Freud. She edited influential volumes of the work of Lacan, Klein, and Balint. In the 2000s, her work on the importance of siblings posed a new research agenda for psychoanalysis and gender theory. The "lateral axis" of the psyche, along which siblings and peers are encountered, is considered by Mitchell as different from and complementary to the vertical axis of parent–child relations and the Oedipal complex. In proposing a "lateral axis" Mitchell has provided a rich new seam of insights and has opened up a new horizon for those wishing to combine psychoanalytical insights with sociological observation.

This volume addresses the contemporary implications of Mitchell's ideas for social theory, gender studies, politics, and psychoanalysis, with a focus on the significance of the lateral axis as a new and powerful theoretical framework for addressing concerns in each of these domains. The development of these themes in the fields of politics, art, philosophy, sociology, gender studies, cultural studies, anthropology, education, peace studies, criminology, and psychology promises rich rewards. This volume takes some of these disciplinary fields and looks at how Mitchell's theory can be applied and developed. Students of these disciplines will find the book a useful source of applied psychoanalytical theory. Readers well versed in Freud and psychoanalytical theory will find that this volume allows the theory to be taken in a new and unexpected direction. The volume provides the readers with the background to the theory, and demonstrates how the lateral axis is of pressing significance for readers from a range of disciplines, and for those interested in the currents that move our social and cultural worlds.

*   *   *

Throughout her academic career, Mitchell has been concerned with explaining the intractable nature of the position of woman as the second sex, oppressed and positioned as inferior. It is from this starting point that she encounters and develops new perspectives on six fundamental issues: equality, violence, collective movements, subjectivity, sexuality, and power. These themes were initially considered through a Marxist perspective in her essay "*The Longest Revolution*," published in 1966. In this text, Mitchell was critical of the overly simple expectation of much socialist theory that with the revolution, and subsequent "freedom" of the working classes, would follow a revolution in the status of women and their own emancipation. Mitchell, unsatisfied with socialist reductions of women's position to that of women position within the division of labor, identified four bases upon which this position rested. These were production, reproduction, sexuality, and the socialization of children:

> The classical literature on the problem of woman's condition is predominantly economist in emphasis, stressing her simple subordination to the institutions of private property. Her biological status underpins both her weakness as a producer, in work relations, and her importance as a possession, in reproductive relations. The fullest and most recent interpretation gives both factors a psychological cast. The framework of discussion is an evolutionist one which nevertheless fails noticeably to project a convincing image of the future, beyond asserting that socialism will involve the liberation of women as one of its constituent "moments."
>
> What is the solution to this impasse? It must lie in differentiating woman's condition, much more radically than in the past, into its separate structures, which together form a complex—not a simple—unity. This will mean rejecting the idea that woman's condition can be deduced derivatively from the economy or equated symbolically with society. Rather, it must be seen as a specific structure, which is a unity of different elements. . . . Because the unity of woman's condition at any one time is the product of several structures, it is always "overdetermined". The key structures can be listed as follows: Production, Reproduction, Sex and Socialization of children. The concrete combination of these produces the "complex unity" of her position; but each separate structure may have reached a different "moment" at any given historical time. Each then must be examined separately in order to see what the present unity is and how it might be changed. (Mitchell [1966] 1984, 26)

In setting out this schema, it seems to us that Mitchell is wrestling with a fundamental concern—of as much pertinence today as when *"The Longest Revolution"* was written. Women continue to be oppressed and positioned as inferior, regardless of major changes in the form taken by that oppression through history and in the relations of production. If more women are in work than ever, then why does there remain a feminization of poverty? If women are free from Victorian sexual mores, then why does a sexual double standard still operate? Mitchell was interested in how continuities in the oppression of women could occur, given overt intentions in individuals and in society to achieve a more meaningful equality. The Marxist answer is ideological subjugation: power does not simply operate upon our conscious intentions, but on our more tacit sense of who we are and how to go about in the world. Mitchell identifies this as an important factor, but suspects that this explanation still cannot account for the continuities in women's oppression over time and across cultures. Mitchell did not reject socialist modes of explanation but added to them a perspective drawn from Freudian psychoanalysis for the purposes of making sense of the entrenchment of tendencies that run counter to the espoused values of individuals and of society. In moving from an analysis of false consciousness to the role of unconscious processes, both the irrational and the intractable nature of women's oppression became much clearer. In Mitchell's words: "The unconscious that Freud described could...be described as the domain of the reproduction of culture and ideology" (Mitchell 1974, 413).

In the second half of *Psychoanalysis and Feminism*, Mitchell defends Freud against the attacks and vilification heaped upon him by the second-wave feminist because of his account of the inferiorized psychic status of femininity. She highlights that this psychoanalytic account is not a prescription of how things should be, but a description of an important and neglected process through which women become the second sex. The different relationship to the Oedipus crisis that forms the pathways to masculinity and femininity for male and female infants, forms, for Freud, the basis of the psychic differentiation into male and female subjectivity. That this drama leads to a state of psychic inferiority for those whose fate is the feminine position is not inevitable: it is a result of patriarchal culture, in which fathers are valorized and powerful, and the power of the woman as reproductive mother is not. The hierarchy implicit in sexual differentiation is not, insists Mitchell, a distortion caused by the patriarchal bias of the man who first described them. The conditions of capitalism have led to a romantic idealization of the nuclear family, and the ideology of patriarchy has led to a position of psychic inferiority for women:

> Freud's analysis of the psychology of women takes place within a concept that it is neither socially nor biologically dualistic. It takes place within an analysis of patriarchy. His theories give us the beginnings of an explanation of the inferiorized and "alternative" (second sex) psychology of women under patriarchy. Their concern is with how the human animal with a bisexual psychological disposition becomes the sexed social creature—the man or the woman..... In each man's unconscious lies all mankind's "ideas" of his history; a history that cannot start afresh with each individual but must be acquired and contributed to over time. Understanding the laws of the unconscious thus amounts to a start in understanding how

ideology functions, how we acquire and live the ideas and laws within which we must exist. A primary aspect of the law is that we live according to our sexed identity, our ever imperfect "masculinity" or "femininity"...Differences of class, historical epoch, specific social situations alter the expression of femininity; but in relation to the law of the father, women's position across the board is a comparable one. When critics condemn Freud for not taking account of social reality, their concept of that reality is too limited. The social reality that he is concerned with elucidating is the mental representation of the reality of society. (Mitchell 1974, 402–406)

Following her encounter with the works of Freud, Mitchell trained and practiced as a psychoanalyst. She continued to write and contribute to feminist debates, collaborating with Ann Oakley and Jacqueline Rose, among others, to produce (single-handedly and in collaboration) books and articles that examined psychoanalysis, feminism, and the relationship between them. With Michael Parsons, she also edited a collection of papers by her training analyst, Enid Balint, titled *Before I Was I: Psychoanalysis and the Imagination* (1998). In 1996 Mitchell accepted a professorial position in Cambridge University, United Kingdom.

Mitchell's next major book, whose full title *Mad Men and Medusa: Reclaiming Hysteria and the Effects of Sibling Relations on the Human Condition* encompasses the full breadth of the work, was published in 2000, a hundred years after Freud's *Studies in Hysteria*. In it Mitchell tackles several related themes, viz. the apparent disappearance of hysteria after the First World War, the lack of recognition of male hysteria, and the neglect of siblings in psychoanalytical theory. The book highlights the psychical significance of lateral relationships through an analysis of the effect of siblings upon the presentation of hysteria. Mitchell argues that the felt sense of "displacement" experienced by the child on the birth of a sibling is caused by a loss of position within the family. In this way, Mitchell carves out a space for attention to siblings within psychoanalytical theory, a topic that had previously received only glancing attention or else omitted and neglected. Mitchell uses the legend of Don Juan to illustrate how male hysteria looks if considered using both the vertical and the lateral axes.

Don Juan's absence from psychoanalytic theory is testimony to the absence of the male hysteric and to the feminizing of hysteria. To read him back into the theory is to shift its centre of gravity, or at least to give it two focal dimensions: an intergenerational one and lateral one; parents as representatives of the vertical axis and siblings as representatives of a lateral axis. Don Juan's story likewise gives phenomenology of male hysteria which is otherwise missing from most psychoanalytic observation. The thrust of his story is the hysterical transmission of lateral jealousy. (Mitchell 2000, 259–260)

In her subsequent book, *Siblings: Sex and Violence* (2003), Mitchell expands upon the importance of siblings in psychic structure. She urges that psychoanalytical theory's insistence on the importance of the vertical axis alone has led to missed opportunities for exploring the effect of sibling relationships. The trauma of a sibling's birth (or the imagined trauma of a sibling in the case of an only child), she argues, leads the child to question its very existence. Displacement leads to questions like "Where does the baby come from?" and "Where am I now that the baby is in my place?" and on the other to the murderous desire to eliminate the usurper. This murderousness is accompanied by narcissistic love, due to the baby being experienced as a replica or extension of the child itself, which can be expressed as incestuous love for the sibling. The challenge for the toddler is to overcome the violence and accept its sibling as like itself but not identical to itself. This leaves room for more than one person to be the mother's child and introduces the concept of seriality. Siblings form the first model for lateral or peer relationships—for the achievement of meaningful equality—and so the success of the attempt to overcome the murderousness of sibling relationships is important for the establishment of social relations with peers and equals.

Mitchell coins the phrase the "law of the mother" for the prohibitions, operative on the lateral axis, against sibling murder and sibling incest. These prohibitions do not operate through negation as do the Oedipal prohibitions, which forbid desire for the mother and permit only a deferred desire for her substitute in adult partners. Instead, they operate through differentiation, in giving each sibling a place. This role is named for the mother, but can be played by any figure—including by the siblings themselves as Freud and Dann's (1951) account of the quasi-sibling group of institutionally raised orphaned children showed. Mitchell argues that the closeness of sexuality and violence, especially in situations where outside controls are weak, such as war, and within the private domestic or intimate sphere, is the psychic root of actions that may seem disconnected, but in fact represent the closeness of sex and violence in sibling relationships. Rape as a weapon of war (sexualized violence), and spousal/intimate abuse (violent sexuality) both result from a failure to fully repress the narcissistic phantasy of being the one-and-only and resolve the trauma that one is not by recognizing difference. Incestuous sex and murderous violence are, on Mitchell's account, are both forms of acting out of the threat from a lack of differentiation. One extreme response to this threat, warding it off, is to stake out the terms of difference by fixating on reproductive possibilities between boys and girls (genital difference) and magnifying its social significance out of proportion to its real effect. This need to emphasize difference as a condition of what is perceived as a fragile existence and the need to murder the potential usurper can support continuities in the denigration of women even through variation in relations of production, over time and between cultures. On the other hand, the successful negotiation of the trauma of displacement and the recognition that there is room for more than one, can lead to self-esteem, tolerance, and meaningful equality.

Siblings and the lateral axis allow Mitchell to theorize gender as separate from sexual difference. For Mitchell, gender is a difference that need not be a binary nor a hierarchy—just like the relationship between siblings. By contrast sexual difference is the place one inhabits in the service of reproduction, which under patriarchy is formulated as of necessity one or other side of the binary phallus/no phallus. As Mitchell has proposed, the sibling relationship asks the question "who am I?" of the subject, to which a key response is differentiation by the manner of gender performance. This differs, Mitchell suggests, from the child's relationship with parents who, on behalf of society's norms, categorize and differentiate children by reproductive sex:

> Because I am arguing that the absolute sexual difference demanded by reproduction is an Oedipal vertical construction, I am instead using "gender" to mark the girl/boy difference as it comes about along the lateral axis....Where the castration complex marks the sexual difference "required" by sexual reproduction, gender difference marks lateral distinctions between girls and boys which include but exceed sexuality.
>
> By differentiating between her children the mother and her law allow for the concept of seriality to be internalised—John has to know that he has lost the possibility of being Jane. One is a child in the same position as one's siblings in regard to one's parent or parents, one's peers in relation to one's teacher or boss, but one is also different: there is room for two, three, four or more. Of this the hysteric in all of us is unaware. Hate for the sibling enables the first move to be made: I hate you, you are not me, is the precondition of seriality. The mother restricts this hate—enjoins its non-enactment. Children's games musical chairs, oranges and lemons, pig in the middle and all the spontaneous play—are about seriality. The mother has enforced, but the lateral relationship itself instigates its own processes of managing sameness through constructing difference. The law of the mother thus also operates between siblings or between siblings and peers. (Mitchell 2003:26, 52–53)

Cultural, psychological, and genital differences in the position of those marked as boys and those marked as girls can taken up or recruited into the struggle to denigrate lateral others; however, they are not intrinsic to the negotiation of that struggle. Mitchell (2003, 219–220) argues that "when the child is overwhelmed by the trauma of one who, in the mind, was supposed to be the same as itself inevitably turning out to be different, it finds or is given ways to mark this difference—age is one, gender another...The cradle of gender difference is both narcissistic love and violence at the traumatic moment of displacement in the world. Gender difference comes into being when physical strength and malevolence are used to make the sister as lesser." When the symbolic and imaginary resources are not available then gender can be deployed in warding off the traumatic moment of lateral displacement though a virgin/whore dichotomy and forms of sexual oppression and violence. However, where such resources are available from experience, support from adult caregivers and from wider culture to allow each subject a recognized and intelligible place, with sufficient meaning and dignity, then the child is able to find a place for themselves:

> With help, the ego is able to bind most of the raging energy—never entirely and sometimes not very well at all. There remains some identification with the violence of the traumatic experience, so that throughout life, rages that echo or repeat the experience will be added to already existent aggression and may erupt in personal violence or be channelled into socially legitimated killing. (Mitchell 2013, 22)

Mitchell's work in distinguishing the lateral axis offers a space for addressing such issues. All too often, to date, attention to the psychical significance of others like oneself in childhood have been neglected or assimilated to parent–child relations as there has been no framework that could contain them and help them be developed. "Observations without theory to crystallize them remain relevant but unintegrated," as Gilmore (2013, 54) observes. Yet with the introduction of the lateral axis, such work from the past—and in the future—can add to Mitchell's own insights. An example is Merleau-Ponty's ([1949–52] 2010) account of how a child learns the distinction between role and individual required for the imperfect tense:

> The jealousy that is manifested at a younger brother's birth can be interpreted as a refusal to accept the change in situation. The arrival of the newborn supplants the previous role. This stage disappears due to the constitution of a kind of past-present-future schema...The child

learns to think of reciprocal relations: he distinguishes between the concept of role and that of individual. He learns to relativise the actions of the youngest and oldest. (Merleau-Ponty [1949–52] 2010, 244)

Merleau-Ponty then gives "the case of a little girl of thirty-five months who was excited by coming across a dog having puppies":

> Two months later, at the birth of her younger brother, the girl suddenly acquired certain linguistic modes, notably the imperfect. A connection exists between the acquisition, the brother's birth, and the past emotion. How can we explain what happened? For the little girl who knows she is about to have a brother or sister, the dog represented a symbol. The future schema: "brother-me-parents" has been anticipated by "puppies-me-dog". To assimilate this schema, the child came to quit her position as the privileged object and took a maternal attitude towards the newborn. It is necessary to move from a captive attitude to an ablative attitude, from a passive attitude to a positive attitude. We thus see the appearance of the use of the imperfect, of the "me", the "I", and four future verbs. The future is an aggressive tense: the subject takes hold in the future and makes projects; the use of "me" and of "I" indicates that the subject adopts a more personal attitude. The use of the imperfect shows that the young girl understands that the present is extended; it is the past, but the past that abides in the present. The imperfect is employed each time the baby is brought up, the baby being what she was until now. (Merleau-Ponty [1949–52] 2010, 245)

Merleau-Ponty suggests that the imperfect tense requires being able to think of reciprocal relations. This is a thought that the child needs in order to negotiate his or her place in relation to others who are alike but different—siblings, potential siblings, or peers. Merleau-Ponty does not imply that the only child will be unable to use the imperfect tense; naturally they will, but they will need to deploy other resources than their actual siblings for thinking about the difference between a person and their role. This process depends upon the experiences and cultural resources the child receives for negotiating the meaning—in this case, the meaning of puppies as a symbol. Merleau-Ponty's account can be further refined by placement in the context of Mitchell's work, since Mitchell suggests that establishing reciprocal relations with the sibling requires identification both with the maternal attitude and with the new child itself—both of which will ultimately be disappointed. However, excavating neglected accounts of lateral phenomena such as Merleau-Ponty's, or developing new work, can add to Mitchell's theory.

In *Siblings* (2003, 44), Mitchell argues, in line with Lacan and Klein, that "representation and hence language relates to absence—what is not there must be signified. Seriality, although it takes place within language, is about numeracy not literacy." Yet more recently Mitchell has highlighted the potential significance of a sibling for language development. She notes that "the sibling arrives when the toddler is mastering speech; it is a time when the frustrations of inarticulacy and inexpressibility occasion rage and despair"; when the child has to address others like themselves but different, at whatever age, "the traumatic nucleus of the experience will be referred to the typical time of two to two and a half years, through deferred or referred action" (Mitchell 2013, 23–4). Further developing this thought, it can be suggested that language can involve the differentiation negotiated by the lateral axis, as well as the relations of absence and presence negotiated by the vertical axis. We have seen with Merleau-Ponty that lateral axis processes can be recognized as significance for the differentiation—rather than negation—of individual and role required for the imperfect tense. The lateral axis opens up a space for placing past insights and for developing further work. This has been our project in *Juliet Mitchell and the Lateral Axis*, in showing the value of engagement with Mitchell's work for contemporary concerns.

*　*　*

In the first chapter of the volume, Susan Walker tracks the development of Mitchell's theory of the etiology of hysteria. It was from this investigation that Mitchell discovered the significance of siblings for psychoanalytic theory, a finding she presented in her book *Mad Men and Medusas* (2000). Walker first sets out Freud's classical theory of the origins of hysteria using the vertical axis and the Oedipus complex. She traces how, as the theory developed, the original traumatic etiology of hysteria was replaced by an emphasis on an incompatible idea of a sexual nature. This shift in emphasis is, Walker notes, reversed by Mitchell who places traumatic experiences back into the origins of hysteria. Walker outlines Mitchell's account of the catastrophic effect, upon the fragile baby-subject, of the arrival of a sibling. This provokes intense ambivalence characterized by murderous hatred, and narcissistic love, for the new arrival who is both nearly identical to and yet a replacement for the baby.

Walker notes Mitchell's fascinating suggestion that the ambivalence and desires first experienced in the pre-Oedipal sibling situation, may be misread, in the necessary reconstruction, which takes place in the analysis of a post-Oedipal adult, as the ambivalence and desires arising from the Oedipal situation. This masks the effect of the lateral axis and conflates it with the effect of the vertical parent–child axis. Walker pulls together Mitchell's reworking of Freud's metaphorical use of the "mystic writing pad" to explain how trauma affects memory, and Mitchell's account of the regressive effect of trauma upon the hysterical adult. These two concepts help the reader to understand Mitchell's clinical observations and explanations of some the symptoms of hysteria, such as bodily enactment and memory loss. Walker then moves on to recount Mitchell's use of the Don Juan myth, to examine the forms that male hysteria may take, and Mitchell's suggestions for why male hysteria is denied or unrecognized, both culturally and within psychoanalytic theory. Finally Walker outlines Mitchell's important emphasis on the presence of death and violence in the hysterical condition. The close proximity of sexuality and death in both the etiology and the enactment of hysterical symptoms are evidence of the presence of violent hatred and love in the sibling encounter. The chapter finishes with some thoughts on where Mitchell's theory of the importance of siblings for the psyche needs to be further explored and developed.

In chapter 2, Daru Huppert explores further Mitchell's innovative theory of the lateral axis. He begins by noting that, prior to Mitchell, siblings had no place within psychoanalytic thought: they were either ignored because they did not fit within Oedipal theory, or were incorporated into that theory without remainder. As Mitchell (2013, 17) states, "in Freud's theoretical superstructure, sisters and brothers are placed in the same category as mothers and fathers, and this amalgamation of parents and siblings is usually followed without concern." Mitchell's work gives sibling relationships a place within psychoanalytic theory, which she calls the "lateral axis" in contrast to the "vertical axis" of parent–child relations. At the heart of Mitchell's account is an image of the older sibling, who experiences the displacement from the position of "the Baby" as an extreme existential threat.

In psychoanalytic terms, the newcomer represents a narcissistic injury. Mitchell proposes that this injury is no less the experience of a younger sibling—who has to find a place in an environment in which their older sister or brother has already made their claim for parental attention and availability. Furthermore, she suggests, the only child too has to face this issue, but on a less favorable terrain: whereas real siblings can negotiate with each other in actuality as well as in phantasy, "the 'only' child is likely to have more, not fewer sisters and brothers than the child with siblings. They are more active in the thoughts and feelings, the unconscious and conscious fantasies, in the inner world of the 'only' child than they are in those of its sibling peers. The 'only' child will ask What has happened? The 'expected' one has not arrived. What have I done wrong?"

(Mitchell 2013, 19). Huppert draws out that in Mitchell's account of lateral relations, the child's first impulse is to presume that a sibling would be more of themselves, a narcissistic extension of self. When this phantasy is disappointed by the fact that the sibling is *like* me but *different*, then feelings of hate will be evoked alongside feelings of tenderness. The issue will be to what extent the child can recognize the other as warranting love not because they are the same, but because of their mix of similarities and differences. Huppert emphasizes that this is a difficult recognition, which is rarely a simple or linear process. However, it is helped when a child has support from adults in making sense of their place and determining "who can stay up latest, have which piece of cake and survive the murderous rivalries to win through to sibling and peer love, a law allowing space for one who is the same and different" (Mitchell 2003, 52).

Having introduced Mitchell's account of sibling relations, Huppert then explores further its logic and implications. He observes that sibling-oriented sexuality differs from the vertical sexuality of the Oedipus complex. Above all, in contrast with some features of the Oedipus complex, a wish for a baby does not form part of our sexual desire for a sibling. He also considers that the taboos that prohibit sibling sexuality are often organized differently. For example, he draws on his clinical experience to suggest that siblings will often include a third child, who is not a brother or sister, in their acts, so as to suspend, obscure, and thereby more easily trespass the incest barrier. He also draws out that we are more likely to have preconscious memories of early sexual wishes and acts with siblings than with parents; Huppert urges recognition that behind these preconscious memories may well remain unconscious events or phantasies of sexual wishes or hate for a sibling. Themes of *keeping promises* or *keeping secrets* in our lives, Huppert suggests, may well receive investment from our early and forgotten sibling relations in which these were in issue. Huppert's chapter closes by raising the question of whether the "sibling complex" can be regarded as on the same level or of the same kind as the Oedipus complex.

Juliet Mitchell's account of the Oedipus complex continues to be at the heart of the issues continued in chapters 3 and 4. Here, a dialogue is presented between Judith Butler and Mitchell. In 2009 Butler addressed a symposium held at the Centre for Gender Studies to honor Mitchell's retirement. Parts of this address were later published in an article for the journal *differences* (Butler 2013), whereas other parts are published here for the first time. In chapter 3 Butler praises Mitchell for the latter's "immeasurable influence" on subsequent feminist and psychoanalytical thought. However, Butler also alleges that Mitchell remains tied to an essentialist account of the difference between men and women, which buys into the organizing assumptions of the oppressive culture it tries to resist. Butler begins by raising the question of the transgenerational transmission of rules regarding identity, and the role of unconscious processes in countering emancipatory political activity. She considers how this issue is treated in the 1999 introduction to the second edition of *Psychoanalysis and Feminism*, attending in particular to Mitchell's interpretation of Freud's ([1933] 2001: 167) remark that "Mankind never lives entirely in the present. The past, the tradition of the race and the people, lives on in the ideologies of the superego and yields only slowly to the influences of the present and to new change…" She argues, however, that Mitchell's interpretation of the role of the unconscious is hamstrung by an inadequate account of gender and of a child's identificatory processes with his or her parent(s). The modes identification and desire through which our identity is formed are always, Butler contends, elaborated in response to the forceful impression, enigmatic and exciting, of the world as we find it around us in its specifically-structured forms of oppression. Drawing on Laplanche's critical discussion of the idea of unconscious communication across generations, Butler criticizes Mitchell, who she reads as "saying that sexual difference is invariably identified with masculine and feminine," and argues that these latter terms cannot be taken for granted as if they were an invariant and universal distinction, with stable and transmissible content.

Mitchell's reply, in chapter 4, begins by clarifying the terms of discussion, showing that Butler's interest in heteronormativity differs from Mitchell's own overriding interest in the oppression of women. This has led them to use terms, most significantly "sexual difference," in diverging ways, and this has caused confusion. Mitchell further suggests that Butler's emphasis on culture at the expense of fantasy misses two universal facets of the human condition—which nonetheless have no set content. The first is that the position of women is shaped, variously, by the psychological consequences of differences in reproductive possibilities. The second is that all human societies require some prohibitions on desire and murder, though the content of these prohibitions can certainly differ. Whereas Butler alleges that Mitchell identifies sexual difference with masculine and feminine, Mitchell argues that this is not her perspective at all. Mitchell observes that biological femaleness and psychic femininity never fully match up; it has always been her argument that we must consider "the way the anatomical male/female data (with all its uncertainties) is mentally lived; the way the physical data, the clitoris/vagina/penis, is phantasized and experienced" (Mitchell 1973, 131). Having clarified the meaning and significance of her invocation of "sexual difference," Mitchell goes on to engage in dialogue with Butler on four fundamental issues: the intergenerational transmission of culture and oppression, the meaning and variability of unconscious prohibition, the relationship between the unconscious and desire, and how to formulate the political task of contesting the oppression of women.

Chapter 4 also includes Rose's reply to Butler on the occasion of the 2009 symposium. Like Mitchell in her reply to Butler, Rose argues that embodiment shapes the discursive construction of sex through the significance of fantasy. This is not to suggest that embodiment legislates what meanings a person will assign to their life, but that the formation of a distinction between men and women will always but contingently invoke anatomy. We cannot therefore solely attend to the discursive limits of "sex," but must also examine the variety of fantasies that can be produced by the universal significance of anatomical differences for the human unconscious. Attention to this issue allowed Mitchell in *Madmen and Medusas* to consider the psychical significance of having or lacking a womb, a significant contribution to psychoanalytic and gender theory. Drawing on her own work in making sense of the Butler–Mitchell controversy, Rose compares the transmission of the oppression of women to the transmission of an ethnic heritage, noting that it is dependent upon the contingencies of cultural performance and the contingent but more enduring ways in which this heritage is sustained by fantasy.

In chapter 5, Robbie Duschinsky proposes that Mitchell's debt to a dialectical mode of thought supports the great value of her ideas for contemporary concerns and for further developing post-structuralist perspectives. He argues that Mitchell's texts have an iridescent quality that allows us, as time passes, to see both particular passages and our world differently. Part of this quality is the result of a core question that animates each of Mitchell's books, and which keeps being reactivated by our concrete personal and political experiences—even as circumstances are reconfigured. This question is: "why are inequalities between men and women so pervasive, even in movements which purport to be primarily concerned with equality?" Duschinsky situates the stakes of this question by considering the dissolution taking place of the Socialist Worker's Party in the Britain, following mishandling of allegations by a young female activist that she had been raped by a leading member of party. Party leaders alleged that those who were concerned by the way the allegations were handled were diluting their socialism with other interests, and gesture to Mitchell as an example of such apostasy a generation earlier in her work for *New Left Review*. At the time, Mitchell described the need to escape a complete severance of socialism and feminism, or losing the latter within the former. She described these two positions as twin sisters. By contrast, she set out that her goal was to find a space that could by those interested in gender theory and feminism, and viewed with suspicion as a science of subjectivity, by a "war culture [which] disavows subjectivity." Nixon charts the reasons for the engagement and later disengagement of psychoanalysis and politics over the last 40 years.

Nixon sees in Mitchell's portrayal of sexualized violence a prescient account of the atrocities that occurred in the Iraq war, and in particular in Abu Ghraib prison, and a belated theorizing of the abundance of violent sexuality, "violence perversion," and "strangely subjective atrocity" in war since the time of the Vietnam war. Nixon's chapter illustrates how these atrocities have been has been portrayed and protested by artists, such as Spero. The final section of the chapter focuses on the challenges of representing seriality (what Nixon terms social subjectivity) and lateral relations, how it has been represented in serial art and minimalism, and includes a detailed account of Yvonne Rainer's protest work Street Action.

Chapter 10, by Gayatri Chakravorty Spivak, also thinks about Mitchell's work and how it can help us think about violence. She considers how the allocation of identities can provide important scaffolding for acts of violence to those whose identities then situate them as violable. In this, she attends particularly to the identities that offer explicit or tacit support to support acts of rape, which make rape in certain regards a collective act. Spivak focuses particularly on the role of transcendent grounds, such as the Kantian a priori, in formulating an image of the human as elevated by reason—and the role of this elevated image of the human in dividing between violable and inviolable, rapeable and nonrapeable subjects in ways distributed by race, class, and sex. Spivak urges us to reconsider the division between transcendental and phenomenal, which has continued to guide our thinking about human life and ethics, and to attend to the significance of rape as formulating and expressing the boundaries that have been constructed for what it is to be human. Such attention brings into view the significance of both the differences in reproductive possibilities between subjects and the role of heteronormativity in organizing, naturalizing, and simplifying these possibilities through tacit appeal to the transcendent grounds of human life: in Spivak's words, "reproductive heteronormativity" can be regarded "as the social account of the transcendental and unconditional discursivity of rape in the general sense." She draws out the implications of her argument by thinking about how redress for rape should be enacted in global contexts without appealing to "humanity." Spivak also engages in a reading of cultural artifacts including in J. M. Coetzee's novel *Disgrace* and the copyright protocols for photographs, raising questions about what counts as meaningful protection from violation.

Also drawing upon cultural artifacts to develop considerations of psychological and political processes, Harkins, in chapter 11, examines representations of the story of Lot and his daughters from Genesis 19. In this story, Lot is living in Sodom when he is visited by male angels. The citizens of Sodom come to Lot's house and threaten to rape his male guests. Lot instead offers his virgin daughters to the citizens in order to protect his guests. As Sodom is being destroyed, Lot's wife turns back to see the destruction and is turned into a pillar of salt. After the destruction of Sodom and the death of Lot's wife, his daughters ply lot with wine and become pregnant by him in order to continue his line. Harkins suggests that this story cannot find adequate psychoanalytic interpretation without Mitchell's ideas regarding the interplay of vertical and lateral relationship, sexuality and reproduction, raw feelings of helplessness, and the need to see or represent. Harkins is interested in the position of the Law of the Mother, and how this function distributes authority and gender within relations of power.

Mitchell asks "Can siblings themselves be each other's lawgiver?" (2003, 53). Harkins develops this question in considering alternative regulatory mechanisms for lateral relations besides the Law of the Mother. Harkins finds in the contemporary discursive figure of the "mean girl" an example of the way in which lateral aggressivity and lateral sexuality between peers can be gendered, regulated, and disciplined in the absence of an authority who offers recognition to each subject. Harkins also considers how the physical space of a house can enact serial differentiation between subjects and its representation in gendered forms. Mitchell identifies the violence and sexuality of the sibling trauma on the one hand, and the role of the law of the mother in differentiating subjects on the lateral axis and prohibiting sibling sexuality and murder on the other. By contrast, Harkins explores the space between trauma and maternal authority, in which lateral relationships and gender can be formulated and represented to produce inhabitable forms of subjectivity with varying forms of security and pain.

Writing in 1932, Melanie Klein describes an interpretation she made to one of her young patients:

> I now made a venture and told Ruth that the balls in the tumbler, the coins in the purse and the contents of the bag all meant children in her Mummy's inside, and that she wanted to keep them safely shut up so as not to have any more brothers and sisters. The effect of my interpretation was astonishing. For the first time Ruth turned her attention to me and began to play in a different, less constrained, way. (Klein 1932/1975, p. 27)

mind, meaning that the person no longer has any conscious awareness of it. The excitation attached to the incompatible idea is transformed into a physical symptom. Freud named this process "conversion," and with this explanation provided a mechanism whereby incompatible or repressed ideas in hysteria can find expression through the body (1894, 48–49).

Freud later adjusted his etiology of hysterical symptoms, from one which suggested an origin in childhood sexual abuse, to one in which the sexual relationship that forms the incompatible idea is a phantasized one, and thus a universal facet of human development (i.e., not limited to victims of childhood sexual abuse) (Freud 1896b, 168, footnote 1; 1917, 370).

> I was driven to recognise in the end that these reports were untrue and so came to understand that hysterical symptoms are derived from phantasies not real occurrences (Freud 2005, 419).

Freud now suggests that it is a prohibited and incompatible idea or desire, not an actual traumatic event, which is repressed.[1] This change marks a shift in the conceptualization of the etiological kernel at the heart of hysterical symptoms, from an actual traumatic experience to a sexual idea or desire, incompatible with the ego. The result of Freud's revision of his ideas was that the emphasis on sexuality remained, but the possibility of actual trauma was less stressed. Importantly Mitchell's theory returns to the idea of an originating trauma in her development of the part that siblings play in the etiology of hysteria.

According to Freud, the developmental time at which the seeds of hysteria are laid is the time of the formation and resolution of the Oedipus complex, when both boys and girls wish to take the role of sexual partner for their mother, and to conceive a baby with her. This wish is prohibited because of the incest taboo. Acceptance of this prohibition is a step in the path toward relatively healthy "normal" psychic development. Rejection of the prohibition sets the young subject on the path of neurosis. For boys and girls the permutations of the Oedipus complex differ, as does the path to its eventual resolution. For boys the Oedipus complex, which contains the desire to be a sexual partner for the mother and to conceive a child by her, is destroyed under the threat of castration, while the wish for a woman and to father a baby is deferred into adulthood. For the girl (who is in Freud's terms, psychically speaking, already castrated) the Oedipus complex is not completely destroyed, but in the face of her mother's rejection, on account of her castrated state, she must redirect her incestuous wishes toward her father, and then defer them into adulthood, when her desire will be fulfilled by a father substitute. She must also accept that she is "castrated" and transform her desire for a penis into a desire for a baby, originally from her father, but again deferred until adulthood, and conceived in partnership with another man (Freud 1917, 329–338; 1924, 395–401; 1925, 402–411).

This formulation, at face value, makes it easy to see why Freudian theory can be used to suggest that hysteria would affect women more frequently than men. The girl child is lacking (a penis), and rejected (by both mother and father as a sexual partner). A failure to accept this state of affairs, and the prohibition which brings it about, and to continue to desire (unconsciously) what she cannot have, leads to classical hysterical symptoms affecting personality such as insatiable wanting, coquettish-ness, and dissatisfaction, which demonstrate a sense of lack, as well as movement between the feminine and masculine positions, in an attempt to be the subject of desire for the mother, or object of desire for the father. The trauma of Oedipal rejection can be reactivated by subsequent perceived rejections or prohibited ideas later in life. The failed repression of the forbidden desire or idea will manifest itself, in hysteria, in conver-sion symptoms that somatically express that which is desired and which is lost or forbidden. This is the template for hysterical symptoms of Oedipal origin in women.

For boys the situation plays out somewhat differently. Given the above explanation of the origins of the hysterical woman's sense of "lack" we might ask "what lack is the hysterical man unconsciously trying to make up for?" Clearly the boy comes to experience his father as a threat and as an obstacle to having his mother. He has a small penis compared to his father (a comparative lack), but he can take his father's place (with another woman), not now but later. The symbolic castration introduces the threat of the destruction of the boy's phallic, narcissistic pleasure, but this is an unrealized threat, unlike the "already carried out" castra-tion of the girl (Freud 2005, 410). However Freud also believed (and Mitchell has emphasized) that children, at and slightly preceding the time of the Oedipal crisis, do not simply want to be the sexual partner of their mother: they want to have a baby as she can (Mitchell 2003, 39; Freud 1909, 1–150). This desire to produce a baby parthenogenically, out of narcissistic plenitude, in identification with the mother, precedes the girl child's wish for a baby as a penis substitute. And for boys and girls this second, somewhat eclipsed, desire is also prohibited as they come to understand the reality of their reproductive positions, but has separate outcomes for the girl and for the boy. This time it is the girl who is told that she cannot have a baby now, but that she can later. For the boy he must accept that fact that he cannot give birth to a baby. This is also a prohibition experienced as "lack." Mitchell coins the phrase the "Law of

Noting the constant presence of death in the accounts of early cases of hysteria, Mitchell argues that Freud's theory of hysteria has been too much concerned with sexuality, and has neglected the importance of death (Mitchell 2000, 76). She attributes this omission to Freud's unconscious reluctance to examine the effect, upon his own hysteria, of the death of his younger brother in infancy.

As Mitchell points out, sibling relationships, while full of love, are also full of death, either as a wish to kill, or as a feeling of being subjectively obliterated, or the actual experience of the death of a sibling, and the ambivalence that may provoke (Mitchell 2000, 76). Mitchell hints that murderousness toward the sibling, over rivalry for possession of the mother, has been overshadowed, in psychoanalytical theory, by murderousness toward the father, with the same goal (the mother's undivided love) driving both.

From the standpoint of the adult analysand and his or her analyst, sibling rivalry can be hidden within aspects of the Oedipus complex (Mitchell 2000, 80). The trauma of a sibling rival regresses the child to a stage where he or she craves unity with the mother, but if the child is beyond the Oedipal stage, that craving for unity has a sexual flavor. Furthermore the problem of the mother's love for the sibling rival, and the craving to "have" the mother/mother's breast, and thus escape annihilation becomes, in the necessary reconstruction of adult phantasies that takes place in analysis, from present to past, the problem of the mother's desire for the father/phallus.

Violence and hatred for the rival can arise in both Oedipal and sibling situations. However, Oedipal violence and sibling violence differ in one crucial respect. In the Oedipal situation the desire is to love/possess one parent and kill/vanquish the other. In the "sibling crisis" the desire to love and the desire to kill are centered upon the same person. As a consequence of this, Mitchell argues strongly that present in hysteria are sexuality and death, love and hate, playfulness and cruelty, which are intertwined, and whose states can be switched rapidly from one to another (Mitchell 2000, 134–5). The presence of the destructive parts of hysteria may account its repulsive nature, in as much as there is a compulsion for it to be assigned to the "other," the weaker, the female, the stranger, which is as apparent in its scientific and clinical treatment, as in its cultural ascription.

Mitchell posits the mobility of the sexual drive, such that it can combine with the life drive, to form unions, but is also activated along with the death drive, in moments of trauma (Mitchell 2000, 141). The sexualization of trauma becomes a means of psychic survival, by way of which, when under threat, the hysteric first hates, then sexualizes the hatred, as a means of asserting his existence, albeit in a narcissistic and auto-erotic way (Mitchell 2000, 145–149). Compulsive, repetitive violent sexuality, either in war or in perversion, signals the effect of the death drive but may also be a means of reaffirming survival against the threat of annihilation (ibid).

The First World War provided a situation in which many soldiers became traumatized. Mitchell's attention to the prevalence and then refutation of the diagnosis of hysteria among male soldiers suffering from "war neurosis," who exhibited aphonia, nonorganic paralysis, and other symptoms virtually pathognomonic of hysteria, reveals the connection between the decline of hysteria as a psychoanalytical diagnosis, and the theoretical omission of attention to the role of death in the traumatic etiology of hysteria.

Mitchell points out that the Oedipus myth recounts the flaunting of two taboos, that against incest and against patricide (Mitchell 2000, 32). In thinking about hysteria, she says that we have tended to concentrate only on the first prohibited desire, that is, incest, and therefore excluded the violence of the condition. The possibility of fratricide invoked by sibling trauma in the lateral axis, which is prohibited primarily by the mother, may form an alternative repressed wish and prohibition, which may also be expressed in hysterical symptoms. Mitchell contends that both the fear of death, preceding and following trauma in war, and the knowledge that the soldier has of breaking the taboo on killing another, can lead to hysterical symptoms, which were renamed or misdiagnosed as traumatic neurosis in the First World War. This new diagnosis concealed male hysteria, and the apparent absence of Oedipal origins in many cases, justified the avoidance of the diagnosis of hysteria (Mitchell 2000, 29).

In summary, Mitchell makes a double claim about the effect of "war neurosis" on the lack of recognition of male hysteria. In the first instance, because Oedipal, sexual elements were overemphasized in the etiology of hysteria, the lack of these in hysterical soldiers, or the impossibility of recognizing these (because of the taint of homosexuality), led to the impossibility of diagnosing hysteria in traumatized soldiers. Concurrently the lack of recognition of the effect of trauma in hysterical etiology, meant that its place in the etiology of hysteria in times of war, could not be recognized, and once again hysteria could not be diagnosed (Mitchell 2000, 128–9).[3]

The prevalence of sexual violence in the context of war underlines the importance of recognizing the sibling qualities exhibited in the fusion of sexuality and violence in hysteria. Without this recognition, the intertwining of sex and death, in the form of sexual violence in war, is

Chapter 2

Siblings, Secrets, and Promises: Aspects of Infantile Sexuality

Daru Huppert

Ever so rarely, we come upon theories that force us to acknowledge what everyone knows, but have somehow been able to disregard. This is the case with Mitchell's work on siblings. While it is a commonplace that siblings are a decisive influence in shaping who we become, this has largely remained an empty assertion with negligible effects on our systematic ideas. Indeed, disregard of siblings is the rule in psychoanalysis, and this is its "great theoretical omission" as Mitchell writes (2000a, xxxiii), though her claim could be extended to psychology and the social sciences more generally.

In psychoanalysis we can discern two lines of approach to siblings. On the one hand, we find that, every few years, a number studies appear on the effects of siblings on some detailed aspect of our psychic lives.[1] These studies, though often of considerable clinical interest, have very little impact on the discipline and soon fall into oblivion. Their neglect, I would suggest, is due to their ill-fit with the Oedipal theory (in its various permutations). It is for this reason that detailed explorations of siblings have remained a "foreign body" within the psychoanalytic literature. The other, far more common fate of siblings within psychoanalysis is that their importance is noted and even carefully described, only to be comprehended almost entirely in Oedipal terms. In this approach, which is so deeply entrenched that it is no longer noticed, siblings are regarded either simply as rivals for the passion of our parents, or merely as parent substitutes. Neither of these of these assertions is necessarily wrong—indeed they may mark essential insights in particular clinical cases—but they do ignore the obvious: sometimes a sibling is only a sibling (or primarily that). So, to date, either studies concerning siblings have been overlooked by psychoanalysis, because the insights that arise from them cannot be assimilated into the Oedipal theory, or, on the contrary, siblings have been completely incorporated into this theory, with the result that insight into the specific effects of siblings *as* siblings is lost.

Mitchell was the first to realize that to overcome this impasse we do not require primarily more studies on siblings, but rather a general theory of sibling relationships, or what she called lateral relations, in contradistinction to the vertical relations between parents and children. She argues that we lose sight of siblings because we do not know how to determine their role—and that what is thereby lost is essential, because the effects of siblings upon the formation and functioning of our minds differs significantly from the effects due to vertical relationships. What is required then is a theory that, in regard to siblings, accomplishes what the Oedipal theory does in regard to parents: it makes their effect on us thinkable and thereby explorable. Such a theory of lateral relations will alter the way we conceive of ourselves, of others, and our reciprocal relationships: as Mitchell (2003, xvi) notes, "bringing in Siblings changes the picture we are looking at."

Sibling Theory

Mitchell's more recent work is an attempt to develop a general theory of siblings and their influence on the formation of our mind. While it is still being articulated, some of its essential contours have taken shape. Mitchell (2000b, p. xi) explains that "when a sibling is in the offing, the danger for the existing child is that he or she, previously—'His Majesty the Baby'—will be annihilated, for this is someone who stands in the same position to parents (and their substitutes) as himself." What is devastating is that another being, too similar to oneself, threatens to usurp the throne of infancy. The subject is not only displaced, deposed, and dispossessed, he is, Mitchell insists, psychically annihilated. The essential response to this annihilation is to try to kill the sibling, who has obliterated the subject (Mitchell 2003, xv). The younger sibling in turn will seek to defend himself, by wishing to annihilate the elder one. Destruction—unilateral or mutual—is averted by different, simultaneously pursued and conflicting solutions.

First there is the possibility of *investing the sibling narcissistically*, as more of oneself or an extension of oneself. This solution, however, founders because the sibling is different and this is felt to be devastating; it reawakens the obliteration initially experienced. There is also the attempt to *invest the sibling libidinously* and with aim-inhibited tenderness, but these solutions are always threatened by the hate arising from the feeling of being annihilated by the sibling. As a result, in infancy and often in adulthood, the feelings of love for a sibling are labile, easily prone to revert into hate and destruction. Yet, in Mitchell's view, siblings do not only have problematic effects. If the obliteration of self, elicited by the sibling, is mourned and the destructive urges against the sibling are sufficiently bound by libidinal and tender impulses, then murderousness gives way to rivalry, competiveness, and eventually to a sense of solidarity not only with siblings, but with other lateral figures. Siblings provide the possibility of grasping ourselves as part of what Mitchell (2003, 149) calls a series—as someone who is like others, but with differences. In this way, we may come to realize individuality based on what we share with others. In the language of classical psychoanalysis we could say the Mitchell describes a development:

1. that begins with the narcissistic injury caused by the advent of a sibling;
2. develops into a crucial negotiation of the narcissism of small differences that mark sibling relations;
3. before then moving toward object love along the lateral axis.

This development is long, complicated, prone to pathological resolutions and regressions—Cain is its constant companion.

Mitchell's theory is the most general and intense portrayal within psychoanalysis of the effects that siblings have on us. Her ideas have crucial implications for thinking about the entirety of our psychic life. In this chapter, I will use some of her concepts to discuss the role played by siblings in the development of important aspects of our sexuality. I hope to outline the particular place and character of sibling sexuality in relation to sexual interactions a child may have with children who are not siblings. This, in turn, will help clarify the relationship between sibling and Oedipal passions.

Infantile Sexuality and Siblings

Although psychoanalysis is still commonly associated with an insistence on sexuality, the days in which this discipline could be mistaken as a teaching of pan-sexualism are now long gone. A casual reader of current psychoanalytic literature could be forgiven for believing that sexuality plays a peripheral role in the discipline (Green 1995). As Mitchell notes, this neglect of sexuality has coincided with a reduced notion of what sex is; increasingly it has come to be understood only in terms of reproduction. Mitchell (2003, 122) remarks that, "the theoretical subjugation of sexuality to reproduction is a hidden version of the repudiation of sexuality itself." This repudiation is baffling given that Freud's notion of libido broke with any necessary link to reproduction; the latter became merely one of its possible aims (Freud 1905). Siblings, Mitchell argues, remind us of the nonreproductive and disturbing features of sexuality. That is because, in contrast with some features of the Oedipus complex, a wish for a baby does not form part of our sexual desire for a sibling. As Mitchell (2003, 22) categorically states: "sibling sexuality is sex without reproduction." There are four core components of Mitchell's claim that the role siblings play in the formation of our sexuality is distinct from, though related to the role played by our parents:

(a) The desire for a sibling is not organized by *sexual difference*, that is, by the *lack* of the phallus (in the girl) or lack of an ability to give birth (in the boy).
(b) Sexual taboos are, in general, less restrictive regarding siblings than parents. As a consequence polymorphous perverse manifestations of the sexual drive are more pronounced in relation to siblings than in Oedipal sexual strivings.
(c) The libidinal investment of the sibling is initially a preponderantly a narcissistic object choice. It is evident, though not trivial, that siblings are more similar to each other than to their parents. Mitchell gives this observation greater poignancy by claiming that, when as children we were awaiting a sibling, we were expecting more of ourselves. Siblings therefore easily take the position of the ideal-ego for each other; the older one for being more capable, the younger one occupying the role of what Freud called His Majesty the Baby. We might say that we love our sibling according to our own image, or, to be more precise, to our ideal image. Yet this narcissistic investment arises is impelled and imperiled by anxiety, as it seeks to fend off the earlier experience of annihilation.
(d) Hatred and destruction, arising from the threat of annihilation, are not differentiated from the sexual longing for a sibling, at least initially. Passionate embraces between siblings quickly give way to strangling; indeed, it can be difficult to distinguish one from the other. Mitchell suggests that parental prohibitions address the violent aspect of children's play more overtly and intensely than the sexual aspect—the fundamental task of parents is to prevent siblings from killing each other. What we must bear in mind is that in the lateral axis it can be difficult to distinguish between sexual investment and destructive proclivities.

This outline of Mitchell's claims suggests that the form and meaning that sexuality will take between siblings will be significantly different and have different effects to those of Oedipal relationships. Since in psycho-analytic theory siblings have been widely disregarded, there have been no attempts to address this issue at a more general level. We can attempt to make up for this lack by introducing siblings into the first of Freud's *Three Essays on a Theory of Sexuality*, which still remains the crucial text on the sexual drive. However, I will not begin by discussing sibling sexuality in particular. Instead I will briefly explore the sexual relationships between pre-latency children, between the age of three and five, even if this means going over territory that may be all too familiar. While this approach may seem circuitous, I would argue that we can only appreciate sibling sexuality if we relate it not only to Oedipal strivings, but also to the sexual activity found among children who are not siblings. Taking a detour will give more precision to later claims.

Perverse Activities

If we follow the first of the *Three Essays* and take heterosexual genital intercourse as our point of departure, we find that the sexual drive shows manifestations that deviate both in terms of the object and in terms of activity. Heterosexual and homosexual object-choices are both possible: a great part, often the greater part, of the sexual excitement involved in play is shared with objects of the same sex. However, animals and other children can also become targets of sexual strivings, and play a salient role in the sexual fantasy and activity of children. Children are fascinated by the open display of copulation or excretion found in animals and it is quite common that children enact sexual desires with each other by assuming the role of dogs, etc. With regard to children as sexual objects, it is evident that they are so for other children. Psychoanalysis has taken this for granted, perhaps too much so, and has instead emphasized the less intuitively apparent Oedipal desire.

Let us proceed to the deviation of the sexual aims, or what we would ordinarily call sexual activities; here Freud distinguishes between ana-tomical transgressions and fixations of preliminary aims; what these cat-egories have in common is that they do not aim at genital intercourse. Anatomical transgressions include the mouth or the anus as sexual organ as well as fetishism. Fellatio or cunnilingus may not be frequent in young children, but the mouth plays a primary role in their excited play, while the mutual inspection and stimulation of the anus is common. The use of toys or objects in these games can have a determining influence on the choice of a fetish (Winnicott 1971). With regard to the fixation on pre-liminary aims, Freud describes the pairs of voyeurism/exhibitionism and of sadism/masochism. In the Bible it required the intervention of the devil for Adam and Eve to realize that they were naked and to develop shame; it befalls parents or other adults to curb the exhibitionism and voyeurism of children. Anyone who has been able to observe a kindergarten knows that for many children furtive journeys to the toilets, to witness each other's genitals and excremental activities, represent the culmination of the day's pleasure. The sexual excitement elicited by rough play and by fights, whether due to suffering or inflicting pain, are unavoidable experiences of growing up, as are the intense and often disturbing pleasures derived from debasing others or becoming the object of another child's degradation.

We have seen that the sexual activity of children shows all aspects that Freud chose to emphasize in his study of the perversions—indeed, he chose to limit his study of perversions to those manifestations that occur universally amongst children. So far, I have discussed this sexual activity without addressing the prohibitions that it may meet. This will now be rectified.

Prohibition

Given conventional wisdom, it seems astonishing that adults generally tolerate, if not explicitly, the often crass sexual activity among children. Reasons for this are manifold. Perhaps most importantly, parents and institutions have no means to hinder this play, unless they wish to put the child under continual surveillance. Moreover parents, due to the repression of their own infantile sexuality, will tend to misapprehend the sexual aspects of children's excited interactions. They will see play, where their children are striving for sexual pleasure. Parents will also feel a mixture of resignation and a dim intuition that such play has a formative role in the development of their child; it may also be that adults wish to grant children experiences they enjoyed themselves while growing up. Yet reasons for the uneasy and mostly unacknowledged toleration of this activity should not be sought in the adults only. Children, of course, will hide their play.

The effects of this sexual play between children are different than those arising from contact that may stimulate sexual feelings in a child in regard to a parent. When Freud in a crucial observation, describes the mother as the first seductress, he is not thinking of sexual abuse, which I will not address in this chapter, but of the mother as providing the necessary stimulation for the efflorescence of the child's sexual drive. Her behavior, at least in the formative influence that concerns Freud, is aim-inhibited: it is delimited by the sexual barriers of disgust, shame, pain, and morality. Amongst pre-latency children these barriers are in the process of being established and intense excitement is to be gained by transgressing the continually shifting boundaries. Consequently, the sexual activities between children are generally less aim-inhibited than that between a child and his parent. It would, of course, be absurd to suggest that children have sexual relationships with each other that are utterly uninhibited. Constraints of libidinal development and aim-inhibited feelings of tenderness for each other impose limitations on their play, as do impositions and control from without. Children know that their behavior is "naughty" and they will have internalized some prohibitions and they will try to avoid being caught, at least in their most flagrant acts. Yet sooner or later—either due to age or the excessiveness of the activities—the parents or someone else will separate the children, cutting them off from their sources of sexual excitement.

Introducing Siblings

This separation also befalls siblings. Aristophanes's parable in Plato's *Symposium* of the round beings that are cut in half by the gods, and since then seek each other, lends itself to being read as depicting the moment in which siblings become the objects of an intense prohibition. Indeed, adults frequently remember a particular moment in which their parents anxiously decided to prohibit them from sharing the same room or bathing with their sibling, etc. The reason for this prohibition is evident: while the extent of overt sexual play and shared excitement with siblings varies considerably, its possibility is rarely entirely absent. All the sexual activities found between children can occur between siblings and frequently do. There is, however, a significant difference: the taboos with regard to sexual acts between siblings are severe, for they concern incest. It may be true that in our culture these taboos are preceded by a period of relative tolerance of sibling sexuality, but eventually the prohibition is imposed, either through parents, other adults, or institutions and the prohibition is highly invested. For this reason, breaking it elicits not only great excitement, but also—potentially—powerful feelings of shame, guilt, or disgust, at least *nachträglich* (i.e., after the child has established the incest taboo more firmly and, due to some later experience, becomes fully aware of the sexual nature of his earlier play). My clinical experience shows that siblings will often therefore include a third child, who is not a brother or sister, in their acts, so as to suspend, obscure, and thereby more easily trespass the incest barrier. In short, among siblings the possibilities of sexual transgression are many—proximity breeds temptation—but the prohibition can have significant and severe consequences.

What emerges from our discussion is a spectrum in which, on the one end, there are prohibited Oedipal strivings and on the other, covertly accepted sexual activities between children. In this scheme the sexual play between siblings represents an *intermediate area*, in which permissiveness and prohibition, ignorance and taboo coexist in an uneasy truce. Since the prohibition on sibling sexuality are less severe than along the vertical axis and children have not fully internalized the same taboos as the adult have, there can be expected to be, in general, both more sexual activity and this activity will be more overtly sexual between siblings than between a child and its parents. The consequences of this last point and the intermediate position of sibling sexuality—between Oedipal sexuality and sexual relationships to other children—raises issues that have not been resolved satisfactorily in the psychoanalytic literature.

Is Sibling Sexuality Preconscious or Unconscious?

In psychoanalytic case studies sexual acts between siblings are often described, but rarely given much importance, because they are subsumed within Oedipal explanations. Mitchell proposes that the reason for this neglect is that Oedipal desires are, as a rule, repressed, while sexual experiences with siblings are often available to consciousness and therefore considered to be of lesser pathogenic force. Mitchell acknowledges that many memories of such acts are, in fact, available to a person, but she does insist that they "contribute independently to the construction of unconscious processes" (2003, 34). Our enquiry may help to clarify this issue. The lesser degree of prohibition and the greater degree of enactment means that, in general, more memories of sexual acts between siblings will be preconscious than would be the case with Oedipal passions. This, of course, does not entail that in regard to siblings we observe no repression.[2] Such a view, if taken without qualification, fails to address the taboo on incest, which distinguishes sexual acts with a brother or a sister from such acts with other children. It also gives too much credence to the preconscious memories. Often preconscious memories will be screen memories, which distort past occurrences by recasting the event or the fantasies associated with it—these remain unconscious. A case in point would be Helene Deutsch's (1932) description of a female patient suffering from compulsive obsessive symptoms, which the patient in part relates to seduction by her elder brother. Deutsch, however, reveals this as a screen memory, diverting from another scene, in which the patient seduced her younger brother (who later, after contracting syphilis, committed suicide). We should keep in mind that even in cases where the memories are accurate, they may nevertheless *function* as screen memories in that they depict certain sexual acts, while both alluding to and covering over other such acts and fantasies with the sibling that have undergone repression. This last claim I wish briefly to illustrate by looking at a particular kind of secret shared between siblings.

Secrets and the Irritability between Siblings

Sibling relationships are marked by an intense, often overwhelming irritability. Mitchell's theory is fundamental in explaining this affect: the sibling is felt to obliterate me and becomes object of my annihilating wishes. Over time this annihilating contest is transformed, among other expressions of affect, into an intense irritability dictated by what Freud would call the narcissism of small differences. We hate the sibling for claiming to possess what we believe are our own qualities or we hate him or her for insisting on privileges the justifications for which we would like to consider baseless. Differences and similarities, as well as privileges, acquire urgent significance because of their narcissistic investment. Conflagrations over these issues can have drastic consequences, at the limit leading to fratricide. Here I want to examine a more obscure source of irritation that can be equally forceful or, at least, augment the force of the narcissistic irritation and even rage.

In the course of a therapeutic treatment we will occasionally hear a patient tells us about a pleasant and innocuous conversation with a sibling that suddenly and inexplicably provoked the patient's fury. Patients will not be forthcoming in trying to explain this sudden irruption of affect. Listening carefully we will find that the irritation may be prompted by a particular word such as "bathroom," which, although it easily fits into the exchange and in this context seems to be innocent enough, elicits a sudden and furious indignation in our patient. We may develop the suspicion that the word "bathroom" has prompted such a reaction because it touches on a secret. I have found that conflagrations of this kind often have their source in sexual exchanges between siblings during their childhood. These intimacies are secret, both in that no one (or hardly anyone) else knows about them and also in that, insofar as the siblings remember such acts, they do not talk about them with each other, or, if they do, the conversation soon leads to painful dead ends, issuing in statements such as: "we were children then," "you started it," "it is not true." If we accept this line of argument and apply it to our example, we find that the irritation erupts when something a sibling says or does is associated with the secret—"bathroom" may refer to the place in which the sexual act took place; sometimes a gaze that is felt to express an accusation or a longing may provoke the furious reaction. In some cases the secret may be unconscious, but in the cases I have encountered they were preconscious, though the patient had no inclination to explore it. This, however, raises a question: Why would the patient, who is able to remember the sexual scene, not recognize that his indignation is evoked by what he takes to be a reference to this secret? The reason, I contend, is that, although the memory is potentially conscious, it is linked with other sexual memories and fantasies regarding the siblings that are repressed. By bringing the memory to attention, the repression of this entire constellation is under threat. We might say that the secret is the guardian of the repressed. The secret, however, can only take on this function so long as it is not examined too closely.

While the secret derives from an interaction between siblings, it can have far-reaching intrapsychic consequences. A patient I treated was once observed by his elder sister when, as a three- or four-year-old, he engaged in a sexual act with another boy. She used this knowledge to continually taunt him and exhort all kinds of painful acts from him until he reached puberty. Later he developed a compulsive-obsessive neurosis, with starkly sexual content, that in many ways was modeled on his interactions with his sister. In yielding to his compulsive commands or revolting against them he was reviving his relationship with his sister and thereby repeating the sexual investment of her exhortations and her taunting of him. This illustrates how siblings can occupy aspects of our psychic structure, here the super-ego, that is commonly assumed to be the sole prerogative of parental figures. It would go beyond the scope of this chapter to ask whether the functioning of this structure is thereby altered. Let us instead return to the intersubjective sphere.

The Promise

One important consequence of early sexual interactions between siblings and of the secrets that arise from these is that they often issue in promises or oaths between the siblings; promises to passionately love each other more than anyone else; promises to avenge any slight or abuse suffered by the other, etc. These promises need not have been verbally articulated to acquire psychical force. Whether kept or broken such promises play an important and underestimated role in sibling relationships and in the clinical material concerning them. Often severe sacrifices are taken on to keep such promises and sometimes a person will seek to punish himself for having broken oaths to a sibling that he has no memory of having made. Such promises may, of course, be conscious, as with the wish to protect the sibling from adversity at any cost. But the reason for this promise taking such a drastic form and gaining such force are unconscious. The compulsive force of such promises derives from repressed aspects of the early sexual interactions and sexual fantasies concerning a sibling. While these promises over time suffer alterations, and are partly disinvested and defended against, they continue to exert a powerful influence. Later they are revived in the passionate oaths that are made to siblings and friends (blood brotherhood) during adolescence. The weightiest expression of such promises is found in the vows exchanged during marriage. It goes some way to explaining the ineliminable tension between marital partners and siblings if we consider that to love a spouse is at once to break a promise to a sibling and to keep it insofar the spouse is a sibling substitute.

I would contend that Antigone is the most implacable depiction of such a promise, even if, or perhaps, because neither the promise nor the secret are referred to explicitly in Sophocles's play. One of the play's main themes is that Antigone sacrifices the pleasures of marriage, indeed her life, in order to bury her brother. But in Sophocles's text, the act of burial is full of sexual imagery and the imagery of marriage, allowing to us to claim that for Antigone the burial place of her brother is her wedding site (Williams 1993). If we assume that Antigone's sacrifice for her brother issues from such a promise, this would clarify the confluence of two otherwise disparate and conflicting trends in her act: her sexual passion and the sense of inexorable duty. This sense of duty is not derived solely, as she professes, from her enacting the "unwritten, solid laws of the gods": it has motives that are carnal, but equally forceful and binding. Antigone, we can say, takes the promise given to a sibling to its terrible extreme.

Conclusion

The themes of the secret and of the promise have helped to bring certain aspects of our sexuality into focus, which are raised with a particular intensity by sibling relationships. In sibling relations there will be more sexual acts and therefore secrets—preconscious guardians of repressed memories—than along the Oedipal line; the promises, I have looked at, arise directly from these secrets. More generally, the material we have discussed gives ample support to the features that Mitchell has emphasized in sibling sexuality. Let us recall that she considers sibling sexuality to be nonreproductive, that it is not organized around sexual differences, that the taboos on it are less restrictive than on Oedipal relationships, that the initial investment of the object are primarily narcissistic and often difficult to distinguish from powerful destructive urges. In Antigone we find the non-reproductive nature of her passion (she rejects marriage to bury her brother), the absence of sexual difference (she does not love her brother passionately because he has what she lacks, i.e., the phallus), its perverse quality (intimations of incestuous desire and necrophilia), its narcissistic force (expressed in Antigone's powerful self-assertion not least against her sister Ismene) as well as its violent moment, culminating in her self-sacrifice. All this would support Mitchell's claim that attending to siblings will help elucidate the perverse expressions of our sexual drive.

Precisely because the scope of my chapter was relatively narrow and addresses issues that are not at the center of Mitchell's ideas, it attests to the truly general significance of her theory. What, however, is still open to debate, is whether the "sibling complex" plays as crucial a role in our mental lives as the Oedipus complex. This I take to be the claim implicit in Mitchell's project. At the beginning of this chapter I discussed the Oedipus complex as the reason for why we have failed to grasp the specific effects of siblings. While this has been detrimental, it also attests to the explanatory power of the Oedipal theory. Its extraordinary significance rests not only on its conceptual depth and cohesion, but on its ability to elucidate a vast array of clinical and social phenomena, in a detail and richness, not conceivable before the articulation of this theory. The other reason for the importance of the Oedipus complex derives from its relation with metapsychology, particularly the structural theory (id, ego, super-ego), of which it is part and parcel. Using the Oedipal theory Freud was able to elucidate both the formation and the functioning of what he called the psychic apparatus. For this reason, within psychoanalysis, the Oedipus complex is not only something we observe, but also a structure informing our observation. While it is probably too early to tell whether sibling theory can become similarly central to psychoanalysis, what is beyond doubt is that Mitchell's theory has made the crucial implications that siblings have on us thinkable. Thereby she has not only changed the picture we are looking at, but also the way we look at it.

Notes

1. See Colonna and Newmann (1983), Volkan and Ast (1997), Colonna and Newmann (1983).
2. I shall here leave out a discussion of other defence mechanisms (denial, projection etc.) that may come into operation when repression fails.

References

Colonna, A. and Newman L. 1983. The psychoanalytic Literature on Siblings. *Psychoanalytic Study of the Child 83*, 285–309.
Deutsch, H. 1932. "Obsessional Ceremonial and Obsessional Acts." In *Psycho-Analysis of the Neuroses*, translated by W.D. Robson-Scott, 175–197. London: Hogarth Press.

Freud, S. 1905. "Three Essays on the Theory of Sexuality." In *The Standard Edition of the Complete Psychological Works of Sigmund Freud Vol. 7,* translated by James Strachey. Hogarth Press, London, *Standard Edition 7.*

Green, A. 1995. "Has Sexuality anything to do with Psychoanalysis?" *The International Journal of Psychoanalysis 75,* 871–883.

Loewald, H. 2000. "The waning of the Oedipus Complex." *Journal of Psychotherapy Practice and Research 9,* 239–249.

Mitchell, J. 2000a. *Psychoanalysis and Feminism.* New York: Basic Books.

Mitchell, J. 2000b. *Mad Men and Medusas.* London: Penguin Books.

Mitchell, J. 2003. *Siblings.* Cambridge: Polity.

Volkan, V. and Ast G. 2000. *Siblings in the Unconscious and Psychopathology.* Madison: International University Press.

Williams, B. 1993. *Shame and Necessity.* Berkeley: University of California Press.

Winnicott, D. 1971. *Playing and Reality.* London: Tavistock Publications.

Chapter 3

Ideologies of the Super-Ego:
Psychoanalysis and Feminism, Revisited

Judith Butler

This chapter and the next presents a dialogue between Judith Butler and Juliet Mitchell. In May 2009 Butler addressed a symposium held at the Centre for Gender Studies to honour Mitchell's retirement from Cambridge University with a paper titled "Ideologies of the Superego." Parts of this address were later published in an article for the journal differences *(Butler 2013); this chapter presents Butler's full address. In the next chapter, Mitchell offers a reply to Butler's account of psychoanalysis and the oppression of women. We hope that, in presenting these texts here, they preserve some of the excitement of the symposium as fundamental concepts of psychoanalytic and feminist theory were discussed and reconceived.*

Judith Butler: It is a daunting task to be here today, to have been invited to address the continuing challenges of Juliet Mitchell's *Psychoanalysis and Feminism*. It is, as you know, a formidable and broad-ranging work whose influence on feminist theory, psychoanalysis, theories of sexual difference, ideology, and kinship, is simply immeasurable. The simple but overwhelming fact is that there was never a book like this book and there has never been one since. Under such circumstances I had then to consider what use I might be on this occasion, how I might take up a more narrow set of challenges, and so I re-read the text along with the quite perspicacious introduction its author offered a decade ago. The introduction was as interesting as the book itself, since it suggested something about the reception of this most important text, including some lamentations about the direction that feminist scholarly work had taken, but also some strong suggestions about what might be some better directions. Let me begin, then, by reviewing that introduction so that we might know better what the author wants of us, and then let me see whether

I can try to meet some of these challenges in ways that, I hope, will prove productive for further thinking on matters of kinship, ideology, and the changing tasks of psychoanalysis.

Let's begin with one of the most basic propositions and consider what it implies for how we think about sexual difference, the unconscious, and the problem of generational transmission. This proves to be a fundamental notion for her since, as she wrote in her 1999 preface, "The superego, with its transgenerational transmission of rules and laws; the id, where drive representatives meet what has been repressed; the ego, which comprises countless other egos—all are concepts which offer a way forward into thinking about ideology as 'how we live ourselves' as sexually differentiated beings." (xxxi). I would like to focus first on the transgenerational transmission of rules. Mitchell insists that sexual difference has largely unconscious dimensions, that these unconscious dimensions are transmitted through time and across generations, and that there is a kind of stasis or "drive to stay put" that characterizes sexual difference understood in this way. If we focus further on what sexual difference is, we find that the following formulations are central: sexual difference has to be included among those phenomenon that "persists" and that remains "incommensurate with the real social situation." As a result, Mitchell tells us, "deliberate socialization is inadequate to explain the structure of sexual difference and the inequalities that always arise from it, despite the fact that there is enormous diversity of social practice." At a certain point she tries to find other metaphors for explaining this "persistence," suggesting that it is perhaps more like a recalcitrance; for instance, she asks, "Why, despite massive social, economic, and legal changes, is there still a kind of *underwater tow* (my emphasis) that makes progress regress on matters of 'gender' equity." I should note here that "gender" is in quotation marks, suggesting that it is a term that Mitchell is provisionally willing to use, but not fully to condone. But I will return to this later as we try and think about all of this in relation to kinship and ideology.

Although sexual difference is not exactly defined (and may well be something that maintains a tense relationship with definition, promulgating metaphors of various kinds), something about its operation is being characterized through a variety of means. It is a kind of persistence; it is "a kind of underwater tow" or, again, a "current" as she writes, "feminism seems to be rowing against a current that is ultimately the stronger force." She concludes here—still the new introduction—with the following remark: "conservatism actually seems inherent in the very construction of sexual difference—as though the difference itself has in its construction insisted on stasis." (xviii) This conservatism is inherent in what Mitchell calls "the psycho-ideological living of sexual relations" and it is distinguished by the fact that "it is women...who become the ascribed repositories of that human conservatism." (xix)

Mitchell tells us that this conservatism is largely unconscious, although she does not try and offer a precise topography of the unconscious. In other words, we would not be able to locate this conservatism in a particular place. Rather, we are asked to understand this conservatism has transmitted across generations. There is a "kind of thought" about masculinity and femininity, understood as equivalent to the thought of sexual difference, that takes place in the course of a transmission, a relay, a transposition, and this would be understood as the particular temporal modality of this thought which, although partially conscious, "is primarily an unconscious process." (xix) This process is a transmitted one, and I am tempted to say that transmission is the mode of its reality, the epistemological modality of the thought of sexual difference itself. It does not belong to a single psyche; when it does belong to a psyche, it is only by virtue of its having been transmitted, and in the course of its further transmission. So any given psyche would be a kind of way station or relay point for the transmissibility of this thought. This point seems to me to be important for Mitchell since she wants to establish what she calls "a shared mental terrain," one which ultimately serves as the condition for understanding the nexus of the psyche and ideology.

It is interesting to note the two examples that Mitchell offers to support her claim about the transmission of unconscious ideas, especially the transmission of unconscious ideas regarding sexual difference. But first, I want to draw attention to the commitment that her position makes to a semantic understanding of masculine and feminine. She not only refers to ideas *about* sexual difference, which would undoubtedly include interpretations and semantic delimitations, but she is willing, throughout, to identify sexual difference with masculine and feminine. I am wondering whether it is not possible, as some psychoanalytic accounts of sexual difference have insisted, to say that sexual difference is persistent, that it works as "an undertow," characterized by a constitutive conservatism, without saying that sexual difference is invariably identified with masculine and feminine. Can there be sexual difference, say, within homosexuality that cannot quite be described as masculine and feminine, and what implications would that have for separating sexual difference, understood as a deep-seated and largely unconscious thought, and specific social ways of determining that thought? In other words, at what point is sexual difference separable from its social determinations? It would seem that we need to assume such a separation when we claim that changes in the social organization of men and women are impeded by a conservatism that seems to be inherent to sexual difference itself. If we define sexual difference as "masculine and feminine," are we not already giving social organization to those terms? And if the "shared mental terrain" established through the generational transmission of the terms is also a social reality, however unconscious, then it seems we are not talking about a psychic reality, presumptively unconscious, and a social reality, presumptively conscious, but two modes of sociality, even two temporalities of the social, one that lags behind, struggles to impede progress, and another that forges ahead, trying to effect social change.

On the one hand, there are progressive social reforms involving gender equity that find themselves impeded by something unconscious, something unconscious that belongs to sexual difference. On the other hand, what impedes such social reforms is itself "a largely unconsciously acquired history," one that presumes "a shared mental terrain." So the social clearly occurs twice, each time in a modality of history, one that is acquired and performs a regressive and conservative function, and another that belongs to a more deliberate orientation toward an illuminated present. As Mitchell, citing Freud, aptly puts it, "Mankind never lives entirely in the present. The past, the tradition of the race and the people, lives on in the ideologies of the superego and yields only slowly to the influences of the present and to new change..." (*SE* XXII, 167). Of course, it is this phrase, "ideologies of the super-ego" that interests Mitchell, and right so. The super-ego belongs to the later topography of Freud, and it is the one that Lacan largely neglects when he considers the conscious (mapping it onto the castration complex almost exclusively). Mankind does not live fully in the present: some history is transmitted at the level of the unconscious, and it has to do with sexual difference. How do we understand this slower and more recalcitrant history, this strange undertow, as part of an ideology of the super-ego?

I am not altogether sure how to make this link, but it seems to me that one of the two examples Mitchell offers to illustrate this point help to shed light on the connection. The first is "the unconscious sense of guilt" experienced by those who have not committed any crime. To use this example to support the idea of "a shared mental terrain" or a generationally transmitted set of unconscious thought, we would have to assume that the guilt actually attached to *past* deeds, and that at some point in history, the guilt was commensurate with a crime. And yet, as we know from Freud's own analysis in "Criminals from a Sense of Guilt" that guilt can be related to a wish or a fantasy, even grounded in a confusion about what is a wish and what is a deed. In that essay from 1916, Freud describes people who relate stories, mainly from their early youth, about committing crimes in order to achieve a sense of "mental relief" from "an oppressive feeling of guilt." (*SE*, IV:332) He concludes that "the sense of guilt was present before the misdeed" and he asks after the "origin of this obscure sense of guilt" that precedes the deed. He concludes that this guilt derives from the Oedipus complex, not to deeds performed, but to "intentions" or wishes to commit incest and parricide. But let us note that even here the guilt pertains to intentions or wishes, but not to deeds done.

The criminal act that follows from a sense of guilt seeks to install a commensurability of guilt and crime where there is none. In other words, there is no reason to infer from crimeless guilt that there was once a crime, but only that there were desires which, if acted upon, would result in crimes; it may well emerge from an anxiety over unacted desire—a desire to have done with the anxiety—and may well be a way that the psyche punishes itself in advance for an act it has not yet committed— and never will. Perhaps guilt is finally more bearable than anxiety or, indeed, fear of punishment, especially if one can orchestrate being punished by one's hand, as it were.

In Kleinian terms, that guilt that corresponds to no act may well be a way of managing an impulse that could possibly destroy an object of love and dependency, and so operates as a prophylactic against destructive aims. In any case, we can see that the existence of an unconscious sense of guilt (or partially conscious one) which seems to correspond to no misdeed may well refer to a possible future just as well as to an inherited past. But one could say that the fear of punishment follows from the awareness of a crime and, so, the prior the awareness of a set of rules or laws. But it could be the other way around. In that same essay, Freud notes that "criminals from sense of guilt" was known to Nietzsche as well. In Nietzsche, the social necessity to curb destructive impulses gives rise to law, even forms part of the very genealogy of law. And for Freud as well, can we really say that law precedes the possibility of crime? Or is it rather that the understanding that certain acts will destroy those relations upon which we depend most fundamentally, we devise law to stop us from acting on those destructive impulses and imperilling the social and intimate conditions of our own survival? So one question that emerges here is whether rules and laws are transmitted, or whether they are, in fact, remade time and again precisely in order to limit and manage the destructive consequences of unimpeded impulse or desire?

Mitchell likens this example of guilt that precedes crime to a second one in order to make the case for an unconsciously acquired history that proves recalcitrant in the face of demands for social change. In the second example, she writes, "a child raised by two parents of the same sex...may make a "'normative' adjustment to heterosexuality..." In fact, the argument suggests that the child emerges into heterosexuality (by which,

I suppose, she means a presumptively normative heterosexuality, what-ever that might be) not simply or only by virtue of biology, educational influences, media, and other environmental factors; rather, some other force has intervened, one that cannot be accounted for by "the actual sit-uation." Mitchell writes, "unconscious thought processes are an impor-tant contribution to these instances of normalization." (xxiv) So here we are meant to assume that unconscious thought exercises its "conserva-tive" force on sexuality, that a set of socially transmitted and acquired thoughts about sexual difference emerge in the heterosexuality of the child where it might not be predicted on the basis of parental influence and identification. In some ways, this confirms what Mitchell argued in *Psychoanalysis and Feminism*, namely, that that "conscious, deliberate socialization is inadequate to explain the structure of sexual difference." And yet, it seems that here the heterosexuality of the child raised by same sex parents is another example of this "persistence" of sexual difference. How are we to understand sexual difference in this instance as exempli-fied by heterosexuality? Is this a paradigmatic exemplification? And if so, does that mean that the persistence of sexual difference, understood as historically transmitted unconscious thoughts, is also the persistence of heterosexuality as the social organization of sexuality?

I am of course reminded here of the late Eve Sedgwick who argued that heterosexuality contains within it all sorts of affiliative links and erotic ties with homosexuality, that sexual acts, including anal inter-course or even kissing, can be relatively indifferent to matters of gender, and that cross-identifications and modes of triangulation often install homosexuality at the heart of heterosexuality. Similarly, we know from various modes of lesbian and gay sexuality that heterosexuality can be rehearsed and restaged in the context of homosexuality, and that we are talking about a nexus here that can and does form complicated con-figurations of sexuality. So if a child of one parent, two parents, or four parents, of different or same sex, or a child with one sibling or six, turns out to "be" heterosexual, that does not actually tell us very much about what that person wants or, indeed, how she or he wants it.

I could go on at length, and maybe I will have a chance to do that later. But I want, as I promised, to use this example to arrive at the questions to which Mitchell has asked us to return: *kinship* and *ideology*. But to do so, I have to ask for some patience as we follow the steps of this argument. First, let us consider the two examples in relation to one another. The child who has done nothing wrong and is not exposed to hyper-critical judgments from his or her parents nevertheless suffers from self-beratement and guilt. The child—who remains ungendered for the purposes of this example—is raised by two parents of the same sex, and turns out to be heterosexual in orientation. We are meant to see incommensurabilities in both instances, and we are meant to infer that only a time lag between the present and the past can account for this anachronistic emergence of guilt or desire. The crime happened earlier, and so the guilt is effectively acquired from another time. That heterosexuality is also somehow transmitted from earlier times, and so emerges now in the child in spite of the homosexuality of his or her parents seems also to be a sign of this conservatism, this "undertow" we call sexual difference.

The first example does not pertain immediately to sexuality, though it certainly could. It could be the nameless or timeless crime of Oedipus transmitted through the ages; or it could be any number of guilt reactions to the potential consequences of living out sexual desire. Taken together, the examples suggest a circuit of guilt and desire, if not a resurgence of Oedipus himself. But whether or not Oedipus gets the last word in this scenario is of less interest to me than some other assumptions at work here.

The first has to do with the emergent or accomplished heterosexuality of this child. To understand the importance of this example as a way of confirming historically acquired unconscious thoughts about sexual difference, we would have to accept sexual difference is not already operative in the home or in the larger circuits of kinship and surrounding social relations. I do not mean to take a fully sociological approach to this question, but rather to consider the peculiar ways in which "transmitting" and "acquiring" take place when it comes to the development of more or less stable forms of sexual orientation. After all, if we were to change the example, and ask how it is that a lesbian is in some ways formed within a family with heterosexual parents, we would not be able to say with ease that some unconscious content regarding sexual difference was transmitted to the child, and that this accounts for the incommensurability between the actual parental situation and the form of that child's sexual desire. Apparently, the straight kid who emerges from gay or lesbian parents acquires a desire that cannot be accounted for by "the actual situation." But the lesbian kid who emerges from straight parents or a single parent may also not be easily accounted for by the actual situation. But this not-accounting, this incommensurability does not seem necessarily to follow from the constitutive conservatism of sexual difference or, indeed, its ostensible corollary, heterosexuality. It may well be the case that sexuality is formed in response to something that is not manifest in the parenting environment, but why would that be any more or less true for the straight or gay kid, or indeed for the bisexual or asexual?

I am not sure that the formation of sexual desire emerges on the basis of a clearly readable mimesis. I want to be like the one parent and to desire the other, so I model myself on the one I want to be like. Maybe, but it could easily be the case that the only way a girl can inhabit a certain feminine position is with another girl, or the only way a boy can inhabit a certain masculine position is with another boy. Or it may be that the adolescent seeks to respond to a maternal demand to be the husband she never had, and the adolescent can in this instance be a boy (and so emerge as heterosexual) or a girl (and so emerge as homosexual). It can be that only within certain sociological framings that fantasy can come alive, and very often there is no commensurability between the sociological framing (queer, straight, gay, bi) and the form of desire, so that we find straight couples with strong queer desires, and queer couples enacting forms of transformed or transposed heterosexuality.

Our vocabularies tend to falter here, since we are no longer sure whether we are to call this straight or gay, and our not being able to call it by the right term may be part of its erotic significance and its social importance. In any case, mimesis is hardly the route to desire, and even if it were, every effort at mimetic doubling risks veering off from its model, functioning through displacement or metonymy. So this allows a lesbian to identify with the father or to find the father in another woman, or not to find him at all, but to construct another fantasy, one that may well be a palimpsest that does not settle into one object or another, even though it takes place at the site of some girl. She may well have more in common with some guy who is doing the same sort of thing in relation to his father or some other masculine figure, but at the site of a girl as well. Indeed, the child of lesbian parents may well end up desiring a girl as a form of identifying with his parents objects, or becoming part of the crowd. This may well be a greater form of loyalty than becoming gay, which would introduce the masculine object of desire in another way, or set up a rival for the lesbian prince who knows he has the absolute and irreplaceable love of both of his mothers. I heard a great story in which a young adolescent girl says to her two dads, will you be disappointed in me if I am not gay, and they respond, listen, if you are gay, you will be like us; if you like men, you will be like us, so in either case, you can't escape us! This may seem to be a strange parental narcissism, perhaps, but one that seeks to give permission to any possible trajectory of desire, which, of course, may function as an interdiction all the same, especially if one considers the potential burden of limitless options.

We could certainly say in all of these scenarios that sexual difference is at play, and I do not have a problem with that claim. But if something about sexual difference persists, how do we describe it? I am not sure that what persists are established semantic ways of organizing sexual difference, already formed legacies of the past that are relayed into the present without translation, transposition, without some loss, without some new twist or turn. For this reason, I am even less sure that heterosexuality is a sure way of confirming sexual difference or providing its paradigmatic instance. But even if both of those speculative propositions proved true (and I am not sure how they could finally prove true), an ever more fundamental problem emerges in my mind. And that has to do with how we understand "transmission" and "acquisition"—and this seems related to the key problem of "communicating unconscious ideas" intersubjectively and trans-generationally or, indeed, any broader thesis about shared mental terrain or, indeed, collective mind.

First of all, we have to ask whether what is communicated actually arrives in the form in which it is sent. In other words, is unconscious communication transparent and effective or does it function a bit more like Kafka's "imperial message," where the message is sent, but circuits through so many detours that its arrival is never quite certain, and no arbiter is really on site to tell us whether or not any message actually arrived. And if the content or the message does arrive, does it arrive in a form that recognizable, or has it undergone alterations and displacements on the course of its journey? What are the operative presumptions behind the idea of communication and acquisition? Does one invariably acquire something other than what was sent? Does one receive something more or less than what was proffered? Through what chains of displacement does unconscious communication occur, if it really can be said to occur at all? And is there not, as Jean Laplanche suggests, always a question of translation? If so, through what language, or set of languages, do such translations occur?

Indeed, for Laplanche the idea of unconscious communication is not finally acceptable, although certainly messages are sent, interpellations are made, and at an unconscious level. There is no guarantee and, indeed, no possibility that the conditions of their reception accord with the conditions of address. In fact, messages arrive in enigmatic form, inscrutable. So, according to Laplanche, we cannot look to the unconscious communication of ideas without first interrogating the conditions of any such communication, and without asking whether content remains intact as it is relayed from one unconscious to another. Importantly, then, if the transmissibility of the laws of culture depend on the possibility of the effective unconscious communication of such laws, then calling into question the transparency and effectivity of that mode of communication has important consequences of thinking about the laws of culture, the laws that are said to be essential to human society, the laws that are generally thought to be the laws of sexual difference, that explain the persistence of patriarchy and the relative intransigence of the symbolic order.

We can accept, for instance, that there is an unconscious operation at work that seems to relay another time into this time, that we are not completely of the present, and that another scene acts upon us as we try to find our way within present time. But even if we accept this time-lag as constitutive of the psyche, it does not follow that we have to accept a universal set of rules or laws as belonging to that other time, or transmitted from that other time. Indeed, that other time may well be an historical time, the times that belong to prior generations, but that is not the same as saying it is the time of cultural law, of the paternal law, of the symbolic, or of the laws that are essential to culture. This structuralist presumption supplements the theory of the unconscious, but it is in no way presupposed by its operation. As Laplanche departs from Lacan, he calls into question the means and mechanisms by which the unconscious desires of the adult world impinge upon the infant; this impingement does not communicate an intact set of laws in clear and effective ways. On the contrary, these enigmatic signifiers become lodged in the psychic life of the infant and initiate the drives as both overwhelming and exciting (these are, in effect, the terms through which Laplanche reformulates the scene of general seduction.

Something of this is given a specifically historical analysis in *Psychoanalysis and Feminism* when Mitchell notes in the final chapter, "The Cultural Revolution," that "the complexity of capitalist society makes archaic the kinship structures and incest taboos for the majority of people and yet it preserves them through thick and thin." So, there seems to be a mandate to preserve an archaism in the face of social reality. How are we, then, to understand this archaism? In 1974, Mitchell wrote, and underscored, the following important claim: "the capitalist economy implies that for the masses demands of exogamy and the social taboo on incest are irrelevant; but nevertheless it must preserve both these and the patriarchal structure that they imply." (409) The argument reminds me of the recent debates in France in which some opponents of gay marriage actively worry that gay marriage will dissolve the institutions of marriage and family even when it turns out that the majority of social arrangements cannot be described as family organized by heterosexual marriage. What is called "demarriage" has already become the norm. And so we might conclude that precisely because, at the social level, demarriage has become the norm, heterosexual marriage must be defended at the ideological level.

a poetic form by throwing the form away. Similarly, I would object if anyone failed to see that even modes of address, such as the famous "hey you there," are themselves citational and ritual moments, and that they assume, carry, and dispel semantic meanings precisely through modes of delivery. (Let us consider that almost all of Brechtian theatre relies on this insight: we can and do change the "message" depending on how it is delivered or performed, and this is because inflection, gesture, bodily, and vocal comportment turn out to be essential to what is being said, are indeed part of the saying.) Thus, the modes of addressing the infant is a way of establishing its semantics, including the use of the proper name, which often installs gender, or any of the interpellations that collect around gender assignment: "what a beautiful girl you are!"

It seems to me that propositional forms cannot be easily extracted from rhetorical modes of address, and that this holds consequences for how we come to think about how the interpellation of gender and, indeed, kinship takes place. One the one hand, I want to seek recourse to Laplanche to insist that whatever generational transmission takes place, it is not the relay of a "human set of laws" considered to be invariant and established, but rather a powerful set of impressions, whose power is not extricable from its semantics, and whose final translation into propositional form is invariably thwarted. On the other hand, I want to counter this view by suggesting that interpellation is its own semantics; it is not just carrying a message, but it is, in its form and delivery, a certain kind of message, and that the particular way its force is stylized has everything to do with the effect it wields.

What propels the displacements of desire is less an effort to evade the murderous consequences of a prohibitive law than an effort to fathom a set of adult desires that have impinged upon, and formed, an internal structure of the psyche. The infant is unknowing and, indeed, helpless, in relation to these overwhelming and confusing messages relayed more or less unconsciously by the adult world. As a result, the sexuality that emerges, understood as a series of displacements from instinct, is a result of this helplessness in the face of the desirous adult world. The infant becomes an investigative theorist on such an occasion, trying to fathom the strange force and direction of his or her own impulses. The problem for infantile sexuality is not how to evade death by punishment, but how to fathom a desire that is, from the start, already the desire of the other.

For those who appreciate how the Lacanian position has been bound up with structuralist models of kinship, this departure from Lacanian doxa is enormously consequential. Let's remember that several analysts and social psychologists of Lacanian persuasion have been active in arguing against gay and lesbian parenting in France (what is called "homoparentalité"), and that they often refer to the symbolic positions of Mother and Father as necessary points of reference for any child who hopes to emerge into the world in a nonpsychotic way. This intense effort to install a contingent form of heterosexual parenting as a precondition of culture itself and even as an invariant norm of psychic health has led to serious legal disenfranchisements and unnecessary pathologizations. It has led as well to a widespread misunderstanding, if not phobia, about the variability of kinship structures, the concrete practices of a *post*-structuralism, and the viability for the infant and child of any number of parenting and care-taking arrangements that provide conditions of love.

Theoretically, Laplanche's departure from Lacan in this regard implies a full critique of the paternal law, linked to the structuralist account of the exchange of women and the universalist premises of "culture." This view of the paternal law is countered by a conception of a non-gendered "adult world" that generates and imposes enigmatic signifiers on an infant who responds with both cognitive helplessness and incitation of the drive. As a result, primary unconscious and sexual messages are impressed upon the child (though "impression" may well be too soft a term). Moreover, those primary others whose desires are communicated through various practices are themselves in the grip of such messages (have themselves been incited unconsciously by such messages). The ones whose desires become the foreign and inciting elements in my own desire are themselves propelled by what is foreign and inciting, and invariably so. In this way, transgenerational transmission probably resembles Borges's story, "Circular Ruins" where one person discovers that he has his reality only in another person's dream, and that the same principle applies to that dreamer, whose reality is secured only in another's dream. This goes on for generations, without end.

Hence, all the characters in the scene are to a large part, and irreversibly, unknowing about the meaning and content of the messages by which they are incited and impelled. They have contracted someone else's dream, or they are themselves living in "the other scene." There is something foreign in desire, and desire makes us always in some ways foreign to ourselves. This is because what is foreign has not only made its way into us, but has become the source of drives, that which incites the very possibility of an "I" who constitutes a subject of desire.

So here we can see that there is a difference between an idea of unconscious communication that presupposes the inevitable transmission of a set of laws or rules that are essential to human society and another mode of sending messages which, via Kafka, Borges, and Laplanche, arrive in forms that were not expected, remain enigmatic or unreadable, or prompt modes of displacement along metonymic lines that establish sexuality in excess of both biological teleologies and social normalization.

The difference between these two views has implications for how we understand the idea of cultural laws and their relation to variable forms of gender and kinship. In Mitchell's chapter, "The Different Self, the Phallus and the Father," she writes, "Before it is born, the child is assigned a name and is son or daughter of...; it has to learn to fit into this already ascribed place. Whatever the child does, whatever the specific accidents of its individual history, all take place within the larger framework of this human order. It is within the Freudian 'unconscious' that the laws of this order speak." (391)

Later, she discusses why the father represents those laws that govern the human society, and here is where she describes such laws as "essential to society." Even in the 1999 preface, Mitchell reconfirms her belief in such an underlying set of laws. She notes that object relations has underscored the importance of the mother "but was uninterested in any underlying laws." She worries as well about those Lacanian efforts to establish the mother in a "pre-Symbolic domain" and argues that both Lacan and object-relations fail to situate the mother "within the laws of the human order." If it is those laws that are supposed to be communicated to us through the stable and predictable mechanisms of unconscious communication, and if the unconscious can work only by translating and displacing any set of injunctions it may communicate, then we cannot rely on such a domain to validate the invariant rules of culture. We can only look to such a domain to find the series of invariant rules, spawned from translation and transposition, that follow the logic of the drive, that is, displacement along routes that are never fully predictable or expected. Of course, we have to be able to account for that recalcitrance, that undertow, that countercurrent that makes our efforts at social change so difficult. This remains a crucial, irreversible insight of *Psychoanalysis and Feminism*. But there is no reason to take that recalcitrance and countercurrent as a sign of the invariant laws of human society; why cannot that conservative undertow be precisely the drag of history, something communicated through the norms of kinship, norms that change, with difficulty, over time?

Mitchell throws down the gauntlet in the 1999 preface when she notes that Lacan's rereading of Freud "is in some ways more dismal for feminist politics than is Freud's original version." Without the super-ego, Lacan cannot give an account of change. Positions can be shuffled in relation to the problem of castration. Her challenge is to get us to return to the second metapsychology, over and against Lacan, but without subscribing to ego psychology. And she worries that recent trends in queer theory and various modes of postmodernism, whatever those might be, are derived from this dismal reading of Freud, bequeathed by Lacan. The idea of "deliberately enact[ing] different stances" seems to follow from the incommensurability between which identificatory relation a body takes in relation to an invariant position; so the phallus can be occupied by this body or another, regardless of gender, or someone may occupy a position of castration, and someone else, the position of the castration threat, regardless of gender. The problem with such positions, variously characterized as the "political practices of 'performance' and 'performativity,'" is that they do not give us "any account of historical change."(xxxii) I would add that such positions, which I think are rather distinct from practices of performativity, presume and ratify an invariant structure to the symbolic order, and make of "agency" and "resistance" a futile, sometimes amusing effort, to simply to work the transposability of the law, but not, finally, its legitimacy or timeless pretensions.

I do not think that theories of performativity were derived from the Lacanian reading of Freud, and, indeed, the "pink Freud" that became so important to critics such as Leo Bersani, Diana Fuss, and John Fletcher represented a return to Freud within queer theory. Indeed, it might make more sense to read Gayle Rubin's (1975) "Traffic in Women" and her particular use of Juliet Mitchell to understand the theoretical moment of departure for queer theory. She thought that by remaking kinship, we could remake gender. In her subsequent work, she sought to establish sexuality as a semiautonomous domain, and this produced a certain tension between feminism and queer theory. But I do not think Lacan was in the picture at that point: Foucault, however, was. My own view is that it was a mistake to leave kinship beyond, since the question of what can and cannot be changed within the rules of kinship became central questions for new modes of association and intimacy. We had not yet answered the question of why it is so hard to change kinship relations, or why it is that experimentation in social organization is so often accompanied by a certain slowness, if not recalcitrance, on the part of the psyche.

The study of kinship has always been linked with the study of ritual, and that this has, after structuralism, given way to historical accounts of changing kinship organizations through an examination of how rituals can and do change; indeed, how rituals must change. The feminist and gay/lesbian work on kinship, including the work of Marilyn Strathern and Cath Weston, has argued not only that kinship arrangements do vary, but that variability marks the very process of transmission. Kinship denotes those web of relations by which we are sustained—or, indeed, in which failures of sustenance are enormously consequential. But kinship can be reduced neither to the family nor to triadic relations. We can surely ask how Oedipalization occurs within single parent families or within gay families or, indeed, in extended kinship networks where there is a distribution of parental function and position. But to ask these questions is precisely to ask how psychoanalysis must be reformulated in light of changing kinship arrangements. It is also to ask how changing kinship arrangements come up against a countercurrent or undertow that is not so easily transformed through purely social means.

If we think about the variable conditions of kinship and what new challenges they pose for psychoanalysis, we may well think about the tasks for psychoanalysis and for feminism differently. To what extent do we operate within certain idealized, if not normative, conceptions of kinship when we describe the initial moments of gender assignment? I mentioned before this example of gender assignment and familial place in *Psychoanalysis and Feminism*: "Before it is born, the child is assigned a name..." Well, that is not always true, especially if the child is born and directly given up for adoption. It can remain nameless in the interim, or be given only a provisional name with the understanding that the name will change. And who is the "one" who makes this assignment? Sometimes a child is left abandoned by virtue of a natural disaster or conditions of poverty. And it may be that the child is in social services, in a series of foster homes, or ends up finally in a family situation where more than one person is occupying the maternal function. Let us remember Winnicott's quite important suggestion that the maternal may not be an object or a person, but, rather, *a field*, and that what one might find in that field are "bits and pieces" of maternal function. So is there an already ascribed place here? Or must we understand ascription and assignment as acts that must be performed time and again, part of an iterable structure with its own risks of failure, derailment, and reformulation?

So if we agree with Mitchell that a return to questions of kinship and ideology are necessary, even a new examination of the "ideologies of the super-ego," and if we are to seek recourse to the theory of ideology through an Althusserian interpellation in particular, then it seems to me we have to be prepared for the fact that interpellation does not just happen once, but time and again, and that the chain of interpellative assignments forms something of the social history within which a particular psychic life is formed and lived. In this way, the infant is not born into a structure, but into a temporally reiterated chain of interpellations or assignments that have to be negotiated in time, that precede and exceed the life of the child, which may well, in the case of adoption, entail a series of geographical, if not geopolitical, and linguistic displacements. No single set of laws replicates itself in the unconscious of that infant, but only a series of transpositions and impingements, never fully conscious, demanding a process of translation that can never fully return to, or grasp, the powerful and enigmatic impression that prompts that largely unpredictable trajectory of the drives.

Let us note here that the act of gender assignment or, indeed, the giving of a name, is one that already carries some enigmatic desire from the adult world. An assignment encodes some inscrutable desire from the adult world. It is carried in the proper name, but also in the assignment of gender. In this sense, some trace of sexuality is already at work in the interpellation of gender, in the sociological practice of gender assignment (a point on which I disagree with Laplanche). One might even say that through gender assignment, "unconscious thoughts are communicated," but there seems to be no nonspeculative way to ground the claim that the laws of human society are precisely what are communicated in and through such unconscious thoughts.

According to Laplanche, communication is invariably errant; what is sent is not the same as what arrives. If this is true, a truth that would also establish something of the relevance of Kafka for thinking about the transmission of sexual difference, then what would that continual misinterpretation and displacement do to the "communication" of sexual difference? Perhaps then we could begin to understand why it is that some people change their assignment, or wish to, and how keeping or refusing the name is bound up with a larger sense of the network of kinship to which one belongs. How else would we understand the claims made, for instance, by the intersex movement that an infant should be assigned a gender, but that the assignment should be subject to re-consideration by that person as she grows older, or the demand for legal re-assignment that has formed the political site of mobilization for so many transgendered people. Or even within genderqueer or butch-femme contexts, when pleas such as "call me a boy" or "let me be your girl" become the site of intense erotic exchange on the part of any number of genders. How else would we understand the violent attacks on transgendered people on the street or the continuing pathologization of homosexual "femininity" in boys within the DSM and other diagnostic tools? And how do we understand compulsory maternity or even anorexia as injunctions that are transmitted as part of a legacy of gender norms? Are they not ways of communicating the "rules" of sexual difference? Are there really rules that are not norms? And what modes do we have to introduce errancy and the unforeseen into such a transmission or communication? And how might we reconceive kinship once this errant and fecund sort of transmission becomes the way that one generation emerges from another, at once bearing the historical weight of what comes before and moving toward something new—what we might understand as the very dynamic of social struggle.

Notes

1. "[Freud] uses instinct in the traditional sense, which designates a behavioural schema that is adapted to a particular end or aim, with a pregiven object…is hereditary and innate, so not acquired…" (23) whereas "drive"—"the more properly psychoanalytic concept" (24), which involve "primal fantasies" understood as "precipitates from the history of human civilization." (23–4) Laplanche, *Essays on Otherness*, tr. John Fletcher, London: Routledge, 1999.
2. "Since we cannot wait for another science to present us with the final conclusions on the theory of instincts (*Triebe*), it is far more to the purpose that we should try to see what light may be thrown upon this basic problem of biology by a synthesis of the psychological phenomenon." (*SE* 14: 19)
3. See Laplanche, "The Drive and its Source-Object" in *Essays on Otherness*.

References

Freud, S. [1915] 2001. "Instincts and Their Vicissitudes." *SE 14*, 109–140.

Freud, S. [1916] 2001. "Introductory Lectures." *SE 15–16*, 1–463.

Freud, S. [1933] 2001. "New Introductory Lectures." *SE 22*, 1–182.

Laplanche, J. 1999. *Essays in Otherness*, tr. John Fletcher, London: Routledge.

Mitchell, J. 1999a. "Introduction, 1999" to *Psychoanalysis and Feminism*. New York: Basic Books.

Rubin, G. 1975. "The Traffic in Women" in *Toward an Anthropology of Women*, edited by R. Reiter, pp. 157–210. New York: Mon Rev.

Chapter 4

Debating Sexual Difference, Politics, and the Unconscious: With Discussant Section by Jacqueline Rose

Juliet Mitchell

The previous chapter presented Judith Butler's address at the symposium held to mark Juliet Mitchell's retirement from Cambridge University in 2009. The first part of this chapter presents Mitchell's reply to Butler. Mitchell identifies misunderstandings, and debates Butler's account of psychoanalysis and the oppression of women. The second part of this chapter presents remarks made by Jacqueline Rose, discussant at the symposium.

Juliet Mitchell: When it was first presented at the Symposium for my retirement from Cambridge in 2009, Jacqueline Rose was the discussant of Judith Butler's paper then called "Ideologies of the Superego," which has been developed and renamed as "Rethinking Sexual Difference and Kinship in Mitchell's Psychoanalysis and Feminism" (2013). On the earlier occasion Rose commented: 'I am sure...that I am not the only person in this room who might have felt at moments that the gap between these two thinkers is too vast to be bridged' (see Rose, below). Rose perceived that, interesting as Butler's work undoubtedly is, its interests are tangential to mine. Rose managed to make something of a bridge across the gap she had perceived but only through offering her own very interesting but different perspective—a third position. Here I argue that Butler's interest in heteronormativity has led her to neglect what is specific to the oppression of women, which leads her to misread my argument.

Her account of gender performativity is a powerful analytical tool and can be helpful politically in contesting essentialism. However, it misses the psychological consequences of sexual differences in women and men which arises, formulated through prohibitions on desire and murder which every subject must face. Butler alleges that I identify sexual difference with "masculine" and "feminine," fatalistically pinning biology to culture. This is quite wrong. Biological femaleness and psychic femininity never fully match up.

I start with a general discussion of why Butler and I might be motivated by problems which overlap on some terrain. Then I move to a dialogue with Butler, through replies to selections from the original talk which include previously unpublished material. This dialogue will address issues of the intergenerational transmission of culture and oppression, the implication of unconscious prohibition, the distinction between the drive and desire, and how to formulate the political task of contesting the oppression of women. It is my hope that presenting the two perspectives together in this way can suggest a contact between them so that disagreements can be grasped creatively.

"Sexual Difference"

Alerted by Rose's perception and considering my own and Butler's work side-by-side, I have come to believe Butler and I are writing with different agendas, different objects, different subject-matter in mind. There is here a déjà vu with the work of Gayle Rubin, famous for her essay "Traffic in Women" (see Rubin 1975; Rubin and Butler 1994).

In 1974 I gave a large public lecture at Ann Arbor. The lecture was a synopsis of the argument of *Psychoanalysis and Feminism*, which was in press with Pantheon and Allen Lane/Penguin, awaiting its publication date later that year. I was asked to meet a student of the eminent anthropologist, Marshall Sahlins; I did. This was Gayle Rubin. Though we have long ago lost touch, I kept much of Rubin's side of our subsequent correspondence. In one of the letters we exchanged, she wrote that our interests diverged—that hers were with the oppression of heterosexual supremacy where mine were with male supremacy. This distinction in our feminisms, she commented, had not been explicit between us.

I think that Butler shares Rubin's concern when she addresses my work. The different concerns of Rubin and Butler on the one hand, and myself on the other, have to date remained *inexplicit*. Yet much falls into place if I now read Butler's critique of *Psychoanalysis and Feminism* as an analysis and an attack on heterosexual supremacy, which contrasts to my concern with the position of women and "sexual difference." The psychoanalytic explanation of women and of homosexuality/heterosexuality are often confused but they are different problematics.

At the beginning of the 1970s I was writing from my practical and intellectual concern about what, at the time, we called the "oppression" of women. In the UK we saw "oppression" as an interim, umbrella term which could be used to signal we were not claiming women were "exploited" in the highly technical sense deployed by Marx. We needed therefore a different analysis and a different revolution. Calling ourselves "women liberationists," we were trying to construct this analysis on the political Left. Butler in her Symposium paper (2009; chapter 3 of this volume) and in her later *differences* article (2013) was critiquing my argument about women as though her field of enquiry—the abuse of homosexuality, and mine—the oppression of women—were the same topic. To have done this is to produce an interesting perspective, but to miss the point of my 1974 book. My insistence on the changing times is to underline a temporal distinction, so as to contextualize my argument. So: different topics in different times.

First things first: we need greater clarity on the term "sexual difference." Butler (2013) writes: "[Mitchell] is willing throughout, to identify sexual difference with masculine and feminine." At no point does *Psychoanalysis and Feminism* do this. The term "sexual difference" refers to Freud's (1933) essay on "Femininity." The line that demarcates where a woman can't be a man and vice versa. All the aspects the line can fall over—such as psychology, culture and anatomy are never in a reflective or one-to-one relationship with each other. "Sexual difference" is a distinction between women and men that as a distinction is universal in human societies: it is also a distinction without any specific or given content whatsoever. Instead, it finds its content in variable ways which relate to the fact that any society must place some prohibitions on sexual desire and murder.

Let me illustrate as best I can. All men possess a penis unless for one reason or another, they are castrated. But the important distinction is not between a penis and a vagina, but between the penis and the phallus. Everyone can at times lay claims to being phallic—for instance, the phallic "mother"; but possession of the phallus is ultimately not possible for anyone: some variable formulation of a universal prohibition on desire and murder stands in the way. Butler's perspective treats universal as if it means "fixed," but this is not a necessary corollary. I distinguish the universality of sexual difference from the variability of gender; concepts which operate on different levels of analysis.

Butler replaces my "sexual difference" with the term "sexual differences," thereby firmly confusing it with gender. Now "sexual differences" is an interesting concept, developed for example by Barbara Johnson (1998), for considering gender. But the use of the plural is never the same as the use of the singular as in *Psychoanalysis and Feminism* and my subsequent writings (2006). In the sense I intend by the term, it does not make sense to describe "sexual difference" as performative.

The universality of the mark of sexual difference and the flexibility of its expressions can be seen in the prohibition on incest and violence that organize kinship relations.

"Kinship" is a far more extensive network of relations than the family. It is, and always has been highly variable. For *Psychoanalysis and Feminism* the exchange of women, as one feature of kinship, was key. I realized that this should be specified as an exchange of rights in women. But overriding this was my concern about the "law" at the center of kinship arrangements: the prohibition on the highly variously classified sexual relationships that go under the classification of "incest" and the forms of killing which go under the classification of "murder." Other diverse laws, "Thou Shalt Nots" accrue to this law which is the nub of the Oedipus and castration complex and their effects on the uncertain construction of sexual difference—on which side of the line women and men in so far as their sexual/reproductive aspects are "normatively" supposed to stand—and never completely do. This theme is central to the argument of *Psychoanalysis and Feminism*.

Butler asks if we can use the terms "femininity" and "masculinity." *Psychoanalysis and Feminism* quotes Freud in its first section at length (27 lines, pp. 46–7) to establish this point which is a fundamental basis for the entire argument:

> It is essential to understand clearly that the concepts "masculine" and "feminine", whose meaning seems so unambiguous to ordinary people, are among the most confused in science ... Every individual ... displays a mixture of the character-traits belonging to his own or the opposite sex; and he shows a combination of activity and passivity whether or not these last character-traits tally with his biological ones. (pp. 46–7)

It is no offence to Eve Sedgewick's important work if we note that Butler in this context credits to her what is the sine qua non of Freud's life-long position. Heterosexuals are always homosexual and vice versa. This is accounted for by the use of the concept of bisexuality. Unlike "femininity" and "masculinity," bisexuality is a psychoanalytic concept.

Butler makes exactly the same shift from "sexual difference" (the mark that all societies make in a million different ways between the sexes) to heterosexuality which underlies Rubin's interest. She then ascribes a negative version of it to me—where it was never a feature of Freud's thinking, nor one I have invented for him in *Psychoanalysis and Feminism*. Butler writes of my argument about the conservation by sexual difference and "its ostensible corollary heterosexuality." A distinction is being read as a relationship. Though it can be taken this way, there is no such corollary in Freud nor in *Psychoanalysis and Feminism*. The contrary is the point of my argument: the object of desire is as wide as the range of human fantasy.

The Freud I used based his work on the fact that the sexual object, and hence its orientation, is always contingent—the sexual drive only seeks satisfaction however this satisfaction might be attained. Freud starts his *Three Essays on Sexuality* with perversions and shows that we are all perverse; he proceeds to claim the child (at the time (1905) officially regarded as "innocent of sexuality") is in fact what he labels "polymorphously perverse." As we have all been children and as our childhood persists in our unconscious life, we all continue as this. Homosexuality is not a perversion—it is an inversion of heterosexuality which is therefore an inversion of homosexuality. In everyday life, sexual orientation is indeed described within existing terms but the theme of Freud's work is to contest rather than abandon them. Freud's is a theory of the subject— the way in which that subject uses its particular parents will be highly various. There is a complex argument at stake about "identification" which certainly takes place and whether this or the bisexuality by which the person is driven is the more important when it finally comes to "object choice," a choice which will contain all the other apparently "unchosen" objects. The same is obviously the case for those parents' parents way back in time. This, indeed, is an aspect of "transmission."

Transgenerational Transmission

Judith Butler: Let's begin with one of the most basic propositions and consider what it implies for how we think about sexual difference, the unconscious, and the problem of generational transmission. This proves to be a fundamental notion for [Juliet] since, as she wrote in her 1999 preface, 'The superego, with its transgenerational transmission of rules and laws; the id, where drive representatives meet what has been repressed; the ego, which comprises countless other egos—all are concepts which offer a way forward into thinking about ideology as "how we live ourselves" as sexually differentiated beings' (Mitchell 1999, xxxi). I would like to focus first on the transgenerational transmission of rules. Mitchell insists that sexual difference has largely unconscious dimensions, that these unconscious dimensions are transmitted through time and across generations, and that there is a kind of stasis or "drive to stay put" that characterizes sexual difference understood in this way. If we focus further on what sexual difference is, we find that the following formulations are central: sexual difference has to be included among those phenomenon that "persists" and that remains "incommensurate with the real social situation." As a result, Mitchell tells us, "deliberate socialization is inadequate to explain the structure of sexual difference and the inequalities that always arise from it, despite the fact that there is enormous diversity of social practice..."

Although sexual difference is not exactly defined (and may well be something that maintains a tense relationship with definition, promulgating metaphors of various kinds), something about its operation is being characterized through a variety of means. It is a kind of persistence; it is "a kind of underwater tow" or, again, a "current" as she writes, "feminism seems to be rowing against a current that is ultimately the stronger force." She concludes here—still the new introduction—with the following remark: "conservatism actually seems inherent in the very construction of sexual difference—as though the difference itself has in its construction insisted on stasis" (Mitchell 1999, xviii). This conservatism is inherent in what Mitchell calls "the psycho-ideological living of sexual relations" and it is distinguished by the fact that "it is women...who become the ascribed repositories of that human conservatism."

Juliet Mitchell: I think "transgenerational transmission" is the nub of a real difference between us. Butler segues into sexual difference as unconscious, the unconscious as what is transgenerationally transmitted, and sexual difference as what I believe persists because of transgenerational transmission. She alleges that, for me: sexual difference has the characteristic of stasis, being unchanging, a permanence which is out of key with the present (or any present) social situation. It is true that I identify an intransigence of the position of women in society, and that this worries me. However the final section of *Psychoanalysis and Feminism* (to which she refers in her version in *differences*) is precisely dedicated to seeing if there might be a way through and beyond this unpalatable position in so far as it affects "sexual difference."

The final section of *Psychoanalysis and Feminism* uses Levi-Strauss to suggest an imbalance of kinship and class regulation for the working-classes that might mean an end to the sway of the former—a sort-of rewriting of Engels through a somewhat poorly grasped Lacanian psychoanalysis and (probably ditto) structural anthropology of Levi-Strauss. My concern here is that, like Butler, just as with the conclusion to "Women: the Longest Revolution" (1966) I wanted to find a way out of what my own argument leads to. But Butler is motivated by a wish to conceive a world without the appalling discrimination against homosexuality and I to imagine one in which the oppression of women is no longer "in-built" to human organization. We share our wishes; the tasks, however, although related, are not the same.

Beyond the divergence of our interest—Butler to homosexuality, me to sexual difference, there is further ground for our "non-meeting." Until she introduces Laplanche's theses of the implanting of enigmatic signifiers in the infant, Butler argues against the idea of transmission. I do not think we have a good or even good-enough understanding of how transmission works—but that it happens and that the good is transmitted with the bad, seems to me beyond doubt. My point is simple: however marked the progress—the vote, sexual freedom, equal pay—something prevents the realization of equality. At the heart of progress there is a deathly stasis or backward lunge. Of course, how something is transmitted and what is being transmitted are linked issues, but they are not the same issue. What today I would call the "inter-subjectivity" that underlies the clinically observable process of unconscious communication may be a sine qua non for this transmission of something that ought to have been eradicated but has not—the "oppression" of women. There is no answer (anyway, as yet) but there are a number of approaches to formulating the question of transmission.

It is relevant to our differences to place conceptualizations of gender in historical perspective. Butler's development of the concept of "performing gender" came 16 years after *Psychoanalysis and Feminism*. It was not that the "performative" (which at that earlier date we had known from Austen) had changed meaning—it was "gender" that had done so. For me "gender" and "sexual difference"—though certainly muddled up inside us—are not analytically the same. In the UK "gender" was introduced by feminism from the work of psychoanalyst, Robert Stoller (*Sex and Gender*, 1968). Early on it was most interestingly deployed by the sociologist, Anne Oakley (1972). However, "gender" in this use was too sociological for me. It implied society adds the construct "gender," which could be changed, to biology's "sex," which could not. For Freud there was never an equation between biology and psychology but nor was there a schismatic separation; biology was one important factor among others that humans relate to in some way or other. I later reviewed Stoller's work on transsexualism at length and had a subsequent interesting correspondence with him around this question until his premature death. Gender in the early feminist use also did not involve a consideration of sexuality and that too was why I would not use it. I changed my ideas about it when its meaning changed.

For me the change was exemplified by Joan Scott's (since self-disputed) use of gender as a category of analysis. Following Scott I thought that although "women" could be an object to analyze, they/we could not be an analytical category. As Scott so well demonstrated, gender could. Since that Pauline moment I have developed gender to refer to the lateral relations of siblings, peers etc. and retained "sexual difference" for the vertical intergenerational ones. Gender, the lateral, would seem to be more fluid and multivalent than sexual difference. I use "gender" then for the polymorphous possibilities and differences to which I had offered a fanfare at the end of "Women: the Longest Revolution":

> Any society will require some institutionalized and social recognition of personal relationships. But there is absolutely no reason why there should be only one legitimized form—and a multitude of unlegitimized experience. Socialism should properly mean not the abolition of the family but the diversification of the socially acknowledged relationships which are today forcibly and rigidly compressed into it. This would mean a plural range of institutions—where the family is only one, and its abolition implies none. Couples living together or not living together, long-term unions with children, single parents bringing up children, children socialized by conventional rather than biological parents, extended kin groups, etc.—all these could be encompassed in a range of institutions which matched the free invention and variety of men and women. (Mitchell 1966, p. 36)

Because Butler is talking about gender, her theory may reflect this great fluidity, and an absence of the potential conservatism/stasis that sexual difference brings to the arena. We now have a plethora of descriptions of the theatres of our minds; "femininity" and its many masquerades, "masculinity," could be performed for sure, but not "sexual difference" which means no more than that one sex is not the other.

The first section of *Psychoanalysis and Feminism*, "The Making of a Lady" part I, starts with a chapter that offers an account of the unconscious; this is followed by one on Freud's still (in 2014) rich and revolutionary understanding of sexuality. Chapter 3 explains masculinity, femininity, and bisexuality. The purpose of this arrangement was to demonstrate that sexual difference must be situated in the basic psychoanalytic concepts of an unconscious mind and a sexually driven body. Throughout the book it is made clear that of the concepts and terms used, only "bisexuality" belongs to psychoanalysis: "we cannot say what a woman is, only how she comes into being from a child with a bisexual disposition." (Freud 1933) Ditto a man.

In 1974 I presented a reading of Freud that was utterly contrary to the ego-psychology that dominated psychoanalysis in the USA. Jacques Lacan had not as yet hit American shores; his "return to Freud" emphasizing the unpalatable notion of the castration complex and penis-envy spoke to the depth of the problem of why women faced "the longest revolution." This is what Rose, at the Symposium of 2009, and today

Gayatri Spivak (in her Juliet Mitchell Lecture 2014) have perceived as the issue that was raised by my book of 1974. Something that despite all the forward moves—prevents women moving forward. For Freud this was recognized in what he observed as a "repudiation of femininity" with its passivity toward a man, by both sexes.

In 1966 when "Women: the Longest Revolution" was published in *New Left Review,* an editorial board member, Quinton Hoare wrote a scathing attack. My memory of first looking into this riposte was of having my breath taken away: Hoare was arguing that women, by definition, have no subjecthood. In countering his claim that the entire history of women had taken place only within the family and that women as such could not be thought about outside its terms, I stated that "not unless women are literally exchange products can they be *identical* with objects and property." Today the discussion has moved on well past these arguments—thank goodness! However, that I can still feel the impossible experience of thinking and acting as a subject while being analyzed as only an object is testimony, unfortunately, to something that persists.

Women, of course, range across all the other social categories with consequently very different effects. However, I still follow a classical line of Freud's that the position the bisexual girl takes up to become her woman self is to be the *object* of another's desire (initially, prototypically, her father's); this differentiates her from the position of the bisexual boy who to become his man-self positions himself as *subject* of desire. "Before" this and in a way that for my theses implicates siblings, forever after as well, both sexes have been both the subject of desiring the mother and the object of her desire. This pre-Oedipal position I call "gender." The person in their gender has subjecthood—the toddler is just insisting on it when it is threatened by separation from its mother if it murders or commits incest with its usurping sibling.

The Law

Judith Butler: We can accept, for instance, that there is an unconscious operation at work that seems to relay another time into this time, that we are not completely of the present, and that another scene acts upon us as we try to find our way within present time. But even if we accept this time-lag as constitutive of the psyche, it does not follow that we have to accept a universal set of rules or laws as belonging to that other time, or transmitted from that other time. Indeed, that other time may well be an historical time, the times that belong to prior generations, but that is not the same as saying it is the time of cultural law, of the paternal law, of the symbolic, or of the laws that are essential to culture. This structuralist presumption supplements the theory of the unconscious, but it is in no way presupposed by its operation. As Laplanche departs from Lacan, he calls into question the means and mechanisms by which the unconscious desires of the adult world impinge upon the infant; this impingement does not communicate an intact set of laws in clear and effective ways. On the contrary, these enigmatic signifiers become lodged in the psychic life of the infant and initiate the drives as both overwhelming and exciting (these are, in effect, the terms through which Laplanche reformulates the scene of general seduction; Butler pp. 20–21).

Juliet Mitchell: This is a misunderstanding; the law is the law of the definition and prohibition of incest. An effect of this desire and its taboo institutes sexual difference but there is no "law of sexual difference." I don't know what Butler has in mind by the suggestion that we should challenge unconscious communication. Does she mean we challenge the fact of its existence or challenge those thinkers who hold it is important? The first is like saying: let's challenge the existence of dark energy and dark matter; the second like saying let's challenge those who think dark energy and dark matter are important and work on understanding them.

Many psychoanalysts have tried different understandings of unconscious communication; I have found it particularly interesting in the psychoanalysis of groups. Many people have argued against the universality of incest prohibitions. But if we see that incest refers only to some forbidden sex then its universal presence and its forbidding seems highly likely. In a variety of ways societies allow and prohibit some killing and some sexual relations. There are *no* laws of sexual difference—the bisexual child is to take up a position in relation to these laws against incest and murder—the laws are the same. Their obedience (or otherwise) to those laws are the same: neither girl nor boy, woman nor man must commit incest or murder. From this misunderstanding comes what follows.

Butler contests my concern that a marker of sexual difference is transmitted down the ages and that I argue that the law from which it takes its always "unsatisfactory" effect—the law against incest and murder—is invariant. This suggestion often annoys people. There of course are only laws because there are what are constituted as "unholy desires." There would otherwise be no need for a law. These laws are that there are some people with whom sex is forbidden, there are some people whom you must not murder. In fact although I keep repeating it, it is a rather obvious claim—referring to nothing much in itself other than its very intractability. The law will always be expressed differently. Again with enormous variation (and frequent breaches) it leads to legislating against maternal incest and paternal murder. With all its different forms, this is,

I believe, an "invariant" stumbling block or small "spot" which will take various forms and be variously transmitted. The persistence of patriarchy is a formulation of these laws, but is not itself by any means invariant.

Against her own claim about the need to contest unconscious communication, Butler accepts that past time can unconsciously impinge on time present. There then seems to be some slippage from the individual historical to the mass historical. This is followed by the assertion that the past can enter the present but the laws cannot. Psychoanalysis claims that the child must fail to resolve, or resolve, never adequately the law against incest/murder and that this resolution/irresolution persists through life. The conflict between the desire and its prohibition in past Oedipal time (3–5 years for us) in the present time of later childhood or adulthood can be manageable or it can produce life-eroding symptoms (neurosis and psychosis) with which psychoanalysis works. We can transfer this understanding of the individual to the larger history but rather as something of a metaphor. This is why literature, art, mythology help construct the metapsychology of psychoanalysis—they apply the individual unconscious to the larger world.

Butler can accept the past in the present so long as it does not involve accepting that the law will be transmitted. However, the law and the desire that prompts it is why this past persists; can you have one without the other? Laplanche, whom Butler argues, is saying something different does not, I think, dispute the desire and the prohibition—only how the desire enters the child. The idea that the laws are transmitted in "intact, clear and effective ways" is supported by no-one.

Drive and Desire

Judith Butler: How we conceptualize the drives has everything to do with how we imagine what it is that drives convey. And what and how drives convey has everything to do with how rules may or may not be transmitted trans-generationally. I am not sure that drives can be effectively separated from the ideation, and that even the effort to define the drive is but a further instance of its operation. My wager is that drives do not loyally replicate the "messages" that initiate them; in fact, the messages, or signifiers, are inscrutable and overwhelming, and they prompt a set of displacements, so that drives, and sexuality more generally, take form through metonymic processes that are not easily foreseen or predicted. The trajectory of displacement is the trajectory of the drive itself. This is why, for instance, Laplanche insists that the drive is not constrained by biological teleologies, including reproduction. In a sense, there is no drive that preexists that metonymic sequence or, rather, there is no drive that is not transformed by the sequence it sets in motion. In other words, what is passed down or, indeed, communicated, is not the same law in the same form, and not the same law in a different form, and not even the traumatic force of law. Rather, what is passed down is a forceful impression, enigmatic and exciting, from an adult world whose libidinal communications are overwhelming and unreadable for the infant. That impression seems to carry a message, but only in encoded forms that remain indecipherable for the infant and child and remain so to some extent throughout adult life. (Butler p. 22)

Juliet Mitchell: This might be some aspect of Laplanche's work with which I am unfamiliar. None of it is what I understand by "the drive" as I used it from Freud in *Psychoanalysis and Feminism*. Drives only drive—they don't convey anything—they force the mind to work in order to avoid unpleasure. They are a hypothesis for a process that is observed but they can themselves only be observed in their effects. Drives are in conflict with each other and have representatives which are in conflict with each other: Sexuality and self-preservation; Life and Death.

As I understand it, Laplanche is talking about enigmatic messages which impinge and create desire in the recipient. I can see that he could dispute Freud's drive model (as many others have done) and substitute his model of enigmatic signifiers. A while back I was Laplanche's discussant at the Institute for Contemporary Art and I recall his delight when I said I saw him as the new Ferenczi—this would still fit. There is room on this earth for both these perspectives—but they shouldn't be confused. Butler uses Laplanche to explain transmission through the infant's puzzled reception and helplessness before the enigmatic signifiers sent out by its desiring parents (and others). I suggest that rather than an either/or proposition (this and not Oedipus) we should see this explanation as one of those both/and scenarios which are the hallmark of psychoanalytic theory. I think of "enigmatic signifiers" as on a par with other both/and accounts.

Rose cites Winnicott's case of a middle-aged man whose many analyses threatened to become interminable and useful but nontransformable because they never reached the fact that the man thought he was also a girl. We could continue with Winnicott's account to think both about transmission and stasis. When the girl is discovered through Winnicott hearing her penis-envy the patient agrees but thinks he will be thought mad; Winnicott answers that is it he, the psychoanalyst (in the transference, the mother), not the male patient, who was mad to hear the speech of a girl coming from a man. Together Winnicott and his male patient construct that his mother had wanted a girl baby—but the story doesn't end there. This girl-in-the-man lying on the couch makes one hell of a scene when the man-in-the-man confronts her. She also has never grown up. Winnicott also did not subscribe to Freud's drive theory—disputing in particular the death drive. I was not a clinician at the time of writing *Psychoanalysis and Feminism* so had no alternative source material as had Ferenczi and Laplanche. I could of course have used other psychoanalytic theoreticians for my feminist aims as Nancy Chodorow (1976) did to great effect a little later. When reading Butler's response to my work, it is important to remember the position I take (Freud/Lacan) is often absent from her critique. My concern is to use Freud and Lacan to show how we have to tackle what seems intractable within the oppression of women—the longest revolution.

Judith Butler: What propels the displacements of desire is less an effort to evade the murderous consequences of a prohibitive law than an effort to fathom a set of adult desires that have impinged upon, and formed, an internal structure of the psyche. The infant is unknowing and, indeed, helpless, in relation to these overwhelming and confusing messages relayed more or less unconsciously by the adult world. As a result, the sexuality that emerges, understood as a series of displacements from instinct, is a result of this helplessness in the face of the desirous adult world. The infant becomes an investigative theorist on such an occasion, trying to fathom the strange force and direction of his or her own impulses. The problem for infantile sexuality is not how to evade castration by punishment, but how to fathom a desire that is, from the start, already the desire of the other.

Theoretically, Laplanche's departure from Lacan in this regard implies a full critique of the paternal law, linked to the structuralist account of the exchange of women and the universalist premises of "culture." This view of the paternal law is countered by a conception of a non-gendered "adult world" that generates and imposes enigmatic signifiers on an infant who responds with both cognitive helplessness and incitation of the drive. As a result, primary unconscious and sexual messages are impressed upon the child (though "impression" may well be too soft a term). Moreover, those primary others whose desires are communicated through various practices are themselves in the grip of such messages (have themselves been incited unconsciously by such messages). The ones whose desires become the foreign and inciting elements in my own desire are themselves propelled by what is foreign and inciting, and invariably so. In this way, transgenerational transmission probably resembles Borges' story, "Circular Ruins" where one person discovers that he has his reality only in another person's dream, and that the same principle applies to that dreamer, whose reality is secured only in another's dream. This goes on for generations, without end.

Juliet Mitchell: Here Butler shifts what she has previously ascribed to the "drive" to "desire" where I think it belongs. However, reading this extract against my account of Freud does produce something quite divergent. Not, I think an unbridgeable gap but a really different explanation of what is going on. This centres on the concept of the drive.

The drive is an ineffable, mythological push forward (the life drive) and urge backward to stasis (the death drive). The drive is a hypothesis of Freud's, conjured up to explain phenomena within psychoanalytic observation and treatment: the psychic conflict. Laplanche suggests that instead of the drives being something hypothesized which drive us; they are established instead within us by the desires of the adults toward us. This is to change the terms—desires drive us. As I said, many analysts have more or less disposed of Freud's theory of the drives. Laplanche, however, is talking about something else—that we are driven by the desires of others. That may be so—it could happen as well. But in itself it does not to get rid of the notion of a conflict between the desire and the prohibition. Certainly, the neonate will not survive if there is no desirous adult to tend it; however to make the desires of others foundational of a drive changes the concept of a drive. Such a drive does not postulate, as does Freud's, that a drive forces the mind to work to get what the body needs and desires. I honestly don't know which hypothesis is correct or whether we still can't have both. In Butler's Laplanche the drive results from communication with its displacements, its translations but it is no less metaphoric, only somewhat more contemporary, than Freud's "mythology." And how Butler describes drives is how Freud/Lacan explain desire. Here for Butler there is apparently intergenerational transmission, so transmission is not the problem—only what is transmitted.

Certainly we are all "ungendered" a good deal of the time—but we are also gendered and sexually differentiated even, at times, in each other's dreams. As a working concept is "ungendered" that different from "bisexuality"? Butler's Laplanche does not need either any laws, or sexual difference. But in not needing these, I cannot see how it offers us anything with which we might begin to grasp the oppression of women. Indeed there seem not to be women. Perhaps the "unbridgeable" gap between Butler and myself and where I started this reply is that she is primarily concerned with developing an understanding of the way out of the abuse of homosexuality as read through sexuality and, while not underestimating this, I remain convinced that something else is going on for women. At least that was my focus in 1974 and still in 1999 and 2014. Is this why Butler and I differ?

Judith Butler: In Mitchell's chapter, "The Different Self, the Phallus and the Father," she writes, "Before it is born, the child is assigned a name and is son or daughter of...; it has to learn to fit into this already ascribed place. Whatever the child does, whatever the specific accidents of its individual history, all take place within the larger framework of this human order. It is within the Freudian 'unconscious' that the laws of this order speak" (Mitchell 2000, 391).

Later, she discusses why the father represents those laws that govern human society, and here is where she describes such laws as "essential to society." Even in the 1999 preface, Mitchell reconfirms her belief in such an underlying set of laws. She notes that object relations has underscored the importance of the mother "but was uninterested in any underlying laws." She worries as well about those Lacanian efforts to establish the mother in a "pre-Symbolic domain" and argues that both Lacan and object-relations fail to situate the mother "within the laws of the human order." If it is those laws that are supposed to be communicated to us through the stable and predictable mechanisms of unconscious communication, and if the unconscious can work only by translating and displacing any set of injunctions it may communicate, then we cannot rely on such a domain to validate the invariant rules of culture. We can only look to such a domain to find the series of invariant rules, spawned from translation and transposition, that follow the logic of the drive, that is, displacement along routes that are never fully predictable or expected. Of course, we have to be able to account for that recalcitrance, that undertow, that countercurrent that makes our efforts at social change so difficult. This remains a crucial, irreversible insight of *Psychoanalysis and Feminism*. But there is no reason to take that recalcitrance and countercurrent as a sign of the invariant laws of human society; why cannot that conservative undertow be precisely the drag of history, something communicated through the norms of kinship, norms that change, with difficulty, over time?

Mitchell throws down the gauntlet in the 1999 preface when she notes that Lacan's rereading of Freud "is in some ways more dismal for feminist politics than is Freud's original version." Without the super-ego, Lacan cannot give an account of change. Positions can be shuffled in relation to the problem of castration. Her challenge is to get us to return to the second metapsychology, over and against Lacan, but without subscribing to ego psychology (p. 26).

Juliet Mitchell: The whole thrust of *Psychoanalysis and Feminism* is to stress the invariance in the framework in order to ask how this might be tackled. Rose has got me completely right when she says of the 1974 book that I argue that "the analysis of the seeming intractability of sexual difference, and the vision for change were inseparable."

Elsewhere in her response to me Butler writes of "the changing tasks of psychoanalysis" and says, "We can surely ask how Oedipalization occurs within single parent families or within gay families, or indeed, in extended kinship networks where there is a distribution of parental functions and position. But to ask these questions is precisely to ask how psychoanalysis must by reformulated in light of changing kinship components." This is to misunderstand Oedipalization—the child of a gay couple or single parent is still not allowed to murder or commit incest. Psychoanalysis is about unconscious processes, the conscious and preconscious material of the clinic will change, different issues will have priority in Tokyo or Timbuktu and different psychic mechanisms will gain prominence. Unconscious processes will be understood differently with further work but this will not be an adaptation to changing social practices.

Unconscious processes come from two directions: there are initiating traumas that are the hallmark of the prematurely born human infant; and there are expressions of desires that arise within the context of premature helplessness with its utter dependence on others. Some of which must be not allowed, these non-allowances are highly variable as are indeed the practices of homosexuality. Sexual difference is an effect of invariant ones. We part company on our dominant concerns not on our attitude to the laws. We part too on our estimation of these laws and what indeed they are.

The Political Task

Judith Butler: If we agree with Mitchell that a return to questions of kinship and ideology are necessary, even a new examination of the "ideologies of the super-ego," and if we are to seek recourse to the theory of ideology through an Althusserian interpellation in particular, then it seems to me we have to be prepared for the fact that interpellation does not just happen once, but time and again, and that the chain of interpellative assignments forms something of the social history within which a particular psychic life is formed and lived. In this way, the infant is not born into a structure, but into a temporally reiterated chain of interpellations or assignments that have to be negotiated in time, that precede and exceed the life of the child, which may well, in the case of adoption, entail a series of geographical, if not geopolitical, and linguistic displacements. No single set of laws replicates itself in the unconscious of that infant, but only a series of transpositions and impingements, never fully conscious, demanding a process of translation that can never fully return to, or grasp, the powerful and enigmatic impression that prompts that largely unpredictable trajectory of the drives.

Juliet Mitchell: Despite its subtle complexity I think Butler's argument makes the political task too easy and too sociological. If the recalcitrance, the "under-tow" always pulling us back, is only the "drag of history" are we just to wait for the end of history?

Now I have written myself into what feels like an understanding, I can properly appreciate and thank Judith for her exciting contribution. Let me summarize; this time speaking for what I hope is Judith as well as myself:

For Judith, the multiple sexualities and internal and external differences can so displace heterosexuality which has hitherto been dominant, so that it just becomes one among many with no hegemonic status either in fact or the fiction about facts. With heterosexuality displaced, psychoanalysis (predicated in its Oedipal centrality) will have to adjust. Laplanche shows the way: we are the recipients of messages we barely can grasp but which set up our drives and desires and which have no absolute status; the transmission is itself a series of displacements without fixed content. These messages establish the drives within individuals so there need be no fixed laws of sexual positions.

For me: in 1974, I addressed psychoanalysis to ask why women, as women, were not perceived as subjects; why there was always a slipping back so that when all the socioeconomic conditions had changed so there was no need for women's oppression, it still persisted. In 1999 with 25 years of clinical work behind me, I *used* rather than *addressed* psychoanalysis. Looking at the question of my 1974 book in this brief new introduction, I thought that maybe the "solution" I had heralded in 1966 ("Women: the Longest Revolution")—sexuality as the weakest link breaking its bounds into multiple different sexualities and hence the end of the "exchange of women" forming the knot of kinship—had instead become part of the problem; as though the end result had been achieved prematurely and the real difficulty of women's oppression, avoided.

Today, as the rich and getting rich reproduce less and less, care-taking has replaced reproduction; as the one declines the other grows exponentially and it is still largely attached to women. For poor everywhere and for the wretched of the earth, reproduction remains central and care-taking is carried out by what for the rich are a declining species: siblings (mostly sisters) and female adjuncts (aunts, grandmothers...). Sexuality without reproduction for the rich may bloom as a thousand flowers, for the rest it is global sex-trafficking above all of women. Within each of the three structures of sexuality, reproduction and child rearing for women that I proposed in 1966, something holds women back and all affect and are affected by the economy where equality eludes them. So I still think we have to take on board the sexual difference of women and men particularly where that is established around reproduction (sex and death) even if the demographic transition to nonreplacement populations for some has displaced pregnancy and parturition on to child-care and socialization by others.

Butler believes oppression will change through the march of history, the slow change of kinship will get us there in the end. I think the problem is larger—at least for women. Feminism must take command of the theory and of the political practice. We need to grasp and remove the rock that blocks the river, to combat the undertow, and move forward.

Discussion Paper: Jacqueline Rose

Judith Butler started her presentation by speaking of the immeasurable significance of Juliet Mitchell's *Psychoanalysis and Feminism* for feminist theory. Let me begin by paying my own personal tribute to the book whose impact on my life and thought likewise is immeasurable. My first activity as a feminist in the 1970s had been a childcare campaign for the mothers of the Cowley workers industrial estate outside Oxford where I was a student. I returned from Paris two years later having read Freud, dismayed at what seemed to be the unbridgeable gulf between feminist activism and the language of the unconscious, a language which had been so profoundly enabling for me. For stating so clearly that feminism was not incompatible with psychoanalysis, Juliet's book—waiting for me as it felt on my return—was the book I needed to be written. It opened a door that has not closed since. I will always be in her debt.

As Judith's presentation makes clear, indebtedness can coexist with the profoundest disagreement. I am sure I am not the only person here who has felt privileged to listen to this dialogue—if that is the right word—between Judith Butler, key theorist of sexuality and gender, and this work which laid down the terms in which any thinker on these questions has to orient herself. I am sure too that I am not the only person in this room who might have felt at moments that the gap between these two thinkers is too vast to be bridged.

Let me try then to summarize how I understand this disagreement whose seriousness I have no intention, nor indeed, desire to downplay. I will try then to say where it might, productively, take us. Taking her reference from the Paris-based feminist group, *Psychanalyse et Politique*, Juliet Mitchell's aim in 1973 was "to analyse how men and women live as men and women within the material conditions of their existence" (Mitchell 1974: xx). Dissatisfied with a normative biologism that made sexual difference the unanswerable consequence of nature- or god-given arrangements, but also the feminist sociology that made femininity a crudely false social imprint on the mind, it was Juliet's intention instead to see how sexual difference entered the psyche and took up residence as an uninvited guest, unwelcome and yet accommodated in the deepest recesses of the mind. To understand the force of that process was to lay down the terms for its transformation—as Lenin said, you must always confront your enemy at its strongest point. To cite *Psychanalyse et Politique* again from the 1973 Introduction, psychoanalysis was to the "ideological and sexual fight" what Marx, Lenin, and Mao were to class struggle—the "only discourse that exists today on sexuality and the unconscious" (1974: xxii). While she was cautious about the analogy: "It has yet to be seen by all of us in the women's liberation movement," she continues, "whether the analysis of ideology is tied as closely to a logic of sexual struggle" (1974: xxiii), the impetus, notably as it emerges in the last chapters of the book, was clear. The aim was nothing less than the overthrow of patriarchy, whose kinship rules, etched into the hearts of women and men, had now been rendered redundant by the organization of work. The first point to make then is that the analysis of the seeming intractability of sexual difference, and the vision for change, were inseparable. The family was in its "slow death throes"; with the end of capitalism, "new structures will gradually come to be identified in the unconscious." In more than one sense, therefore, *Psychoanalysis & Feminism* was—and I use the term advisedly—a revolutionary book.

By 1999, something, for Mitchell, has gone astray. Let's leave aside for a moment the way the introduction to the new edition of *Psychoanalysis and Feminism* (Mitchell 1999) sounds at moments like a chastising of undutiful daughters or perhaps I should say siblings (from which I myself incidentally do not escape). The point Juliet makes in 1999 for today's debate, and for the brilliant intervention we have just heard from Judith, is key—that a focus on the instabilities of sexuality and desire in the feminist theory that came after, has risked dethroning the law of sexual difference from the mind, and with it, paradoxically, the possibilities of transformation which depended on first recognizing its force. It has introduced a type of short-circuit into the system—as if the variety of the sexual lives we lead, so much more openly now than then, and of the fantasies that accompany them, was being taken in and of itself to have dispensed with the question of the law. Unconscious instability became a type of bid for freedom, lifted out of the depths of the mind to do service for a better world. What this means among other things, I would want to add, is not just an idealization of the unconscious, but also that the gap between our unconscious and conscious lives has been closed.

I see everything Judith has said today in terms of this move, which is not to say that I think it is a fair, or perhaps I should say full, representation of that later thought (of course Juliet I consider you to have completely misread me, but that is beside the point!). But it is clear that for Judith, the inexorability of symbolic law, the idea that sexual difference is transmitted with such power into the unconscious, offers us all a grim unanswerable destiny. Hence, as I see it, the two central planks of her critique today. First, that the law is not an inheritance but an endlessly renegotiated process: the law does not take precedence, it does not necessarily predate desire, but can instead be thought of, as she suggests Klein for example thought of it, as the always imperfect response to our most dangerous inner drives. Secondly, that even if there is such a law, its transmission into the minds of new generations will be as precarious, distorted, reworked, and enigmatic as the logic or rather illogic of the unconscious. Freud insisted that unconscious thoughts were normal, but the processes of the unconscious were another matter: the unconscious does not, he said, "think, calculate or judge in any way." "I am not sure," Judith writes, "that what persists are…already formed legacies of the past into the present without translation, transposition, without some loss, some new twist or turn." And taking her cue from Jean Laplanche: "Messages arrive in enigmatic form, unscrutable." "What is passed down is a forceful impression, enigmatic and exciting, from an adult world whose libidinal communications are overwhelming and unreadable for the infant."

And if—as I understand it—there is no infallible transmission of the law, but rather—I quote again—"a powerful set of impressions," then no immutable sexual difference. In fact I will risk pushing it, if the transmission of the law is "invariably thwarted," then no law. We have entered—I quote—a "non-gendered adult world."

As I was reading this response, I have to say that there was something about the very force of the disagreement that struck me as odd. I have no doubt that Judith is right to point to the conservative positions occupied by some analysts toward homosexual parenting and other new organisations of sexual life—I would however want to stress "some," having met on Saturday a Paris-based woman analyst who signed a recent petition against the legalization of surrogacy in France but whose friend, another eminent feminist thinker and psychoanalyst, had refused to do so. In fact she had signed it not out of hostility to surrogacy—she was happy with the idea of artificial uteruses—but because she believed sexuality should not in any form fall under the remit of the law. Nonetheless the inherent conservatism of psychoanalytic institutions on these questions should never be underestimated. I also agree that the 1999 Introduction stresses the invariance of the law with renewed force.

But I fail to see in anything Juliet writes a tribute to or call for what Judith referred to this evening as "accomplished heterosexuality." What Juliet is talking about it, as I understand it, is precisely the law of sexual difference—that cruel, arbitrary, and unjust law— "unjust" as Freud explicitly termed it—which requires of all human subjects that at some point they reorder a polymorphous perverse bisexual disposition into a diacritic opposition between male and female according to an anatomical distinction which becomes as obligatory as it is a travesty of everything that went before, and that will subsist for ever in the unconscious. The basic Freudian premise, as I say to my students when I am teaching psychoanalysis, is that we all know, anatomically speaking, if we are a man or a woman, but, if the unconscious knows this as Juliet would insist, it also knows better. The moment is as fraudulent as it is inexorable. Or as the mother of feminist theorist Constance Penley put it to her as a child, you can be a boy if you can kiss your elbow. What happens next is anybody's business. You cannot legislate for the after-effects of any one subject in terms of their subsequent sexual lives. But that is not the same thing as to suggest—and this is the rub as I see it—that the multifarious experiences of sexual life have in and of themselves dispensed with the law.

Two extraordinary moments from psychoanalytic literature can I think make this point clear. The patient of D. W. Winnicott (1971) described in "Creativity and its Origins," who Winnicott analyzes as experiencing penis-envy toward himself from the position of an unconscious girl: "I know perfectly well," Winnicott observes, "that you are a man, but I am listening to a girl, and I am talking to a girl. I am telling this girl: 'You are talking about penis envy.'" "If I was to tell someone about this girl," the patient responds, "I would be called mad." Or the famous patient from Robert Stoller's (1973) case study *Splitting* who was convinced she had a penis. Wanting to acknowledge the force of that fantasy while disintricating it from the body sitting before him, Stoller observes: "Look, physically, biologically, according to a doctor's examination, there's no penis. Right?" To which the patient replies: "I don't know that I've ever been examined that closely" (1973: 13). What to make of these extraordinary moments if not to point to the stunning disparity between the inner experience of these two patients and the inexorable law of sexual difference to which they both do and do not submit themselves?

Judith is surely right therefore to point to the disparity between unconscious desires, lived social arrangements, and the injunctions of a heteronormative world. But perhaps you weaken your case by requiring that those forms of errancy and experimentation subsist outside or beyond the reach of the law which they endlessly contest. At the same time, as we indeed watch the law close around the subject in Juliet's thought, perhaps we should also remember how far her argument in *Psychoanalysis and Feminism* rested on just such a disparity between reality and norm: In her brilliant critique of Shulamith Firestone, for example, who, in order to read penis-envy in terms of power, had to make the mother powerless. Whereas, as you insisted, the mother is psychically all-powerful for the infant. Happily there is no perfect match between the law of culture and how we experience each other and ourselves. We cannot therefore dispense with either side of this equation. We have been presented with a false alternative. I would like to effect a reconciliation of sorts since it is, for me, in the gap between the law and its failing that transformation takes place.

On this, a correction vis-à-vis Lacan might be in order. As much as it refers to kinship, Lacan's account of the law stresses its inherent perversion as well as the utter fraudulence of anyone who claims to embody it (the law and the super ego are the specific focus of his Ethics seminar of 1969). He also lifted from Freud—although Freud never quite articulated it as such—that there has been no adequate account of the origins of law. Similarly, the emphasis on language as structure gave way in his thought to the idea of an inherent failing of meaning: meaning, he stated in Seminar XX, always indicates the direction in which it fails. That Lacan ignores the superego or freezes the subject into the laws of language—the one point perhaps on which you seem agree—is therefore, perversely you might say, something I would wish to contest.

A final point from my own recent thinking. I could not help but be struck by how closely this discussion of the transmission of the law, as the key issue for both Juliet and Judith, mirrors the preoccupation of Freud with the question of the transmission of his own Jewish legacy. To say Freud's inheritance on this matter was complicated is an understatement. Passionately affiliated to what he referred to as the "essence" of Judaism, at the same time he dissociated himself from the lore and language of his fathers, the injunctions of Holy Writ, and the nationalist aspirations of his people. I see traced out in this struggle, the same tension as the one rehearsed here today between recognizing the force of an inheritance and discarding or reworking the worst of its effects. Today Freud's difficult negotiation of that trajectory has become for me one of the most powerful and effective models for thinking about how to avoid the most dangerous components of ethnic and group identities at the same time as we have to acknowledge, so frighteningly in the new century, their continuing force. I would like to conclude by suggesting that we could do worse than to think about the persistence and undoing of sexual difference in similar terms.

References

Butler, J. 2009. "Ideologies of the Superego." A paper presented at the Symposium for the retirement of Juliet Mitchell. University of Cambridge, May 2009.

Butler, J. 2013. "Rethinking Sexual Difference and Kinship in Mitchell's Psychoanalysis and Feminism." *differences* 23(2): 1–19.

Freud, S. 1905. "Three Essays on Sexuality." In *Standard Edition of the Complete Psychological Works of Sigmund Freud*, Vol. 7, translated and edited by James Strachey. London: Hogarth. *SE7*, 123–246.

Freud, S. 1933. "On Femininity." In *Standard Edition of the Complete Psychological Works of Sigmund Freud*, Vol. 22. Translated and edited by James Strachey,112–135. London: Hogarth.

Johnston, B. 1998. *The Feminist Difference: Literature, Psychoanalysis, Race and Gender.* Cambridge, MA: Harvard University Press

Mitchell, J. 1966. "Women: The Longest Revolution." *New Left Review* 40: 11–37.

Mitchell, J. 1974. *Psychoanalysis and Feminism.* New York: Basic Books.

Mitchell, J. 1999. "Introduction." In *Psychoanalysis and Feminism.* New York: Basic Books.

Mitchell, J. 2000. *Psychoanalysis and Feminism.* New York: Basic Books.

Mitchell, J. 2000. "The Different Self, the Phallus and the Father." *Psychoanalysis and Feminism*, 382–298. New York: Basic Books.

Mitchell, J. 2006. "Procreative Mothers (sexual difference) and Childfree Sisters (gender)." In Browne, J (ed.). 2007. *The Future of Gender.* Cambridge University press pp. 163–188

Rose, J. 2009. A discussant reply given at the Symposium for the retirement of Juliet Mitchell. University of Cambridge May 2009.

Rubin, G. 1975. "The Traffic in Women." In *Toward an Anthropology of Women*, edited by R. Reiter, 157–210. New York: Mon Rev.

Rubin, G. and Butler, J. 1994. "Sexual Traffic." *differences* 6(2–3): 62–99.

Stoller, R. 1968. *Sex and Gender.* New York: Science House.

Stoller, R. 1973. *Splitting.* New Haven, CT: Yale University Press.

Winnicott, D. W. 1971. *Playing and Reality*, London: Routledge.

Chapter 5

Dialectic and Dystopia: "This might come as a shock..."

Robbie Duschinsky

Each of Juliet Mitchell's texts has an iridescent quality that allows us, as time passes, to see both particular passages and our world differently. Part of this quality is the result of a core question that animates each of Mitchell's books, and which keeps being reactivated by our concrete personal and political experiences even as circumstances are reconfigured: Why are inequalities between men and women so pervasive, even in movements that purport to be primarily concerned with equality? Mitchell has been described as a "conservative" by scholars such as Lynne Segal (2001) for even asking this question, since it seems to presume sexual difference as a single, natural, and immovable binary along reproductive lines (see also Grosz 1990; Chiland 2004). Yet in fact Mitchell's interest has been to interrogate why genital and reproductive differences between human beings, which in themselves imply little at all about how our lives or our society should be structured, have been figured with a significance that allows them to support the entrenchment and naturalization of inequalities.

In a tract for the Fabian society, asking what values a socialist should hold, Bernard Crick (1984, 13) proposed that "only equality is specifically socialist in itself; liberty and fraternity, however, take on a distinctively socialist form when the three are related to each other." This analysis helps highlight the commitment to exploring meaningful equality, which links together Juliet Mitchell's early work on liberty (exploring women's liberation for the *New Left Review*) and her more recent, psychoanalytic work on fraternity (exploring sibling relationships and gender). "This might come as a shock," Mitchell (2011, 2) notes, "but I never actually stopped thinking of myself as a Marxist." Drawing out this "red thread" of continuity between Mitchell's early and late work, this chapter will focus on her enduring attention to a particular moment in the dialectic: the emergence of the most minimal difference between subjects. An examination of the way this minimal difference is organized in relation to sex has been crucial to Mitchell's theorization of meaningful equality, as a set of relations along the lateral axis.

Socialism, Women, and *New Left Review* Syndrome

Mitchell is well known for her commitment to psychoanalysis and feminism as analytic frames and as movements. However, for Mitchell, psychoanalysis and feminism also need a third point as mediator and catalyst, to avoid quietism or fatalism. Here lies the importance of a socialist thread in Mitchell's analysis, which works to counter the way in which "the independent forces of conservatism in psychoanalysis and in feminism at times interlock and reinforce each other" (2002, 218). This is not to say that socialism is devoid of conservative currents. In particular, Mitchell's early work considered the lack of recognition of sexuality and reproduction as issues within socialist theory, resulting in an inadequate account of the condition of women. Whereas socialist theory had considered the role of production and socialization in shaping the modern subject, Mitchell was concerned that leaving reproduction and sexuality out of the picture had resulted in a neglect of the position of women, making women's liberation seem like a distraction from true socialist struggle and causing ongoing problems for female members of the socialist movement. Her conclusion was that "the liberation of women can only be achieved if all four structures in which they are integrated are transformed—Production, Reproduction, Sexuality and Socialisation" (1971, 120).

The iridescent quality of Mitchell's analysis means that it reads differently, though no less insightfully, today. The relations between socialism and feminism have changed a good deal since the early 1970s. Yet difficulties with placing reproduction and sexuality in socialist theory are played out on a new front, in the context of increased pressure on young women to walk the tightrope of showing themselves to be free, self-possessed in their desirability, "sexy but not a slut." Mitchell's concern for the effects of female members of a movement that treats women's liberation as a distraction from class struggle thus gains new resonance.

The renewed pertinence of Mitchell's reflections on the difficulties socialism has in finding a place for women can be illustrated with a contemporary case. The Socialist Workers Party is the largest far-left organization in the UK and a major political force within the Left—for instance, it was integral to the Stop The War Coalition, which staged a demonstration of two million people against British involvement in the Iraq war. In 2012, the organization received an allegation from a young female activist (W.) that she had been raped by Comrade Delta, a leading member of party, in repeated incidents over a period of six months. Rather than reporting the allegation to the police, the claim was dealt with by the Party's Disputes Committee, made up of friends and close colleagues of the accused. Comrade Delta was unanimously acquitted by the committee. Consideration of the case, as was usual for the Disputes Committee, took place in private, over four days; at the SWP Conference on January 5, 2013, the Disputes Committee chairman reported on the deliberations and decision:

> We heard from W and from Delta, who gave us two very different accounts of what had taken place in 2008 and 2009. We heard from and questioned a number of other comrades. They were people who had been brought as witnesses, either by W or by Delta. However neither of them were witnesses to the actual events...
>
> We didn't think that Delta raped W. And it was not proved to the disputes committee that Delta had sexually assaulted, harassed or abused W. We found it difficult to rule on these issues, because the versions of events differed substantially and there were no witnesses. The disputes committee didn't recommend any disciplinary action against Delta...
>
> We discussed, debated, considered, changed our minds, listened to each other, and then we came to the best conclusions that we could, to the best of our abilities, and it's on that basis that I put this report to you and to the conference. (applause)
>
> (transcript of the Disputes Committee Report to Conference, CPGB 2013a).

Members at the SWP Conference voted narrowly to accept the Disputes Committee Report. However, during and after the conference concerns were raised that the SWP leadership had mishandled the allegations. Sadia Jabeen spoke on behalf of W. during discussion of the report, explaining why she did not approach the police and relating the experiences of W. with the Disputes Committee:

> She thought that if she put a complaint to the party that it would be dealt with in line with the party's politics and our proud tradition on women's liberation. Sadly her experience was quite the opposite...She was questioned about why she went for a drink with him, her witnesses were repeatedly asked whether she'd been in a relationship with him, and you know, she was asked...about relationships with other comrades including sexual relationships. All this was irrelevant to the

case...She felt she was being interrogated and felt they were trying to catch her out in order to make her out to be a liar. She did not accept the line of questioning, saying "they think I'm a slut who asked for it"...she feels she's been treated as this non-person. The disgusting lies and gossip going round about her has been really distressing and disappointing for her to hear, and the way her own witnesses have been treated in Birmingham hasn't been much better.

(transcript of the Disputes Committee Report to Conference, CPGB 2013).

A second women (X) also presented allegations of sexual harassment again Comrade Delta. At the conference she spoke of losing her position within the SWP because "in many meetings and appeals to the central committee I was repeatedly told that I'd disrupt the harmony of the office" (transcript of the Disputes Committee Report to Conference, CPGB 2013a). After the conference, the Communist Party of Great Britain (2013) announced that "with the best will in the world, the SWP's Disputes Committee is clearly ill-equipped to deal with serious criminal charges. Such matters belong in the courts." Yet major figures within the SWP argued in defence of the actions taken. Addressing accusations of institutionalized sexism in their March Bulletin, the Central Committee of the SWP (2013, 10) responded that "historically the fate of women is tied to the fate of the working class. This is not about the working class leading a struggle on behalf of women or other oppressed sections of society. Instead it is within the organised working class that the mass of women find their power." Alex Callinicos (2013), a leader within the SWP and professor at Kings College London, specifically defended the procedure by which this "difficult disciplinary case" was handled, which "scandalously, a minority inside the SWP are refusing to accept." Callinicos urged recognition that "democratic centralism," the idea that the voting members of the party can produce a unity of opinion from which members cannot subsequently deviate, is "what our critics dislike most about us—how we organize ourselves—is crucial to our ability...to punch above our weight." Callinicos's defence was e-mailed to all members of the SWP, as well as published in the journal *Socialist Review*. Callinicos subsequently described those who have criticized the SWP as the equivalents of Perry Anderson and his editorial team at the *New Left Review* a generation ago—that is, Juliet Mitchell, Tom Nairn, and Robin Blackburn—who claimed to speak for socialism while diluting their commitment out of, Callinicos suggested, "political ambition" (cited in CPGB 2013b; cf. Matthews 2002). Callinicos termed this debasement of socialist commitment "*New Left Review* syndrome" (ibid.).

The mishandling of the rape allegations has prompted many members to leave the SWP, suggesting that the failure to adequately respond to the rape allegation was inseparable from wider gender norms within the organization. For example, the University of Manchester Socialist Worker Student Society disaffiliated from the SWP en masse. The author and SWP member China Mieville (2013) describes this crisis of legitimacy and exodus of members as "the biggest crisis we have ever faced," leaving the "party on the brink of political annihilation." In his resignation letter from the SWP, Ian Walker (2013) expressed concern that "party workers are being spoken to individually, and if they refuse to give a guarantee that they will never so much as mention the case again, they are being told they must leave their party jobs. Some have already gone, others may be going as I write." He added that "it may shed some light to learn that 'feminism' is used effectively as a swear word by the leadership's supporters...it is being used today against young, militant anti-sexists coming into the party. In fact it is deployed against anyone who seems 'too concerned' about issues of gender." The SWP incident was placed in broader context by Laurie Penny (2013). Writing in the *Guardian*, Penny identified that the mishandling of the allegation was one in a string of incidents that reflected not just sexism within the Left, but also a particular, characteristic response to and justification of sexism. She observed that "the past years have been dispiriting for anyone who believes that feminism should be at the heart of any struggle against oppression...women on the left, along with those brave men who support our fight against abuse and exploitation, find ourselves accused of being 'bourgeois media stooges' or, worse, police informants. To hear such ugly nonsense from people with whom you had expected to find common cause isn't just depressing, it's painful. Sexism and misogyny are by no means unique to the left, but the response is—the angry, self-justifying implication that little things like rape allegations against male leaders can be dismissed in the context of the 'wider struggle.'"

Twin Sisters

In discussions of her work by younger scholars, Mitchell's tale is often recounted: "I remember sitting at a table with all the men of *New Left Review*, and going round the table with people saying 'Well, I will think about Algeria', 'I will think about Persia', 'I will think about Tanganyika', as they then were, and I said, 'Well, I'll think about women'—and there was silence" (1995, 74). Mitchell went on to write *Women: The Longest Revolution*. As already mentioned, Callinicos has characterized such works by members of the *New Left Review* editorial team as a debasement of true socialism, motivated by political opportunism. An actually plausible and far more common reading has been that this story represents the moment that Mitchell's socialist concern with ideology and inequality were "quietly abandoned" (Lovell 1996, 322), as the lack of a responsiveness in socialist circles to the issues she was raising meant that Mitchell instead became drawn to pursue psychoanalytic rather than political lines of inquiry. Swindells and Jardine (1990) offer an acute and detailed account of the period, but they are not correct when they imply that having had the socialist door shut in her face when she raised the issue of gender, Mitchell simply went off to do something else. Mitchell's tale is, I wish to contend, better regarded as the recollection of a fracture within a continued socialist commitment, which has sustained an analysis of ideology and inequality in a new and evolving form. It is true that Mitchell did not flag her socialist commitments after the 1970s by "wearing sandals and burbling about dialectical materialism" (Orwell [1937] 2001, 208)—but even without caricature markers, the commitment remained and is visible in her texts. Its fracture did not degrade but reorganized the vitality of Mitchell's socialism as a spur toward an analysis of how the way in which sexual difference is configured in our society relates to the possibility of meaningful equality.

Mitchell and Oakley (1976, 381) came to perceive that "equal rights are an important tip of an iceberg that goes far deeper. That they are only the tip is both a reflection of the limitation of the concept of equality and an indication of how profound and fundamental is the problem of the oppression of women." The concept of equality alone was insufficient: it required supplementation and regeneration from sources beyond socialism. Reflecting on the shift in practice this required, Mitchell (2011, 2) has described her trajectory from protesting on the streets for "equal work, pay and conditions" to clinical and theoretical reflection as a movement "off to the hills to rethink what needs to be done politically. It is, as Adorno says, like putting messages in a bottle. I will remain in the hills until the streets, where there is still radical work going on, welcome me back." Mitchell's socialist interrogation of the meaning of equality, though little noted by commentators for decades, has not been left behind: "looking at it from the point of view of a clinical psychoanalyst, thinking as a feminist about its gendering, and, as a socialist and social scientist, reading about it historically and cross-culturally—for me all are interlinked" (2002, 218). Whether in a socialist, a feminist, or a psychoanalytic frame, Mitchell's work can be understood as animated by an interrogation of how differences between subjects—whether how much they are paid or their capacity to give birth—are recognized or misrecognized as signs of equality or inequality.

The topics of siblings and of place have served as among Mitchell's most privileged themes for rethinking the dynamics of equality. Note the appearance of both in *Women's Estate*, as Mitchell argues against either allowing socialism to subsume other oppressions or of giving up on socialism because of its inadequacy:

> The rejection of socialism by radical feminists is only the other side of the same coin as the over-hasty rush into revolutionary socialism by those left-wing sisters who have always hovered around the edges without a "place" within it—either theoretically or practically. The demand that "what we've got to understand is the relationship of Women's Liberation to socialism" is twin-sister to "socialism has nothing to offer us." (1971, 92)

Identifying the axes of identity and difference between these twin sisters, Mitchell suggests that radical feminism is utterly correct to analyze the role of sexism in positively forming our subjectivity itself, rather than solely its material conditions of possibility. Ideology shapes what we perceive and who we are as sexed subjects, not just the conditions and divisions of the labor conducted by men and women. This trains attention on the importance of experience, and "starts to grapple with the ideological and psychological oppression of women" (1971, 95). Yet Mitchell incisively observes that "the notion of undifferentiated male domination from the earliest to the latest times simply gives a theoretical form to the way oppression is usually experienced," and is therefore insufficient on its own. An undifferentiated "full presence" of patriarchy is interpreted by Mitchell as a conceptual trap, with no escape possible. Likewise, Mitchell observes that a socialist orientation is required because "the unequal distribution of wealth and ownership" provide the context "from which all lack of freedom and of possibility for realisation of individuality follows as night the day" (1971, 177). Yet to lose attention to the diversity of oppressions by, for example, presuming they run in ways neatly homologous or subordinate to class, serves to "evade the specific oppression of women and idealise the role of the oppressed" (1971, 94). To presume an undifferentiated "full absence" of patriarchy within a socialist orientation forecloses attention to the intersection of oppressions, including within organizations committed to the attainment of meaningful equality.

Dialectics

Fundamental to Mitchell's movement within/beyond socialism has been the theme of dialectical processes. A dialectical perspective, which explores the interplay of "sameness and difference, the subject and the other," was one she first encountered "when as a student I read Simone de Beauvoir's *The Second Sex* and discovered that I was, as a woman, the very site of a primal alterity" (Mitchell 2006, 35). The widespread and crude reduction of the "Hegelian dialectic" to a static and totalizing process of thesis, antithesis, and synthesis was an interpretation already ridiculed by Marx and Lenin as "wooden trichotomies," and utterly dismissed by Hegel, who specifically describes this "triplicity" as "nothing but the merely superficial, external side of cognition" (Hegel [1832] 2010, 746). A more acute interpretation understands dialectics as social ontology in which monism or dualism are necessarily precluded by the ongoing weave of our existence out of contradictory relations within and between phenomena. Hegel identifies that "the being as such of finite things is to have the germ of this *vergehen* [spatial transgression/passage of time] in their in-itselfness" (ibid., 101); the reason for this is that for a phenomenon or form of subjectivity to "positively" exist, it must establish determinate relations of exclusion and "negation" with other phenomena. However, this means that their very existence depends upon maintaining a contradiction with these other phenomena. This places contradiction and otherness, and therefore some degree of change and sensuous motion, into the beating heart of each "positive" phenomenon or subject: "The positive, since implicitly it is negativity, goes out of itself and sets its alteration in motion. Something is alive, therefore, only to the extent that it contains contradiction within itself" (ibid. 382). The implication is that where apparent unities or simple oppositions occur as characterization of human experience or relations, such characterizations require critical investigation as deflections or containers of contradiction (ibid. 416; cf. Jameson 2010).

Mitchell likewise affirms that "there is a contradiction *within* anything that can change and one *between* it and its relationships to other things" ([1974a] 1984, 91). Yet against any caricatured and crude "Hegelian demands" (1967, 82), the dialectic for Mitchell never reaches a moment of closure, beyond historicism and change. In *Woman's Estate* (1971, 90), she describes the concept of dialectics as positing "a complex (not dualistic) structure in which all elements are in contradiction to each other; at some point these contradictions can coalesce, explode and be overcome but the new fusion will enter into contradiction with something else. Human society is, and always will be, full of contradiction." Whether the idealism is familialist (Marie Stopes) or radical (Shulamith Firestone), Mitchell perceives that any "notion of transcending the divisions that plague our world," ending the dialectic in a closed shape, form, and established limitation, can only be illusionary; deploying the idea of "ultimate union no more solves divisions than it explains them" (Mitchell 1973, 125). To Mitchell the operation of this dialectical process of contradiction certainly did not imply, as it did for Engels, that universal laws of history can be discerned or exist. Yet neither did it imply that, because individual particularity would always be too singular, social and psychological processes could not be described (a stance reiterated in Mitchell and Spigel 2003). Like her colleagues in the *New Left Review* editorial team (e.g. Blackburn 1972), Mitchell was influenced by Althusser ([1962] 2005) for whom dialectics implied a world structured and disturbed by multiple determinate contradictions, each capable of affecting and partially constituting the others. Ideology would attempt to hide these contradictions but it could also further cause them; humans would experience these contradictions as bearable and unbearable everyday difficulties but could also organize using them to achieve social and political change.

The conviction that apparent unities within ideological formations can be interrogated as masks for determinate objective contradictions underpins Mitchell's analysis of femininity and the family as natural and inevitable in their apparent purity and unity: "It is the function of ideology to present these given social types as aspects of Nature itself. Both can be exalted, paradoxically, as ideals. The 'true' woman and the 'true' family are images of peace and plenty; in actuality, they may both be sites of violence and despair" (1966, 11). Mitchell analyzes how the femininity and the family can appear as images of natural purity, when in fact both are organized in concrete practice by disjunctures and contradiction:

> The contemporary family can be seen as a triptych of sexual, reproductive and socialisatory functions (the women's world) embraced by production (the man's world)—precisely a structure, which in the final instance is determined by the economy. The exclusion of women from production—social human activity—and their confinement to a monolithic condensation of functions within a unity—the family— which is precisely unified in the natural part of each function, is the root cause of the contemporary social definition of women as natural beings. (1966, 34)

Her analysis suggests that it has above all been "the woman's task" to sustain femininity and the family as ostensibly natural unities. She concludes that "women in the family are used to deflect the tide and implications of social labour" (1971, 161), masking determinate contradictions in society as merely the flaws of particular women who deviate from the imputed "truths" of femininity and the family. Yet, Mitchell also observes that precisely the strain of trying to contain the movement of dialectical contradictions within the monism of femininity and the family has resulted in the Movement for Women's Liberation, since "out of the increasingly numerous contradictions of their position, a sense of their oppression is growing" (ibid.).

Mitchell's analysis places the subjective experiences of women as both an expression and as a containment of contradictions in the objective relations between production, reproduction, sexuality, and socialization in society and the family. In this she is aligned with studies using the concept of "the dialectic of negativity as the moving and generating principle" (Marx [1844] 1977, 101), which have presumed that the trials of subjectivity will co-vary with objective contradictions—until this subject comes to recognize the contradictions it faces are common to a whole group of subjects, and in doing so achieves the possibility of freedom from them. Within this dialectical approach, the examination of contradictions at the level of subjective experience and at the level of objective conditions in society must be considered together, as part of the very same event occurring at two different levels in potential support or disjuncture with one another (cf. Williams 1973). In Mitchell's usage, this approach offered a method for investigating the interrelation between contradictions at the level of both the personal and the political, treated as one event—but not necessarily as mirroring one another. This agrees with Marx and Engels ([1846] 1994, 130), who argued that so long as there exists any form of division of labour "the productive force, the state of society, and consciousness"—each of which themselves will be threaded by contradictions— "can and must come into conflict with one another."

A dialectical movement in which contradictions within a particular form lead both deeper within and beyond it characterized both Mitchell's own *relationship* with socialism (which entered into a productive contradiction with feminism) and her *analysis* of the position of women under patriarchy (as masks and containers for ultimately unbearable contradictions between production, reproduction, sexuality, and socialisation—as the four bases of sexism in society). This was concerted. From the time of 'Women: the Longest Revolution," Mitchell (1967, 82) insisted that her work could not be understood if readers were to enact any "separation of methodology from content. I consider that the two are correlatives"; indeed, perhaps the only accurate comment in Hoare's (1967, 79) vituperative critique of Longest Revolution is to note that Mitchell's "method is more than a method—it demonstrates her whole ideological orientation." Precisely a combination of a dialectical relationship with socialism and a dialectical analysis together led Mitchell to integrate socialist analysis with further insights from feminism and from a further intellectual movement, psychoanalysis.

Despite what she perceived as the degradation of psychoanalysis in normalizing therapeutic practices, Mitchell discerned that "the last thing Freud meant this to be was the adaptive process prevalent today. He saw psychoanalysis as revolutionary, shocking, subversive—a plague that would disrupt society" (1971, 167). She emphasized Freud's ([1933] 2001, 116) claim that "psychoanalysis does not try to describe what a woman is—that would be a task it could scarcely perform—but sets about enquiring how she comes into being," pointing out the potential value of an analysis of unconscious processes for making sense of how gendered inequalities can remain entrenched even within institutions and movements bent on social change in the name of equality. Mitchell ([1974c] 1984, 228) argued that "opposition to Freud's asymmetrical history of the sexes...may well be more pleasing in the egalitarianism it assumes," but it neglects to "realise that it was exactly the psychological formations produced within patriarchal societies that he was revealing and analysing." Looking back, Mitchell (1999a, xvii) has explained that "psychoanalysis seemed to offer some way into the question of how, along with social changes, something persists that is incommensurate with the real social situation," which organizes "the structure of sexual difference and the inequalities that arise from it." That is to say, "if equal rights are accepted in principle, what is the stone in the stream of progress? What obstacle prevents the move forward to equality between what was then the sexes, and now is gender? The turn to psychoanalysis was to think through that question" (1999b, 186). The appalling vibrancy of the unconscious, in which the "the logical laws of thought do not apply...and this is true above all for the law of contradiction'" (Freud [1933] 2001, 79), meshed well with Mitchell's existing critique of monism or static dualism within human experience and social structures. In Freud's ([1933] 2001, 176) analysis, "dialectical evolution" from contradiction to closed synthesis is certainly no "natural law" dominating all of human life: within human development he identifies a disjuncture between early life—preserved in unconscious processes in which all the various "contradictory" reactions to experience survive—and later development and conscious thought in which "the power of synthesis" is stronger ([1938] 2001, 229; see also Milner 1969, 241 and Green 1999).

In her book opening a rapprochement between *Psychoanalysis and Feminism*, Mitchell (1974b, 402) would emphasize again: "the principle of dialectics is contradiction, not simple unity: elements contradict one another, resolve themselves, join together, and enter into further contradictions with other aspects—any 'unity' is a complex one containing contradictions." In her later work, as the recourse to psychoanalytic reference points became more overt and to socialist reference points less frequent, Mitchell would not abandon this use of a commitment against monism or static dualism as an tool for analyzing practices and phenomena. In particular, from *Psychoanalysis and Feminism* onward, this analysis has been framed as a discussion of how a "minimal difference" is founded and structured. Mitchell's attention to "difference" is a far cry from vague notions of social diversity; the term comes—probably through Marx, de Beauvoir, and Lévi-Strauss—from a specific moment within the dialectic, a moment of emergence, and recognition, which "negates the simple, [and] thereby posits the determinate difference of understanding" (Hegel [1832] 2010, 10, 535). Specifically, for Mitchell, attention to "minimal difference" orients analysis to the movement that must found and structure any inhabitable subjectivity and which is denied in ideologies and fantasies of the achievement of simultaneity and full unity—such as that which may at times animate the SWP's "democratic centralism," in which the voting members can produce a view for the party that fully binds its members. For it is, Mitchell (2000, 312) insists, only through some degree of acceptance of the "play of presence and absence, existence and non-existence" that our lives and encounters with others are bearable and sustainable without the deployment of neurosis or psychosis to block or circumvent what we know or feel. This agrees both with Hegel and with psychoanalytic accounts of symbolisation as requiring loss; Lacan ([1953] 1977, 69), glossing both, claims that any form of individual or social subjectivity "without dialectic" can only be a "delusion," whether of a form "fabulous, fantastic, or cosmological; interpretive, demanding, or idealist." A person or a group may long for the plenitude of full unity, or to retreat into full nothingness; in fact these longings are, Mitchell (1983) argues, the precise terrain that distinguishes psychoanalytic inquiry. Yet she perceives that to achieve or inhabit the object of such longing is not possible "without in the process setting in motion its own dissolution" in our mixed-up and differentiated world—except in phantasy, or symptom, or mystical experience or death ([1974a] 198, 106). As Mitchell ([1982] 1984, 293) explains, "'Oneness' is the symbolic notion of what happens before the symbolic; it is death and has to be death." The reason for this is "the necessity of incompleteness" in our lives; as a result, plenitude "would be omnipotence—the concept of God is the concept of total fullness" (1988, 82).

    A sustained example of these processes for Mitchell, from her early to her more recent writings, relates to the dream of simultaneity and full unity associated with the feminist discourse of "sisterhood," which have in part been animated by "a love of sameness" (2006, 39). While fully acknowledging that "sisterhood can undoubtedly be a relationship of solidarity and support," Mitchell and Oakley express particular concern that the concept of "sisterhood" has worked against attention to other forms of oppression, such as class and race, within the feminist movement:

> When the present phase of the women's movement established itself in the second part of the sixties, there was a need for a unifying ideology while ideas were being worked out or rediscovered. "Sisterhood" served the rhetorical purpose of political under-development; it was a useful rallying-cry. But its implications were not thought out and it seems to us now to mask both an absence of any real unity beneath it and to ignore the highly problematic relationships that in itself it implies. We do live in hierarchical world; the women's movement does not just combat structures of dominance, it is also surrounded by them and embedded in them. (Mitchell and Oakley 1976, 12–13)

Mitchell (1986, 44–5) recalls that "with torturous arguing in the early days, we tried to see whether we could call ourselves a class, a caste, a social group, and so on. The point it that, calling ourselves "sisters" operated effectively as a polemic against the hierarchies between men and women and among women. However, it did so in a way which risked underestimating the reality of these hierarchies, through a "polarity that disguised other distinctions by the comprehensive, all-embracing opposition" of sisterhood and patriarchy. In this way, "we helped to produce the ideological notion of a 'classless' society," which has subsequently been so important to neoliberal ideology.

Siblings and the Lateral Dialectic

Through an investigation of hysteria, Mitchell came explicitly to a conclusion already present in latent form from her work in the 1970s: that sibling relationships are an integral (and neglected) site for understanding the social and the psychological relations that organize sex into an entrenched absolute difference. Indeed, "recognition of siblings as the same but different seems to me to be the Ur, or primal situation, that underlies the particular problematic of sameness and difference" (Mitchell 2002, 227). The reason for this, Mitchell proposes, is that the "sibling is the concrete embodiment of a general condition in which no human being is unique—he can always be replaced or repeated by another" (2000, 26). This substitutability and displacement includes within it, from the very start, the possibility of the absence of the subject—a possibility that is denied in hysteria, in which the lateral other is phantasized as a repetition and extension of oneself.

Lacan ([1956] 1997, 179) had asked "Can we now spell out the factor common to the feminine position and the masculine question in

hysteria—a factor that is no doubt situated at the symbolic level, but perhaps isn't entirely reducible to it? It concerns a question of procreation."
Mitchell specifies this link between hysteria, procreation, and imaginary
forms that unsettle symbolic thought, offering a new interpretation of
the "primal scene" to which Freud assigned such importance. In doing so
she deploys her ongoing attention to reproduction—criticized by theo-
rists such as Segal (2001) as crude gender essentialism. In fact, Mitchell's
perspective is subtle, firmly eschewing both "biological determinism"
and "socialisation" theories. Mitchell's analysis suggests that "biological
femaleness and psychic femininity in certain but by no means all situations are co-incident. Even in these instances we should remember that
there is never a perfect fit" (1988, 88–9). This perspective leaves open
the possibility of attending to "the way the anatomical male/female data
(with all its uncertainties) is mentally lived; the way the physical data, the
clitoris/vagina/penis, is phantasized and experienced; the way these are
lived in people's heads and in their experiences" (1973, 131). This subtly
allows Mitchell to identify the fantasies of the primal scene and parthe-
nogenesis (the birth of another exactly like oneself from oneself), which
address the question of how difference occurs or does not occur within
the reproduction and birth of new identities. This question, Mitchell
insists, is *shared* by men and women, since "giving birth is no more psychically gendered than is dying. It is, however, actually gendered—as
is having a penis, which, because it can be cut off, can also represent
the annihilation of the subject" (2000, 200–1). Since reproductive intercourse between the parents "is a perfect image for an originary absence
of the subject at the very place where he comes into being—we are not
present at our own conception. It is, however, the catastrophe of the sibling displacement which occasions a retrospective imaginary perception
of this 'unimaginable' event. Hysteria protests this displacement, this
absence of the subject" (Mitchell 2000, 24).

Mitchell suggests that, for both sexes, themes of sexual and parthe-
nogenic reproduction as well as death predominate in the experience of
hysteria, because each is a fundamental site that can be used to "represent the annihilation of the subject" (2000, 200–1). This potential for
an experience of annihilation in the threat of substitutability and displacement, Mitchell theorizes, is a threat that every subject must either
surmount or try to evade in hysteria and which is necessarily evoked by
the potential for a sibling who is not merely an extension of the subject.
Whether through the advent of a new sibling, a potential sibling, or the
intrusion into mother-baby of the needs and demands of an older sibling,
there appears "a black hole where we thought we stood" (Mitchell 2003,
42). Together with the parent–child vertical axis, the horizontal axis of

possible siblings draws out the dimensions of a frame within which every subject is established in a matrix of relations of similarity and difference. Perpendicular to the dialectic through which a child emerges from a relationship with an adult caregiver, in *Madmen* Mitchell therefore identifies another horizontal dialectic in which "the minimal difference between brothers and sisters is the difference that must be socially established" (2000, 324–5). The idea of an identity which could be a self-enclosed point is a necessary phantasy but is not a sustainably inhabitable form of subjectivity, Mitchell proposes, because it is precisely through the matrix of relations along the vertical line and the lateral line that we first find our place in the world:

> The sibling experience organises narcissism into self-esteem through accepted loss—through a mourning process for the grandiose self, the "death" of His Majesty the Baby. This is the necessary acceptance that one is ordinary, which does not mean that one is not unique—just that all those other brothers and sisters are also ordinary and unique. Without this gradual and never fully established transformation of the self, the distress and disruption of the anti-social child or the maladies of madness are on the cards. The shock of the sibling trauma will also be repeated and have to be reworked through in any future event that displaces and dislodges a person from who and where they thought they were. (Mitchell 2003, 205)

To restate Mitchell's analysis of the threat of sibling substitutability and displacement for the subject in explicitly dialectical terms: any point occurring within our differentiated world is, regardless of whether we want to conceptualize it as self-contained, already and irreducibly situated by its relationship with others outside of it. Whether they like it or not, their dialectical relationship means that siblings "hinge on each other" (Wandschneider 2010, 35). For this reason, the human who wishes to be a simple and totalizing point can only ever do so in phantasy, since the world will continually provide experiences of troubling continuity and contradiction from and with others in the world: the single point, as Hegel ([1832] 2010, 100) says, is inexorably and faced by "the transition as it occurs and has already occurred into the line." A parallel dialectic occurs in relation to time, framed as birth order on the lateral axis. The subject understood to come "first" is not independent and outside of dialectic if it stands in relation to a potential second, even if that second is yet to appear. The first must negotiate a loss of narcissistic primacy. The second (and any subsequent additions) will be subject to a different but parallel task in trying to establish itself as an identity with respect to others, including at least one who antedates her. To overlay the dynamic of birth-order and the moments of the dialectic directly: "Because the first or the immediate [the first-born] is the concept in itself or implicitly [as 'the Baby'], and therefore is the negative also only implicitly [because the next child may only exist as a possibility], the dialectical movement in it consist in the positing of the difference that is implicitly contained in it [learning of difference, grieving for parthenogenesis]. The second [child] is on the contrary itself the determinate, the difference or relation [faced by always being 'the Baby' in relation to an older 'relation': the sibling]; hence the dialectical moment consists in its case in the positing of the unity contained within it [and the younger sibling has to find its identity within a relationship coeval with its birth]" (Hegel [1832] 2010, 745). In particular, as Mitchell ([1964] 1984) observes of Heathcliff in her commentary on *Wuthering Heights*, the child loaded by their caregiver as a replacement for or in the shadow of a dead sibling has among the more acute and rocky forms this task can take (see also Guntrip 1975). Even the only child must negotiate the issue of substitutability and displacement, and Mitchell's analysis agrees with that of Klein (1932, 73) that "an only child suffers to a far greater extent than other children from the anxiety it feels in regard to the brother or sister whom it is forever expecting…because it has no opportunity of developing a positive relation to them in reality."

Attention to sibling relations as a site for the negotiation of sameness and difference helps Mitchell identify why genital and reproductive differences have been figured with a social significance that allows them to support the entrenchment and naturalization of inequalities. Unless the subject is provided with the symbolic and imaginary resources to negotiate their place within the matrix of vertical and horizontal relations, the threat posed by the difference comprising the lateral axis remains active as a destabilizing trauma. Then genital and reproductive differences are picked up or suggested as symbols to staunch the trauma of substitutability and displacement, which provides an impetus for sexual oppression, which will take different forms depending on culture and context. Mitchell (2003, 219–220) argues that "when the child is overwhelmed by the trauma of one who, in the mind, was supposed to be the same as itself inevitably turning out to be different, it finds or is given ways to mark this difference—age is one, gender another…The cradle of gender difference is both narcissistic love and violence at the traumatic moment of displacement in the world. Gender difference comes into being when physical strength and malevolence are used to make the sister as lesser" (2003, 219–220). When the symbolic and imaginary resources are available from adult caregivers and from society to allow each subject a recognized and intelligible place, with sufficient meaning and dignity, then genital and reproductive differences are registered and given social meaning. However, they do not need to be deployed in warding off the traumatic moment of lateral displacement though a virgin/whore dichotomy and forms of sexual oppression and violence: "When this recognition is missing then either idealising love or demolishing hate or a love without boundaries (incest) or a hate without boundaries (murder) become rampant and social relations predicated on equality cannot be established. De Beauvoir's thesis on men and women in *The Second Sex* now sounds to me like unresolved sibling relations" (2003, 132). Though Mitchell is not fully clear on the particular conditions that would lead to incest as opposed to murder when trauma on the lateral axis is not contained, her overall point is that the unbound sibling trauma instigates unbounded behavior, whether idealizing or callous—or both.

When oppression is reduced to vertical axis, such important dynamics are missed. Mitchell (2006, 36) notes that "our explanation of parental abuse rests on an assertion of how the abusing adult was previously the abused child—vertical explanations. [Yet] in England the most prevalent abuse of all is older brothers to younger brother or sister." A parallel can be drawn with the SWP Disputes Committee, which reported that they decided to assess the rape allegations of W. against her comrade Delta themselves—party big brother against younger sister—rather than passing the matter to the police because of concern for the oppression W. would experience if she took her case to the patriarchal state legal system. To the extent that meaningful recognition of each other as the same but different is absent within socialist organizations, Mitchell (1971, 84) reports, the result for women is likely either to be a sham of "respect" or else something more overly malevolent: "where socialist groups have apparently 'respected' the position of women, the 'respect' has had all the implications of paternalism and mystification with which its meaning in capitalist society is redolent. Again, as in contemporary society, where 'respect' is absent, thuggishness takes its place: the wife and the prostitute."

It must be insisted, however, that what Mitchell means by "recognition" on the horizontal axis is quite distant from much contemporary usage, for example in the work of Axel Honneth (1996), in which Hegel is read as suggesting that difference—including sexual difference—can be reconciled by respect and understanding between peers (see McNay 2007). Mitchell's use of the term "recognition," throughout her writings, has always highlighted the need to dig beneath formal recognition of equality to achieve the meaningful equality, which requires attention to social and economic inequalities and to differences between and among men and women. Her "socialist...perspective suggests that 'equality' in capitalist society is based on class inequality; in a classless society there will still be differences or inequalities, inequalities between individuals, strengths or handicaps of various kinds. There will be differences between men and women, differences among women and among men; a truly just society...would take these inequalities into account and give more to he who needed more and ask for more from he who could give more. This would be a true recognition of the individual in the qualities that are essential to his humanity" (1976, 397).

Mitchell's concept of "recognition" also highlights the importance of the external framework within which lateral encounters are folded and situated. In her earlier writings (addressing equality primarily in relation to liberty), this external framework is necessary because any adequate "recognition" along the lateral axis is likely to require more redistribution, collective provision, and curtailment of the capacity for exploitation than society currently employs. In her more recent work (addressing equality primarily in relation to fraternity), Mitchell uses the figure of the mother distinguishing between siblings as equals, but as different (for example in their capacity one day to gestate a child), to depict a form of recognition modeled on seriality and space: "one, two, three, four siblings, playmates, school friends...tinker, tailor, soldier, sailor. There is room for you as well as me—something of which the hysteric in all of us has no cognisance" (2003, 44). In contrast to any notion of recognition as reconciliation through respect and understanding, Mitchell's attention to the external framework of recognition gives her a container in which hate and conflict can be acknowledged and have a place. She firmly criticizes as a form of theoretical repression and as unproductive any perspective that sees the possibility of lateral relations reconciled and devoid of conflict, including "Hegel's perception of the sister-brother relationship as ideal because of its closeness without sexuality" (2003, 232). Whereas Hegel ([1807] 1977, §457) suggests that "between brother and sister" lies a relationship, outside of dialectic or other social relations, in "a state of rest and equilibrium" in which "they do not desire one another," Mitchell's analysis treats the sibling trauma of substitutability and displacement as directly tied to a dialectic of sex and violence and love, and as a paradigm of later lateral relations outside the family. The materialized, embodied aspects of the psychical dynamics of sibling squabbles and affection are also always described by Mitchell: in this, her account of the sibling dialectic is distant from Hegel's tendency to abstract conflict from its sensuous and physical dimensions.

Mitchell theorizes the sibling trauma of displacement and substitutability as a black hole within subjectivity, a disappointment with qualitative difference to which the first response is hate and sexual aggression; this agrees with Freud's ([1915] 2001, 139) claim that "the relation of hate is older than that of love" as the subject registers difference, because this difference is only registered on the occasion of frustration. Yet Mitchell argues that it is not a problem that difference is first recognized in hate—if this hating subject acknowledges the other as discrete from the subject, with their own place within the relations that tie them together: "hate for the sibling enables the first move to be made: I hate you, you are not me, is the precondition of seriality" (2003, 53). The concept of seriality has two components: it is "the unity of these moments, of continuity and discreteness" (Hegel [1832] 2010, 154). One component of seriality is continuity—all the units are the same in some relevant sense, and as such are commensurable and can be recognised together. Another component is discreteness—each unit is separated off from the others as having a meaning, even if this meaning is partly shaped by its context in continuity. Two takes its meaning in part from one, but is irreducible to one, and both can be situated within the frame of integers, though this frame does not fully capture their possible senses and uses. To deploy the configuration of continuity and discreteness of seriality is a new and, I think, ingenious move within social and political theories of difference and equality. Each subject takes its meaning in part from another, but they are irreducible to one another, and each can be situated within frames of recognition, though these frames are always potentially reversible and do not fully capture any subject.

Part of the concept of seriality situates the differences between subjects as a matter of quantity, since they partially exist in continuity. Yet each subject is also discrete, with properties that cannot be assimilated to mere continuity and rather mark some degree of qualitative difference. Siblings may be situated on the continuum of age, but this does not capture their possibilities: the continuum of age variously means that some can stay up that bit later, some can bear children, and some can drive a car. As Marx ([1867] 2011, 338) notes, any dialectical perspective must acknowledge that "quantitative differences beyond a certain point pass into qualitative changes." The dimension of sameness will under some conditions be disrupted by some "becoming-other that interrupts gradualness and stands over against the preceding existence as something qualitatively other": for instance, in the perception of those who are in some sense the same as oneself, "every birth and every death, far from being a protracted gradualness, is rather its breaking off and a leap from quantitative to qualitative alteration" (Hegel [1832] 2010, 322). Mitchell's concept of recognition, symbolized by the mother organizing sameness and difference and privilege and future reproductive capabilities among her children (the Law of the Mother), does not attempt to reconcile these qualitative differences and retains a place for the conscious and unconscious conflicts inherent to qualitative differentiation. Rather, it provides a framework within which conflicts become both manageable and productive. A framework of recognition is set out by the Law of the Mother in which lateral dynamics such as differentiation and envy are not experienced or enacted as annihilating, and a meaningful place can be found in "who can stay up latest, have which piece of cake and survive the murderous rivalries to win through to sibling and peer love, a law allowing space for one who is the same and different" (2003, 52). Mitchell's account therefore grants no quarter to any tendency to end contradiction and activism: "Rhetoric and anger have their place—[and] that place is within political strategy" (1971, 163). Since she perceives that "there has to be conflict somewhere" (1988, 87) within any social relations, Mitchell criticizes claims to have ended social contradiction between peers as themselves an ideological strategy for managing relations along the lateral axis.

Dystopia and the Lateral Axis

One of the first claims of *Siblings* (2003, 4) is that "the sibling, I believe, is the figure which underlies such nearly forgotten concepts as the ego-ideal—the older sibling is idealised as someone the subject would like to be." Freud introduced the concept of the ego-ideal in *On Narcissism*. There he suggested that, as the child grows up, he has to leave behind any ideal of perfection he had sustained in infancy: "he is disturbed by the admonitions of others and by the awakening of his own critical judgement, so that he can no longer retain that perfection, he seeks to recover it in the new form of an ego ideal," an image of who the subject should be ([1914] 2001, 94). Freud conjectures that there is some "psychical agency which performs the task of seeing that narcissistic satisfaction from the ego ideal is ensured and which, with this end in view, constantly watches the actual ego and measures it by that ideal... recognition of this agency enables us to understand the so-called 'delusions of being noticed' or more correctly, of *being watched*... A power of this kind, watching, discovering and criticising all our intentions, does really exist. Indeed, it exists in every one of us in normal life" ([1914] 2001, 95). In *Nineteen Eighty-Four*, Orwell describes Britain in a dystopian future in which the ideology of the state is Ingsoc, a contraction of "English Socialism." Under this system, "in the eyes of the Party there was no distinction between the thought and the deed." With this distinction suspended, the intrasubjective dynamic between ego and ideal and persecutory agency can be elaborated for the reader, to the extent that one is captured by the novel and subjected to the party, as a form of social organization.

In the opening pages of the book, Winston Smith describes how "you had to live—did live, from habit that became instinct—in the assumption that every sound you made was overheard," and in which, always and inexorably for any member of the party, "Big Brother is watching you" (Orwell 1949, 6). Panoptical surveillance works to ensure not only outward conformity, but inward and unthinking allegiance. Any internal dynamism—whether triggered by contradiction between reality and perception, or between desires and social injunctions—is potentially dangerous since "any nervous mannerism that could possibly be the symptom of an inner struggle is certain to be detected" (1949, 168). With the generative tension of conflict with reality or the id foreclosed, the ego is at the mercy of its ideal. Big Brother as "an invincible, fearless protector" is opposed in Ingsoc ideology to Goldstein, "the commander of a vast shadowy army, an underground network of conspirators dedicated to the overthrow of the State. The Brotherhood, its name was supposed to be"; it is the responsibility of every member of the party to feel, confronted with an image of Goldstein, "a hideous ecstasy of fear and vindictiveness, a desire to kill, to torture, to smash faces in" (1949, 14–5).

Over the course of the book, Winston has two visions, which begin at the same time and progressively develop over the book. The first is a sequence of "memory, which he could not pin down, but which was powerful and troubling" (1949, 100). The first hint is the undue resonance he finds in a media image of a mother and small child, from a convoy of ships to England which had been bombed (an image also with resonance to Mitchell's biography). The vision then appears to Winston more sharply as a dream in which "his mother was sitting in some place deep down beneath him, with his young sister in her arms. He did not remember his sister at all, except as a tiny, feeble baby, always silent, with large, watchful eyes...they were being sucked down to death, and they were down there *because* he was up here. He knew it and they knew it" (Orwell 1949, 27). The sequence of memories gradually comes into focus. He remembers, from late childhood, "the fierce sordid battles at meal-times. He would ask his mother naggingly, over and over again, why there was no more food...His mother was quite ready to give him more than his share. She took it for granted that he, 'the boy', should have the biggest portion; but however much she gave him he invariably demanded more. At every meal she would beseech him not to be selfish and to remember that his little sister was sick and also needed food...He knew that he was starving the other two, but he could not help it; he even felt that he had a right to do it" (194, 132). The big brother's sovereign egoism at the expense of his younger sister is consciously felt as entitlement; and this entitlement is enacted as Winston's mother gives him more because he is "the boy" and because the family's intense poverty and his mother's depression undermines her capacity to firmly establish any frame for recognition between the siblings. Even though he gets the food he desires, Winston is aware that he is starving his mother and sister with his demands, though the associated guilt is sufficiently unconscious as to allow his behaviour to continue.

After stealing her share of a chocolate ration, "his sister, conscious of having been robbed of something, had set up a feeble wail. His mother drew her arm around the child and pressed its face against her breast. Something in the gesture told him that his sister was dying. He turned and fled down the stairs, with the chocolate growing sticky in his hand. He never saw his mother again" (1949, 133). Winston tells his lover Julia that because he had not had access to this memory until now, "until this moment I believed I had murdered my mother" (1949, 131). What is curious, and which has not been picked up by commentators on Orwell, is that Winston's guilt is organized by a confusion of the vertical and lateral axes through the link between the two. Klein ([1928] 1998, 190) observes that "the tendencies to steal and destroy are concerned with the organs of conception, pregnancy and partuition," and she associates these tendencies with a desire to "appropriate" the mother's existing children into oneself and by "jealousy of the future brothers and sisters whose appearance is expected." As a result, "the boy fears punishment for his destruction of the mother's body...he fears that his body will be mutilated and dismembered, and this dread also means castration." Winston did not murder his mother, but rather drove her away because his selfishness was killing or speeding up the death of his younger sister. Like Klein, he presumes that stealing and appropriation are ultimately directed toward the mother, rather than identifying the relationship between big brother and little sister as capable of its own psychical dynamics and consequences, its own processes of love and guilt. In his society, there are no symbolic resources usable to make sense of lateral complexity and ambivalence: only love for Big Brother, and hate for the Brotherhood. In another context in the novel, Winston dismisses the working-class Proles because instead of having political vision they only "remembered a million useless things, a quarrel with a workmate, a hunt for a lost bicycle pump, the expression on a long-dead sister's face" (1949, 78).

As the book closes Winston has a further memory from his childhood:

His mother was sitting opposite him and also laughing. It must have been about a month before she disappeared. It was a moment of reconciliation, when the nagging hunger in his belly was forgotten...the tiddlywinks climbed hopefully up the ladders and then came slithering down the snakes again, almost to the starting point. They played eight games, winning four each. His tiny sister, too young to understand what the game was about, had sat propped up against a bolster, laughing because the others were laughing. For a whole afternoon they had all been happy together, as in his earlier childhood. He pushed the picture out of his mind. It was a false memory. (1949, 238)

In identifying this memory as false, Winston circumvents mourning. The relationship with reality is given up, as the ego ideal succeeds in winning the ego's love away from lost objects and towards itself: "the final, indispensable, healing change had never happened, until this moment...the struggle was finished. He had won the victory over himself. He loved Big Brother" (ibid. 239). These are interesting lines for Orwell to write, bedridden and dying of tuberculosis and cared for in a remote farmhouse on Jura by his younger sister Avril, choosing to finish the book rather than receive treatment at a sanatorium (Ingle 1993).

At the same point in the novel that this sequence of memories first begins to return to him, Winston also has a second vision. This second vision, written about in his diary, is of a time in the past or the future "when men are different from one another and do not live alone" (1949, 26). These two elements are in counterpoint to the psychical economy of Big Brother's Ingsoc, in which each human is isolated and homogenized with respect to a lateral ideal, separating each individual in the form of their equality. For the Panopticon to exist, Foucault ([1975] 1977, 219) observes, "it must neutralise the effects of counter-power that spring from...anything that may establish horizontal conjunctions." Winston's vision of a time when humans are different from one another and do not live alone has been understood as praise of the capitalist ideologies of individualism and familialism (Goldstein 2000), but this is to ignore that liberty and fraternity are being rethought against the dominating background of a false equality, and as an attempt to revise it. Orwell's attention to the false equality and dystopian dimensions of the lateral axis is not an attempt to collapse it into sovereign egoism: "every line of serious work that I have written since 1936 has been written directly or indirectly against totalitarianism and for democratic socialism, as I understand it" (Orwell 1947 [2002], 1083; see Williams 1982).

The themes of liberty, fraternity, and equality come into focus in the form of the tract "The Theory and Practice of Oligarchical Collectivism," which is described to Winston by its coauthor O'Brien, a member of the Inner Party, as true "as description." It can therefore by degrees be trusted as an explanation of what Ingsoc believes it is doing. The tract explains that the idea of brotherhood, of political relations modelled on sexed sibling relations, "had haunted the human imagination for thousands of years" (1949, 164). Ingsoc was not a direct outgrowth of English Socialism, but a new political programme that subsumed it and wears its cadaver—because "wealth and privilege are most easily defended when they are possessed jointly" in the name of "fraternity" (1949, 164). Ingsoc "systematically undermines the solidarity of the family, and it calls its leader by a name which is a direct appeal to the sentiment of family loyalty…these contradictions are not accidental, nor do they result from ordinary hypocrisy: they are deliberate exercises in *doublethink*. For it is only by reconciling contradictions that power can be retained indefinitely" (1949, 172). The difficulties in lateral relations experienced by Winston in his past and in dealing with his memories in the course of the novel are not distinct from the political system within which he lives. These difficulties are a concerted consequence of Ingsoc, in which actual horizontal ties are systematically isolated and displaced in order to purify the relationship between ego and lateral ideal of any dialectic, and capacity for change.

Freud's "Rat Man" had a *Zwangsneurose* (obsessional neurosis—but, literally, a neurosis of coercion) in which he was tormented by the image of rats gnawing into the anus of his father and fiancé-cousin. When discussing this torture with Captain Novak, the "Rat Man" has a compulsive need to prevent discussion of his beloved cousin, but in fact ends up interjecting her name into the conversation. In his case-notes, Freud suggests that this rat phantasy was shaped by a matrix of desire and aggressive relations "derived from his several sisters," in relation to whom his erotic life had first been kindled (Freud [1909] 2001, 273). Winston, left by his mother as a child, too has an "unendurable" phobia of "carnivorous" rats; the phobia is localized around the idea that rats are so insatiable that "a woman dare not leave her baby alone…the rats are certain to attack it" (Orwell 1949, 229). A key difference lies in the fact that the "Rat Man" has an obsessional neurosis with an anal erotogenic organization: if he does not satisfy the demands of the super-ego, then the rat torture will happen to others. By contrast, Winston's phobia is oriented by a concern with "incorporating or devouring—a type of love which is consistent with abolishing the object's separate existence": an oral erotogenic organization, in which the very constitution of the self is at stake (Freud [1915] 2001, 139). During his torture in Room 101, Winston finally gives up his opposition to Big Brother when confronted with his deepest fear: a cage is attached to his face so that the rats within are constrained to gnaw away at his mouth and devour his tongue. He interjects "Do it to Julia! Not me!" believing "there was one and only one way to save himself. He must interpose another human being, the body of another human being, between himself and the rats" (1949, 230). Political resistance to the coercive state is given up by Winston at the moment at which he is forced to repeat interposing a particular body between himself and an image of his sordid hunger. This body is that of Julia, a "young girl" who loved him and who "stirred up some memory which he could not pin down" when she shared chocolate with him (1949, 100).

In describing this ultimate betrayal of Julia with images that resonate with Winston's earlier relations with his younger sister, Orwell dramatizes the psychical effect of a society in which lateral relations have been systematically undermined and warped. A socialist, Orwell ([1946] 2002, 1005) argues, "is not obliged to believe that human society can actually be made perfect, but almost any socialist does believe that it could be a great deal better than it is at present, and that most of the evil that men do results from the warping effects of injustice and inequality." Commenting on dystopian writing as socialist meditation, Williams (1980, 206) observed, "it is within a complex of contemporary tendencies—of efficient and affluent capitalism set against an earlier capitalist poverty and disorder; of socialism against capitalism in either phase; and of the deep divisions within socialism itself...that we have to consider the mode of dystopia" as a genre of modernist fiction generally, and Orwell's *Nineteen Eighty-Four* specifically. In this way, Winston's dream of a time when humans are different from one another and do not live alone dramatizes the possibility, explored in Mitchell's work, of change in the social and psychological configuration of liberty and solidarity as the condition of advance toward meaningful equality.

Concluding Remarks

Mitchell has described that "I find the question of 'othering' as an abstract concept vertiginous, and my contribution here is consequently prosaic, down-to-earth" (2006, 35). In contrast to such vertiginous analytical tools for examining social and psychological forces which disrupt the practice of meaningful equality, Mitchell explores "the minimal difference that needs to be set up between sisters and brothers for replication to turn into seriality" (2003, 151–2). She deploys sibling relationships as a lens on the dialectic that must organize lateral relations if they are to escape twin dangers: collapse into the callous sovereign egoism lauded by capitalist ideology; or warping into dystopian isolation and homogenization. In contrast to post-structuralist thinking in which difference and multiplicity are held up as a counter to capitalist and socialist totalities,

Mitchell's critical theory is animated by a commitment to socialism without totality since she believes that "difference doesn't oppose the One, dialectic does" (Mitchell 2008). This position opened both her *relationship* with socialism into a productive contradiction with feminism and psychoanalysis, on the basis that they each have their differences but they also have a certain axis of continuity and potential equality:

> My own background had been in Marxist-Feminism; dialectically the thesis and antithesis move into a position of synthesis—war becomes peace and this new unity in which each has changed into the other, becomes a new point of antithesis or thesis. The theory implicates movement and change; the practice was one of polemic and argument between those with the same concerns. There has to be some common ground to start with; a giraffe and a stone can never form any part of a dialectical relationship. (Mitchell 2007, 203)

Socialism, feminism, and psychoanalysis are not giraffes and stones to Mitchell. Rather, as she suggests in an interview with Angela McRobbie, psychoanalysis and feminism can be regarded as "twin births" of the nineteenth century (Mitchell 1988, 80); socialism, in that case, would be a somewhat older sibling. As ever eschewing any "separation of methodology from content," her work engages the three movements in a way which models the Law of the Mother, facilitating a manageable and productive organization of lateral relations and their conflicts. She argues against any tendency toward reciprocal annihilation between the three movements, manifest in "inapposite polemic, however mordant or caustic" when weighing up the value of their theoretical positions (Mitchell and Rey 1975, 80). Such annihilatory polemics do not benefit even the position being argued for, since without interplay or mediation our thought risks losing opportunities to "give and receive one another back from each other" and the production of "lifeless" positions (Hegel [1807] 1977, 114). As Feuerbach ([1843] 1986, §62) also emphasises, "the true dialectic is not a monologue of a solitary thinker with himself; it is a dialogue between 'I' and 'Thou.'" Yet dialogue within recognition (rather than annihilation of the other) along the lateral axis is not at all perceived by Mitchell as implying a pacified end to conflict or anger. Rather, it implies the productive containment of conflict and dialectic. Mitchell models this in making space for "one, two, three…room for you as well as me" between socialism, feminism. and psychoanalytic thinking—and between liberty, fraternity, and equality. "There is a place for oppositional perspectives that respect each other but also can confront each other," Mitchell (2007, 204) argues, since "to transcend these loses the dynamic of historical change which only comes about through their confrontation." Over her career Mitchell has sustained a dialectic between the three siblings—socialist, feminist, and psychoanalysis—in using their ideas to interrogate oppression, contradictions, and possibilities in society. This analysis both enacts in itself and critically considers relations of lateral recognition, presenting an advance in conceptualizing the conditions for meaningful equality.

References

Althusser, L. [1962] 2005. "Contradiction and Overdetermination." In *For Marx*, translated by Ben Brewster, 87–128. New York: Verso.

Blackburn, R. 1972. *Ideology in Social Science*. London: Fontana/Collins.

Callinicos, A. 2013. "Is Leninism finished?" *Socialist Review*, January 13, 2013.

Central Committee of the Socialist Workers Party 2013. "The SWP and Women's Oppression." http://socialistunity.com/wp-content/uploads/2013/03/SWP-internal-bulletin-special-conference-march2013.pdf

Chiland, C. 2004. "Gender and Sexual Difference" in *Dialogues on Sexuality, Gender, and Psychoanalysis,* edited by Iréne Matthis, 79–91. London: Karnac.

Communist Party of Great Britain 2013a. "Transcript of the Disputes Committee Report to Conference." http://www.cpgb.org.uk/home/weekly-worker/online-only/report-of-swps-disputes-committee-and-conference-debate

Communist Party of Great Britain 2013b. "Callinicos threatens 'Lynch Mobs'." http://www.cpgb.org.uk/home/weekly-worker/online-only/callinicos-threatens-lynch-mobs

Crick, B. 1984. *Socialist Values and Time, Fabian Tract 495*. London: The Fabian Society.

Feuerbach, L. A. [1843] 1986. *Principals of the Philosophy of the Future*, translated by Manfred Vogel. New York: Hackett & Co.

Foucault, M. [1975] 1977. *Discipline and Punish*, translated by Alan Sheridan. London: Penguin.

Freud, S. [1909] 2001. "Notes upon a Case of Obsessional Neurosis," *Standard Edition, Volume 10,* edited by James Strachey, 153–318. London: Vintage.

Freud, S. [1914] 2001. "On Narcissism: An Introduction," *Standard Edition, Volume 14,* edited by James Strachey, London: Vintage.

Freud, S. [1915] 2001. "Instincts and their Vicissitudes," *Standard Edition, Volume 14,* edited by James Strachey, London: Vintage.

Freud, S. [1933] 2001. "New Introductory Lectures." *Standard Edition,* Volume 22, edited by James Strachey, London: Vintage.

Freud, S. [1938] 2001. "Findings, Ideas, Problems," *Standard Edition, Volume 23,* edited by James Strachey, 299–300, London: Vintage.

Green, A. 1999. *The Work of the Negative*, translated by Andrew Weller, New York: Free Association Books.

Goldstein, P. 2000. "Orwell as a (Neo)conservative: The Reception of 1984." *Journal of the Midwest Modern Language Association* 33(1): 44–57.

Grosz, E. 1990. *Jacques Lacan: A Feminist Introduction*. London: Routledge.

Guntrip, H. 1975. "My Experience of Analysis with Fairbairn and Winnicott." *International Review of Psychanalysis* 2: 145–156.

Hegel, G.W.F. [1807] 1977. *Phenomenology of Spirit*, translated by A. V. Miller. Oxford: Oxford University Press.

Hegel, G.W.F. [1832] 2010. *The Science of Logic*, translated by George Di Giovanni. Cambridge: Cambridge University Press.

Hoare, Q. 1967. 'Discussion on "Women: The Longest Revolution." *New Left Review* 41: 78–81.

Honneth, A. 1996. *The Struggle for Recognition*. Cambridge: Polity.

Ingle, S. 1993. *George Orwell: A Political Life*. Manchester: Manchester University Press.

Jameson, F. 2010. *Valences of the Dialectics*. New York: Verso.

Klein, M. [1928] 1998. "Early Stages of the Oedipus Complex." In *Love, Guilt And Reparation, Writings of Melanie Klein 1921–1945*, 186–198. London: Vintage.

Klein, M. [1930] 1975. "The Importance of Symbol-Formation in the Development of the Ego." In *Love, Guilt And Reparation, Writings of Melanie Klein 1921–1945*, 219–232. London: Vintage.

Klein, M. 1932. *The Psychoanalysis of Children*. London: Hogarth Press.

Lacan, J. [1953] 1977. "Function and Field of Speech and Language." In *Écrits: A Selectio*, translated by Alan Sheridan, 30–113. New York: Norton.

Lacan, J. [1956] 1991. *The Seminar of Jacques Lacan: The Psychoses 1955–56, Book III*, edited by John Forrester. New York: Norton.

Lovell, T. 1996. "Feminist Social Theory." In *The Blackwell Companion to Social Theory*, edited by Bryan Turner. Oxford: Blackwell.

Marx, K. [1844] 1977. "Critique of Hegel's Dialectic and General Philosophy," In *Karl Marx: Selected Writings*, edited by David McLellan. Oxford: Oxford University Press.

Marx, K. [1846] 1994. "The German Ideology." In *Karl Marx: Early Political Writings*, edited by Joseph O'Malley. Cambridge: Cambridge University Press.

Marx, K. [1867] 2011. *Capital, Volume 1*, translated by Samuel Moore and Edward Aveling. New York: Dover.

Matthews, W. 2002. "The Poverty of Strategy: EP Thompson, Perry Anderson, and the Transition to Socialism." *Labour/Le Travail* 50: 217–241.

McNay, L. 2007. *Against Recognition*. Cambridge: Polity.

Mieville, C. 2013. "The Stakes." http://www.leninology.com/2013/01/the -stakes.html

Milner, M. 1969. *The Hands of the Living God: An Account of a Psycho-analytic Treatment*. London: Hogarth Press.

Mitchell, J. [1964] 1984. "Wuthering Heights: Romanticism and Rationality." In *Women: The Longest Revolution*, 127–144. London: Virago.

Mitchell, J. 1966. "Women: The Longest Revolution." *New Left Review* 40: 11–37.

Mitchell, J. 1967. "Reply to Q. Hoare." *New Left Review* 41: 81–83.

Mitchell, J. 1971. *Women's Estate*. London: Penguin.

Mitchell, J. 1973. "Female Sexuality." *Journal of Biosocial Science* 5(1): 123–136.

Mitchell, J. 1974a. "Aspects of Feminism." In *Women: The Longest Revolution*, 77–126. London: Virago.

Mitchell, J. 1974b. *Psychoanalysis and Feminism*. New York: Basic Books.

Mitchell, J. [1974c] 1984. "On Freud and The Distinction Between the Sexes." In *Women: The Longest Revolution*, 221–232. London: Virago.

Mitchell, J. and Rey. 1975. "Comment on 'The Freudian Slip.'" *New Left Review* 94: 79–80.

Mitchell, J. and Oakley, A. 1976. "Introduction" to *The Rights And Wrongs of Women*, 7–16. London: Penguin.

Mitchell, J. & Oakley, A. 1976. "Women and Equality." In *The Rights And Wrongs of Women*, 379–399. London: Penguin.

Mitchell, J. [1982] 1984. "Femininity, Narrative and Psychoanalysis." In *Women: The Longest Revolution*, 287–294. London: Virago.

Mitchell, J. 1983. "Psychoanalysis and Child Development." *New Left Review*, 140: 92–96.

Mitchell, J. 1986. "Reflections on Twenty Years of Feminism." In *What is Feminism*, Oxford: Blackwell, pp. 34–48.

Mitchell, J. 1988. "Angela McRobbie: An Interview with Juliet Mitchell". *New Left Review* 170: 80–91.

Mitchell, J. 1999a. "Introduction, 1999" to *Psychoanalysis and Feminism*. New York: Basic Books.

Mitchell, J. 1999b. "Feminism and Psychoanalysis at the Millennium." *Women: A Cultural Review* 10(2): 186–191.

Mitchell, J. 2000. *Mad Men and Medusas*. London: Penguin.

Mitchell, J. 2002. "Reply to Lynne Segal's Commentary." *Studies in Gender and Sexuality* 3(2): 217–228.

Mitchell, J. and Spigel, S. 2003. "The Power of Feelings." *Psychodynamic Practice* 9(1): 87–89.

Mitchell, J. 2006. "From Infant to Child: The Sibling Trauma, the Rite de Passage, and the Construction of the 'Other' in the Social Group." *Fort Da* 12: 35–49.

Mitchell, J. 2007. "On Asking Again: What Does a Woman Want?" In *The Claims of Literature: The Shoshana Felman Reader,* edited by Emily Sun, Eyal Peretz, and Ulrich Baer, 201–209. New York: Fordham University Press.

Mitchell, J. 2008. "What Do We Mean by Gender Studies?". Multidisciplinary Workshop at the University of Cambridge Centre for Gender Studies, January 22, 2008.

Mitchell, J. 2011. "Emancipation in the Heart of Darkness: An Interview with Juliet Mitchell." *Platypus Review* 38: 1–6.

Orwell, G. [1937] 2001. *The Road to Wigan Pier*. London: Penguin.

Orwell, G. [1946] 2002. 'What is Socialism?' In *Essays*. New York: Everyman.

Orwell, G. 1949. *Nineteen Eighty-Four*. London: Penguin.

Penny, L. 2013. "The SWP and Rape: Why I Care about This Marxist-Leninist Implosion." *Guardian*, March 12, 2013.

Segal, L. 2001. "Psychoanalysis and Politics: Juliet Mitchell, Then and Now." *Studies in Gender & Sexuality* 2: 327–343.

Swindells, J. and Jardine, L. 1990. *What's Left? Women in Culture and the Labour Movement*. London: Routledge.

Walker, T. 2013. "Why I am Resigning." http://www.cpgb.org.uk/home /weekly-worker/944/swp-why-i-am-resigning

Wandschneider, D. 2010. "Dialectic as the "Self-Fulfilment" of Logic." In *The Dimensions of Hegel's Dialectic*, edited by Nectarious G. Limnatis. New York: Continuum.

Williams, R. 1973. "Base and Superstructure in Marxist Cultural Theory." *New Left Review* 82: 3–16.

Williams, R. 1980. *Problems in Materialism and Culture*. New York: Verso.

Williams, R. 1982. "George Orwell." In *Culture and Society*, 285–294. London: Hograth Press.

Chapter 6

Marked by Freud, Mitchell, and the Freudian Project

Daru Huppert

Juliet Mitchell is considered to belong to the Independent School of British Psychoanalysis, in which she was trained. Such claims necessarily involve simplifications and soon require amending. One qualification of is that, while psychoanalysts of the Independent School of Psychoanalysis often have a loose, even sometimes a cavalier relationship to Freud, this is not at all the case with Mitchell. Among the prominent figures of the Independent School she is arguably the most deeply immersed in Freud. Indeed within British psychoanalysis her relationship with him is one of the distinctive features of her work.

While Mitchell has desisted from raising her relationship to Freud into a doctrinal position, we cannot escape noticing the deep and constant concern with his work that runs through all her psychoanalytic writings. Since *Psychoanalysis and Feminism* she has attended to his texts, with a fertile sense of their unsettling, but unarticulated implications. Over the course of her work Mitchell has brought him to bear in a fundamental way on two different issues, which he did not envisage or would have necessarily endorsed: feminism and siblings. Indeed, what is compelling about Mitchell's work is that is has been innovative, while retaining an allegiance to and living sense of Freud's conceptions. In this she is an exception. We find that the majority of the innovative work done in Britain and elsewhere, such as the deeper exploration of pre-Oedipal relationships by Kleinian psychoanalysts and attachment theory, was advanced by ignoring central tenets of Freudian theory. While the importance of this later work is beyond question, the price has been excessive. Giving up Freudian tenets has contributed to a loss of conceptual cohesion within psychoanalysis (Green 2005; Turnheim 2007). To give two examples that shall be of concern later on: if Freud's conceptions of the unconscious or of sexuality are overly diluted, psychoanalysis becomes unintelligible, insipid, or both.

This neglect of Freud has led to a series of responses that seek to reclaim the central meaning and actuality of his work—I am thinking, among others, of authors as diverse as Glover (1947), Lacan (1966/2006), Matte-Blanco (1975), Laplanche (1979), or Green (2000). While these responses claim his centrality for different and in part conflicting reasons, they nevertheless coalesce around certain general points that are worth outlining and that allow us to emphasize their "family resemblance" (Wittgenstein 1984), rather than the narcissism of small differences. What these authors would agree on is the unique power of the Freudian corpus. Freud not only established the fundamental concepts of psychoanalysis; these notions make psychoanalysis possible, so that neglecting them inevitably leads to conceptual disarray. The above authors would further agree on that contemporary work within psychoanalysis should satisfy the conceptual and procedural requirements that are found in Freud's texts. What I mean by the conceptual requirements can illustrated by the basic example of pleasure. Freud (1920g) proposes a notion of pleasure that is experienced as unpleasurable by the subject who has it. This idea is deeply incoherent from a phenomenological perspective, in which pleasure is considered to be an irreducible phenomenon, which can refer to only to what is experienced as such. Freud's notion becomes intelligible, though still unsettling, if we assume, among other things, that the pleasure he refers to, issues from the satisfaction of a repressed wish that, due to the effects of repression, now produces not pleasure, but aversion, pain, or an anesthetized sensation, etc. This account becomes particularly unsettling if we assume, as Freud does, that the pleasure involved is of a sexual kind, but which, for reasons akin to the above, is experienced without the sexual charge becoming conscious. A procedural requirement that psychoanalysts would have to satisfy is to show how these notions play out in a specific psychic phenomenon, such as a dream, a symptom, or a slip of tongue. This effort will only carry conviction, if the analysis is born out in detail (a requirement I discuss later), and also, if it addresses the points that are urgent to the person, that is, if it takes up those issues that are deeply invested in terms of ideas and affects and lastly in terms of the drives, which the ideas and affects represent. We find then that the conceptual requirements of Freud's thought are both disturbing and original, while the procedures he developed are painstaking; it would seem that the powerful effect of his writings depends on these, among other qualities.

Accepting this does not entail an idolatry of Freud's texts; the very same requirements have been critically applied to Freud (Laplanche 1979). Yet it is also true that his writings fulfill these requirements to a degree that have rarely, if at all, been reached again. That is one reason why his texts are exemplary. Their unique status within psychoanalysis, however, depends on something more basic: most of the central concepts found in this discipline derive from Freud. Those who seek to reclaim the central meaning of his work for psychoanalysis are keenly aware that their work takes place within his concepts. In the view I wish to propose here psychoanalysis is a development of his thought; in other words, it is a Freudian project; the authors named above offer different and partly conflicting versions thereof. Although this outline of the Freudian project may seem overly abstract and will only gain in detail as we proceed, it can nevertheless serve as a foil to the dominant view of Freud within psychoanalysis, expressed with particular clarity by someone like Ferro (1999, p. 1–19), though shared by many, perhaps the majority of psychoanalysts. In this view Freud is treated (if at all) with a deference due to a great figure of the past, who points to the progress that has been made since him and, to a large degree, independently of his work. Such a view unwittingly turns Freud into an antiquarian figure, whom we must "go beyond." In contrast, within the Freudian project, his writings remain of acute and immediate importance. One reason for proposing this project is, precisely, that efforts to go beyond Freud, in general, fall far behind him. The challenge, rather, becomes to develop the strange and unsettling originality of his thought and to extend it onto new areas.

In this chapter, I will discuss Mitchell's work as a successful version of the Freudian project, though not without some critique. Given her long-standing engagement with Freud, any attempt to show how she thinks with him and within his conceptions will necessarily be selective. Three points will be taken up. I will first address her initial encounter with his writings, then her allegiance to his concepts in her later texts, and finally I will compare Mitchell's and Freud's analysis in more detail with reference to a sadomasochistic fantasy. Throughout the purpose of this chapter is twofold: to describe what is distinctive about Mitchell's work and to flesh out the demands of the Freudian project.

Marked by Freud

Mitchell's entry into psychoanalysis was through Freud and she is still probably best known for introducing him as a crucial thinker for feminism within the English language. Yet this was not the intention she initially pursued. In her introduction written for the 25th anniversary edition for *Psychoanalysis and Feminism* Mitchell (2000, xv) remarks that she had actually planned to write a book on the family:

> For my book on the family I had intended to read a few articles of Freud's on "femininity" and, with this in mind, had entered the British Museum reading room at the start of a university long vacation. I emerged at the end of the summer having read all twenty three volumes of the standard edition of Freud's complete works. The projected work had changed and something in me had also. I had been deeply marked by my reading Freud, and probably it is this that carries the book, twenty-five years later, I am no less impressed by Freud, although somewhat more independent from him. (Mitchell 2000 [1974], xv)

This passage, which may seem anecdotal, reveals some of the features that have made Mitchell's relationship with Freud compelling. Moreover, it will serve to show what is required from us, if we wish to engage with Freud. Since my focus here is on her relationship to Freud, I will not enter into the other theme of her engagement: feminism. It is important to note that Mitchell's encounter with Freud was unexpected. With this I do not mean primarily that she was planning to read only a few articles of his, instead of writing a book in which he was to become the main protagonist. I mean rather, that she was seized by Freud in a manner that nothing could have prepared her for. One of the reasons for this captivation is that Freud's object and mode of inquiry takes up the most pressing matters of infancy. More precisely, his thought takes up the repressed investigation of sexual questions in childhood.[1] That is why, while reading his texts, we are overcome by an uncanny sense, of following a line of exploration that is deeply familiar, but which we have become estranged from, due to the repression (never total) it has suffered. Freud's writings affect us deeply, because they provide developed forms of thought that take up our inchoate explorations of sexual questions in infancy, of issues, such as sexual difference, that continue to confuse and excite us. A main virtue of *Psychoanalysis and Feminism* is that Mitchells does not try to asphyxiate what Freud has stirred up in her, instead she uses this effect to give a stirring, lucid, and committed account of his thought.

What is required by such an account is shown by Mitchell reading the twenty-three volumes of Freud's complete works. A point that she repeats throughout *Psychoanalysis and Feminism* is that Freud is not reducible to any of his assertions, whether considered scandalous and absurd, by detractors, or essential, by some of his followers. For Mitchell his assertions can only be comprehended by assessing their position within his thought. That is why *Psychoanalysis and Feminism* does not begin with Freud's conceptions of the feminine, but with his ideas about the unconscious, which, he considered the "true psychic reality" (Freud 1900a, 617), from which the strange originality of his conceptions derive. Implicitly she argues that if we wish to comprehend the particulars of Freud's thought, we need to engage with all of it—he is not to be had for less. A reason for this, which is often overlooked, is that throughout his work, Freud maintains a holism of our psychic lives. He is more commonly associated with dividing the psyche into different systems (for example, into the unconscious, the preconscious, and into consciousness) and with emphasizing that, to a considerable degree, they function independently of one another. Yet when discussing a particular psychic phenomenon, such as the dream, he does so by examining the interaction of these systems. Thus, while the entirety of the psychic forces at work within a dream is never available to the dreamer or to the analyst—too many features are unconscious—these forces are nevertheless present structurally in the dream. This holism of Freud's theory, albeit a complex holism, has a deep influence on his writings, so that his discussion of sexuality only take on their full meaning if we relate it to his ideas of the unconscious, etc. I would argue that this has nonintuitive implications for how we should read Freud: while it is, of course, important to read his theories in terms of their historical development, they should also be read as if they existed all-at-once. This may be something that we can only strive for, yet Mitchell reading all his works represents an exemplary approximation.

What can sustain this kind of commitment? In the passage quoted above Mitchell writes that she has been deeply marked, indeed changed by Freud. This is a distinctive feature of his writings, which is not given due consideration in most academic discussions of him. I would argue that unless Freud changes us, our encounter with his writings is merely incidental. This is due to the impetus that sustain his texts that is perhaps best expressed in the epigram by Vergil that Freud (1900a, ix) chose for *The Interpretation of Dreams*, "Flectere si nequeo superos, acheronta movobo," which might be translated as, "If I cannot move the heavens, I will stir up the underworld." We may take the "underworld" here to mean the repressed wishes that stir up the unconscious. In other words, wishes that are indestructible, imperative, and constantly active, but that we can neither become conscious of, nor satisfy. Freud's writings are sustained by an overriding desire to analyze and change this state of affairs. I would suggest that Mitchell's ability to translate this impetus onto another field—a feminist discussion of sexual difference—and to do so with such impact stems from her having been deeply marked by Freud. This is, perhaps, the primary subjective feature that all proponents of the Freudian project share, though, evidently, to differing degrees.

Still Marked by Freud?

While *Psychoanalysis and Feminism* could have been called "Freud and Feminism," this cannot be said about her later writings. As quoted earlier, Mitchell (2000, xv) writes "...twenty-five years later, I am no less impressed by Freud, although somewhat more independent from him." There are, of course, many differences between Mitchell's early and later engagements with Freud. Here I will take up only the most significant one: she has developed a theory that emphasizes the central importance of siblings. This position arose partly out her criticism of the neglect of siblings within psychoanalysis, a neglect that began with Freud. Yet her critique develops from an allegiance to his thought, implying that, given his claims and mode of thought, he should have given siblings a central position within his theory. In Freud we frequently find passages about the Oedipus complex such as the following:

> It is the complex which comprises the child's earliest impulses, alike tender and hostile, towards its parents and brothers and sisters, after its curiosity has been awakened—usually by the arrival of a new baby brother or sister. (1909d, 207)

I will only comment on the first part of the sentence, in which he makes no distinction between "tender and hostile" wishes to parents and to siblings, which suggests that the Oedipus complex would seem to encompass both. But while Freud provides a painstaking account of the passions involving the parents, siblings receive a downgraded treatment. This is where Mitchell's work sets in. As we shall see, her writings on siblings arose within the context of her commitment to his concepts.

Fundamental Concepts

It is a difficult task to specify Freud's influence on Mitchell's later texts, since, in some sense, he pervades all of it. An anecdote, however, may provide a more specific orientation. About a decade ago I attended a postgraduate seminar in Cambridge, in which Mitchell asked the students to write down three concepts that they considered to be the most important within psychoanalysis. She participated in this exercise and her choice fell on sexuality, the death drive, and the unconscious. I shall briefly discuss the role these concepts play in *Mad Men and Medusas*, the book in which introduces both her theory of hysteria and of siblings. This will allow me to point to commitments that distinguish her from the majority of British analysts.

Sexuality

One of the themes Mitchell inherited from Freud is her insistence on the central importance of sexuality, in the extended and unsettling meaning of the term that he first articulated. This notion, to name but some of its aspects, entails that sexuality aims at pleasure (rather than at reproduction); this pleasure is derived from diverse and therefore perverse objects and activities, with the excitement arising from specific erogenous zones (such as the eyes) and impelled by component drives (such as the visual component drive). To refer to a programmatic sentence in regard to this view, Mitchell (2000b, 140) writes, "Insofar sexuality seeks satisfaction rather than an object...it is in a sense necessarily perverse." This position also entails seeing sexuality as central to psychic conditions, which is attested to by another sentence, "Masturbation, auto-eroticism and narcissism are core states of hysteria" (Mitchell 2000b, 157). (To comprehend the full meaning of this last statement, we need to remember that in psychoanalysis narcissism means the libidinal investment of the ego.) Mitchell's stance on this issue contrasts with the reticence often found among the proponents of the Independent School of Psychoanalysis, who concede importance to sexuality, only to emphasize something else as more fundamental, such as maternal care (Phillips 1998). It also contrasts with another view of sexuality found among many Kleinians, the other dominant stream of psychoanalysis in Britain, in which libido is relegated to the function of a defense against primary destruction or against psychosis; what interests in sexuality is then not sex, but aggressive or reparative fantasies (Spillius 1989). The issues raised by these two schools are significant in their own right, but they entail a movement away from Freud's insight into the irreducible importance of sexuality in shaping who we are. Tellingly, both positions also revert to a more conventional understanding of what sexuality is (Green 2000). One of the many advantages of retaining the Freudian understanding of libido is that it enables us to see more clearly the continuity between ordinary and perverse sexuality. This, for example, allows Mitchell (2000b, 134–158) a critical but nonmoralistic view of the perversions. It was one of Freud's great accomplishments to have established such a perspective, which, within psychoanalysis, is becoming rare.

The Death Drive

Another point of convergence with Freud is that Mitchell maintains the category of the death drive as analytically distinct from aggression or a destructive drive. For Freud (1920g) the death drive aims at turning the organic into the inorganic and finds expression in the repetition compulsion as well as in the search for anesthetized states and the disinvestment of objects (Green 2001). This concept has been the bête noire of psychoanalytic theory, rejected by the vast majority of analysts, British or otherwise, with the notorious exception of the Kleinians, who, however, conflate the death drive with an urge to destruction, which Mitchell does not. She writes, "The death drive is a 'drive' precisely, because it drives an organism into a state of inanimacy, or inertia, to stasis or even literally death" (Mitchell, 2000b, 140). The role this concept plays in her analysis of hysteria is discrete, but fundamental. We find that hysteria has been abandoned by psychiatry and partly neglected by psychoanalysis, due to the advent of the so-called personality disorders. What was considered to be hysteria has been largely absorbed into the categories of the histrionic and the borderline personality disorder. This development was facilitated by a view of hysteria, in which it is considered to be a relatively benign condition and therefore of lesser relevance. Using the concept of the death drive, or having it as a background, allowed Mitchell to emphasize the repetition compulsion (2000a, 136–7, 146–7), states of emptiness (ibid. 203–232), and feelings of annihilation (ibid. p. 298–315) in this condition. Thereby she alerted us to the severity of hysteria and argued against it vanishing into other categories. Insisting on hysteria also enabled Mitchell to emphasize another concept that has been brushed aside by the triumph of the personality disorders: the unconscious.

The Unconscious and Hysteria

Freud (1926e) defined psychoanalysis as the science of the unconscious, even after his introduction of the structural theory (ego, super-ego, id) and it may seem unnecessary to emphasize this issue. Yet his concept of the unconscious has been sidelined—some have even claimed that it has suffered repression (Blanco 1975). One reason for this is that much of the progress in psychoanalysis has been made in relationship to early development, in which the distinction between the unconscious, the preconscious, and consciousness is being formed. According to Mitchell (2000a, xxiii) this has led to these crucial distinctions being blurred even in texts that refer mainly to adults. In general, we find that Freud's (1915e) notion of the unconscious—as the system with particular laws that are entirely different and partly oppose those of consciousness—has over time become sidelined by the vaguer and descriptive term "unconscious processes" (Huppert 2014). The central importance that Mitchell gives to hysteria in *Mad Men and Medusas* takes on a particular significance within this context. Of all psychical conditions it is hysteria that was most closely associated with Freud's discovery and articulation of the unconscious. By reminding us of hysteria's centrality, Mitchell was insisting that the unconscious remains the distinctive and fundamental perspective of psychoanalysis.

This list of positions that Mitchell has taken up from Freud is certainly not exhaustive. Yet it shows clearly that she has prioritized concepts that are indispensable to the Freudian project and that have suffered neglect by the majority of British analysts. Her allegiance to Freud's notions also leads to a similar set of preoccupations (with psychoanalysis as the discipline concerned with the unconscious) and a shared sensibility (a nonmoralistic sense of the perversions). What is particular about Mitchell's adherence to Freud is her lack of polemic against other positions; indeed she is rare among the proponents of the Freudian project in that she has not used him as a weapon against differing views. It seems that she is more concerned with what Freud enables her to do. Her conceptual commitment to Freud in *Mad Men and Medusas* is important, because in this text she proposes one of the more significant shifts in the development of psychoanalysis, by urging us to make siblings central to our thinking. We may conclude that allegiance to the Freudian project need not, as is often implied, issue in conservatism and inhibit psychoanalytic development, but, rather, can enhance it.

A Child Is Being Beaten

Yet Freud not only serves to a stir further development; his texts also offer a critical measure for the newer work. Emphasizing this aspect of his role within the Freudian project entails a certain reversal of Mitchell's claims. While she has maintained that Freud has left siblings out of his theory, my emphasis, will be on what she has, so far, left out of Freud in her analysis of siblings. The aim of this critique is to point toward areas that require further attention and development in her writings. To do this end I shall compare Freud's interpretation in *A Child is Being Beaten* with Mitchell's (2003, 83–110) account thereof. Since the fantasy discussed therein is very intricate, I will consider it only as it occurs in women. My emphasis will be on the procedural aspect of the Freudian project, that is, on how Freud and Mitchell develop their claims rather than on the claims themselves.

The Fantasy

A Child is Being Beaten is Freud's most sustained analysis of a sadomasochistic fantasy, which is found very frequently in both women and men.

Its manifest content is of a child or several children being beaten by a teacher or some person of authority. The fantasy, which is first imagined before the age of six, has been reproduced countless times; initially it takes place voluntarily, but later in spite of the fantasist, acquiring a compulsive character. It is accompanied by masturbatory activity and culminates in orgasm. During psychoanalytic treatment this fantasy is confessed only with great hesitation and this confession is accompanied by a powerful sense of shame and guilt. Through interpretation Freud reveals the Oedipal structure of the imagined beating scenes. As the fantasy is very common and is entertained not only by neurotic patients, his analysis marks a significant step in establishing the Oedipus complex not only as the core of the neuroses, but also as the central structure organizing our psychic formation and functioning. Mitchell's interest in this essay seems to arise from a similar set of concerns: if she can show that siblings play a crucial role therein, this supports her claim about the general significance of her sibling theory (for a discussion of this theory, see my chapter 2 in this volume).

Phases

Freud stipulates that the fantasy undergoes three transformations or developments, before it is experienced in the manner confessed to during analysis. Of the first phase, which occurs in infancy, he writes, "The child being beaten is never the one producing the phantasy, but is invariably another child, most often a brother or a sister if there is any" (Freud 1919e, 183). Freud wavers whether to call this a fantasy or a recollection; he is tempted to call it sadistic, but he cautions us to note that it is not the child who does the beating. In each case, analysis reveals that it is the father who performs this act. So the first phase of the fantasy could be stated as: "*My father is beating the child*" (Freud 1919e, 185). We are led to understand what motivates this scene, if we add that the child being beaten is a hated child. The scene can be rendered as: "My father is beating the child whom I hate." In the second phase the person who is doing the beating is still the father, but the child being beaten has changed: it is now the fantasist herself. The corresponding sentence would be: "I am being beaten by my father." The fantasy is now unmistakably masochistic. For Freud this second stage is the core of the beating scenarios, it is the scene that elicits the greatest pleasure, yet it is irretrievable to consciousness, even in psychoanalytic treatment. This scene is what he calls a "construction," that is, a necessary assumption. We find that the third phase, which is the one confessed to during psychoanalytic treatment, is again nearer to the first. In it the person beating is not the father, but a substitute of some form, such as a teacher, and instead of the fantasist there are several children being beaten. This last stage can be embellished and varied, but its sadistic character remains in all variations.

Transformations

Let us now look in greater at detail the three transformations that the fantasy undergoes. As Freud (1919e, 187) notes, the mother is not the only rival of the child in regard to the Oedipal love of the father; siblings must also be contended with and they are hated with the "wild energy characteristic of the emotional life of those years." If the sibling is younger, it is despised as well hated, yet it nevertheless attracts a share of the affection from the parents. In this context the beating signifies a "deprivation of love and a humiliation" (ibid) and it means, "My father does not love this other child, *he loves only me.*" The term "love" here is meant genitally, that is, it expresses an incestuous fantasy. However, this fantasy succumbs to repression, in the wake of which arises a sense of guilt. For Freud the second phase of the fantasy, in which the fantasist is being beaten, is a direct expression of the girl's guilt (the beating acting as punishment). But guilt alone cannot explain the masochistic, that is, the sexual character of the second phase. He notes that the genital impulse of the first phase not only suffers repression, it also undergoes regression to an anal sadistic stage. That is why the beating expresses a distorted version of a coital fantasy. As Freud (ibid, 189) summarizes, "This being beaten is now a convergence of the sense of guilt and sexual love. It is not only the punishment for the forbidden genital relation, but also the regressive substitute for that relation..." The third phase of the fantasy primarily serves to substitute the second, deeply repressed phase. Now the child appears as spectator and is represented by the several children, while the father takes shape as a teacher or some authority figure. The fantasy has become sadistic and can once again be rendered by the sentence: "My father is beating the child, he loves only me." Yet the stress is now only on the first part of the sentence, while the latter part has undergone repression (Freud ibid, 190).

Before turning to Mitchell's work, I would like to underline the density of Freud's psychological analysis. He not only describes the transformation that the beating fantasy undergoes, but also specifies the mechanisms by which these changes are accomplished. This ability to explain the minutiae of psychic life is one of the characteristics of Freud's thinking; his penetration of detail remains a measure for any attempt to develop or even to transform his thought. Psychoanalytic insight is always an insight into a particular constellation.

Siblings and the Beating Fantasy

While Mitchell (2003a, 89) is deeply appreciative of Freud's essay and maintains its structure, she criticizes what could be called his Oedipal-monism, "I believe that this interpretation...occludes the siblings in favour of the exclusive desire for parents." To amend this she provides a complementary account from the perspective of her sibling theory.[2] Before entering into the detail of her dense and suggestive interpretation it is worth noting that she chose to analyze a sexual fantasy, whose fundamental meaning is deeply unconscious. The issue of the death drive is more complicated, as Freud had not yet articulated it when writing this essay; in Mitchell's work on siblings the presence of this drive is, as we shall, see, primarily discrete.

Mitchell (ibid) writes, "The first stage [of the beating fantasy] involves an eradication of the other." This suggests that the fantasy satisfies the wish to annihilate the sibling whose existence is first felt to eradicate the subject. As with Freud the attack on the sibling is experienced sexually and has a sadistic quality. Yet the objective of the aggression has changed: it is no longer the aim-inhibited beating scene, but the kill-or-be-killed of sibling survival (ibid, p. 94). We also find that the scene also is no longer primarily about the father's love; he seems to have been downgraded to the executor of the child's destructive wishes. What makes my comments tentative is that these issues are not explicitly addressed by Mitchell, what is also left implicit, is how the scene of eradication is turned into or transferred onto the beating scene.

Of the next and decisive phase Mitchell (ibid) writes: "The middle stage is an eradication of the ego as a prelude to autoerotic orgasm." An assumption that runs through Mitchell's interpretation is that the initial excitement at having the sibling beaten—or obliterated—persists in the second stage. It would seem that what facilitates this transfer is an identification with the other sibling; an identification which is more encompassing than with the parent, because of the greater similarities between the siblings and, more deeply, because the siblings is first invested narcissistically, as an extension of the subject. However, my interpretation remains tentative, for the reason named above. At this point we also come upon an ambiguity in the term "eradication." While in the first stage of the beating fantasy, this term denotes an imagined destructive attack on the sibling, now it seems to mean something else. I would suggest that the eradication of the ego implies an activity of the death drive, which here acts to disinvest the ego, just as it may, in other contexts, disinvest an object. If this line of interpretation is correct, if only approximately, we are nevertheless, left with the question of how the eradication of the ego relates to the unconscious—among Freud's female patients this second phase remains deeply repressed. Addressing this matter would require more speculation than warranted here. Mitchell's (ibid) characterization of the third stage of the beating fantasies broadly coincides with Freud's, "The third stage sees to the diffusion of the first stage of one 'other' into a number of others." This allows for the satisfaction of both sadistic and masochistic trends of the fantasy.

We find then that Mitchell's interpretation does more than merely complement Freud's, by placing the emphasis on the sibling rather than on the Oedipal axis; her essay shifts the focus from a genital interpretation of the fantasy onto a more archaic scene of killing and being killed, which is experienced both sadistically and masochistically. Thereby the first phase of the fantasy becomes greatly valorized, and even more so the archaic stage that is hypothesized to precede it. I would suggest that in the context of the beating fantasy, this more archaic scene is deeply repressed.[3] Yet such ascriptions of defense mechanisms must remain tentative, as they are left largely implicit Mitchell's account. Indeed, though highly suggestive, her interpretation of the beating fantasy involves less psychological detail than Freud's analysis. I would suggest that her relative lack of emphasis on defense mechanisms is also found in her general sibling theory, with the effect that this theory, although very persuasive, does not yet carry the convincing force that would make it an undisputable part of psychoanalytic theory. As stated earlier, the aim of this critique is to point out areas in which work is necessary, particularly if Mitchell (2000a, x) is to bear out her claim that siblings are "half of the picture" that Freud leaves out in his account of the psyche. Such a project, of course, requires time. Freud took twenty-four years from his introduction of the Oedipus complex in the *Interpretation of Dreams* (Freud 1990a) to his comprehensive statement thereof (Freud 1924d)—and psychoanalysts have been working on this insight ever since. There is little reason to believe that it would be different in the case of siblings.

What the comparison between Mitchell's and Freud's interpretation of the beating fantasy has shown at the level of procedure, is that his work remains not only a template, but also a challenge to any new theory in psychoanalysis. In this view Freud is not only the past, but also the future of psychoanalysis.

Conclusion

During the course of this chapter Mitchell's version of the Freudian project has, to an extent, taken on shape, as have some of the general features entailed by this project. What is distinctive about Mitchell's work is the degree to which she has been able to translate the powerful effect that the Freudian writings have had and continue to have on her onto the areas in which she engages. Her allegiance to Freud's concepts comes with a sense of common concerns and has honed a shared sensibility. At the level of procedure we have seen that the Freudian project compels us to show our ideas in the minutiae of psychic life. While Mitchell's sibling theory requires more detailed working out, it promises to become deeply important to psychoanalysis. This importance is due, not least, to her taking the Oedipus complex as the model for what she seeks to achieve with siblings, a challenge that is formidable and that, more generally, gives us a sense of the challenge that Freud's work represents to anyone thoroughly engaged with him. I began this chapter, by saying that Mitchell is considered to belong to the Independent School of Psychoanalysis, but it may be more apt to call her an independent Freudian—insofar as anyone can be a Freudian and not simply strive to become one.

Notes

1. See Freud's (1905d) development of this issue.
2. Mitchell's chapter dedicated to the fantasy touches on an extraordinary array of issues—ranging from Madame Bovary, to war and gender—which I cannot touch on here.
3. Repression should be understood as acting within a particular context, so that a theme, which may be conscious in one context, such as the relationship of mutual obliteration between siblings, may be unconscious in another context, such as the beating fantasy.

References

Bion, W. R. 1984. *Attention and Interpretation*. London: Karnak Books.
Ferro, A. 1999. *The Bi-Personal Field*. Routledge: London.
Freud, S. 1905d. "Three Essays on a Theory of Sexuality." In *The Standard Edition of the Complete Psychological Works of Sigmund Freud Vol. 7*, translated by James Strachey. Hogarth Press, London, *S.E. 7.*
Freud, S. 1909d. "Notes Upon A Case of Obsessional Neurosis." *S.E. 10.*
Freud, S. 1915e. "The Unconscious." *S.E. 14.*
Freud, S. 1918a. "The Taboo on Virginity." *S.E. 11.*
Freud, S. 1919e. "A Child is Being Beaten." *S.E. 17.*
Freud, S. 1920g. "Beyond the Pleasure Principle." *S.E. 18.*
Freud, S. 1924d. "The Dissolution of the Oedipus Complex." *S.E. 19.*
Freud, S. 1926e. "The Question of Lay Analysis." *S.E. 20.*
Glover, E. 1947. Basic Mental Concepts—Their Clinical and Theoretical Value. *Psychoanalytic Quarterly* 16, 482–506.
Green, A. 2000. *Chains of Eros*. London: Karnack.
Green, A. 2001. *Life Narcissism and Death Narcissism*. London: Karnak.

Green, A. 2005b. The Illusion of a Common Ground and Mythical Pluralism. *International Journal of International Psychoanalysis* 86, 627–632.

Huppert, D. 2014. Die Eigenschaften des Unbewussten. In *Sigmund Freud Vorlesungen 2014*. Vienna: Mandelbaum.

Lacan, J. 1966/2006. *Ecrits*. New York: Norton.

Laplanche, J. 1976. *Life and Death in Psychoanalysis*. Baltimore, MD: John Hopkins.

Matte-Blanco, I. 1975. *The Unconscious as Infinite Sets*. London: Duckworth.

Mitchell, J. 2000a. *Psychoanalysis and Feminism*. New York: Basic Books.

Mitchell, J. 2000b. *Mad Men and Medusas*. London: Penguin Books.

Mitchell, J. 2003. *Siblings*. Cambridge: Polity.

Phillips, A. 1988. Winnicott. London: Fontana Press.

Spillius, E. 1989. *Melanie Klein Today*. London: Karnak.

Turnheim, M. 2007. "Über die innere Spaltung der Freudschen Geste und die Frage der Rückkehr." In *Freudlose Psychoanalyse?* Vienna: Turia und Kant.

Wittgenstein, L. 1984. "Philosophische Untersuchungen." In *Werkausgabe Band 1*. Frankfurt: Suhrkamp.

Chapter 7

Hysteria between Big Brother and Patriarchy

Paul Verhaeghe and Eline Trenson

Like many others, I (Verhaeghe) discovered Juliet Mitchell via her first book, *Psychoanalysis and Feminism* (1974). The way she extended psychoanalysis, from the individual to family and society, was an eye-opener to me. In the two decades that followed, I studied Freud and Lacan, but just after the new millennium, Anglo-Saxon psychoanalysis was brought back again under my attention when I attended Juliet Mitchell's lecture on siblings in New York, and later, in Vienna, her lecture on gender. I read *Mad Men and Medusas* and *Siblings*, which reminded me of the necessity to place psychoanalysis in a much broader framework than only a family frame, and to assign psychoanalysis an explicit political and social dimension (Verhaeghe, 2014a).

In this chapter we will discuss two interconnected subjects, which we perceive as the core themes of Juliet's books: hysteria in relation to gender, and siblings in relation to contemporary politics. It is not the intention of this chapter to provide the reader with an exposition of or a detailed comment on Mitchell's theory—other chapters in this volume do this work, and in any case the reader is best informed by studying her books. It is our intention here to present a Freudian–Lacanian perspective, as we have developed in the Department of Psychoanalysis in Ghent (www.psychoanalysis.ugent.be). Juliet Mitchell's theory and our Freudian–Lacanian framework are not the same. Lacanian psychoanalysis is more structural than the empirical clinical approach of Anglo-Saxon psychoanalysis. Yet our work and Mitchell's share the same extension beyond previous psychoanalytic theory, as they take into account the importance of the Other: siblings, society, and the symbolic order.

Hysteria and Femininity?

The conviction that hysteria is essentially a female disease dates back to ancient times and is etymologically defined by the term itself—*hysteros* meaning the uterus or womb. Juliet Mitchell distances herself from this reductionist perspective and presents us with convincing clinical descriptions of hysteria in men. The original denomination was coined by male authors, and especially by men whose position as master more often than not was subject to challenge by women. Lucien Israël, in his description of hysteria in a medical setting (1984), taught me the following lesson: it takes two to create hysteria. Lacan's structural view added an extra element, and taught that a third party is needed as well. Hysteria does not exist by itself, it needs an audience, someone who is looking, while a certain relationship toward a master figure is brought on the scene. As we will explain later, the hysterical subject demonstrates to the Other both the master and the failure of the master.

Relationship is not an apt expression to characterize the dynamic played out in hysteria, as it suggests a concrete interaction and directs attention away from the significance of the unconscious and fantasy. Relational structure is a better term because it permits us to take a necessary distance from an all too concrete biological understanding of men and women in terms of the penis (or the womb) and its absence. For Lacan, gender differentiation is based on the position that the subject takes with regard to the signifier of the phallus and the castration complex (Lacan, 1975). In this line of reasoning, a biological male may take the "feminine" position, and vice versa, a biological female may take the "masculine" position. The latter will be considered as a phallic woman, the former as a hysterical man. Hysteria is no longer synonymous with femininity.

In Lacanian psychoanalysis, the idea of a structural lack is central. Castration is considered as its phallic reading (see Verhaeghe, 2001). The *symbolic* phallus denotes the supposedly final answer to desire, and hence, the lack of the Other because there is no final answer. The neurotic subject is precisely neurotic because he or she believes in the *imaginary* phallus. "Hysterical" denotes the subject who believes in the phallic omnipotence. That is, he or she believes that there is someone who has or is the phallus, meaning that there actually is a final answer to every desire. The origin of this belief is the Oedipal complex, with the father in the position of the master. In contrast to the Freudian solution for the Oedipal complex, that is, its repression or destruction, the Lacanian solution is symbolic castration, that is, the acceptance of a structurally determined lack for everyone of us. In short, acceptance of existential limits (sexuality, birth, death) is a basic human condition. This implies a totally different stance towards the phallus and the Other, because the not-All is recognized and considered. In "Encore" Lacan (1975) will identify that position with femininity.

Yet in his elaboration of the lack of the Other, Lacan remains within a phallic paternal reasoning and a paternal prohibition. Juliet Mitchell adds a maternal dimension missed by Lacan. "If the phallus is the upright 'I', the womb is the round 'me'" (Mitchell, 2003, p. 72). Mitchell identifies the wish of both male and female children to give birth (parthogenesis) as a wish for the womb, that is, "for a cavity within." The processing of this wish as a result of their acceptance of the "law of the mother": the mother's prohibition ("it is I, the mother, not you the child, who gives birth") results in the formation of a symbolic space: "an inner space can be symbolized—a place from which thoughts come and in which representation can be held 'in mind'" (Mitchell, 2003, p. 72). What Lacan conceptualized as symbolic castration is here enlarged: the lack of a penis in women and the lack of a womb in men are both elevated to a lack in the symbolic.

According to Lacan, the hysterical subject is quite particular in this respect. Being convinced that he or she has/is not the phallus, he or she will put all hope in a phallic master. This is Lacan's reading of the Freudian Oedipal complex: the father, as phallic master, is expected to provide the final answer to the lack. Traditionally, one expects a man in that master position, but, as we are talking about a signifier, biological gender is only relevant to the extent that it can be made to signify. As mentioned above, in Lacanian theory, "feminine" and "masculine" are replaced by the position someone takes toward the phallus. A phallic woman elicits hysteria in neurotic men, just like a phallic man, a master, provokes hysteria in neurotic women. The phallic woman and the master man have one thing in common: both of them pretend to possess the (imaginary) phallus in relation to someone who is looking for final answers. Let us not forget that desire (Lacan) or wanting (Mitchell) is a key feature of hysteria. This relational structure works the other way around as well: a hysterical subject in his or her search for the phallus promotes a master figure. Consequently, the meeting between a hysterical subject and a phallic master creates a structural bond, specified by Lacan (1991[1969–70]) in his theory on the hysterical discourse and the discourse of the master.

On the surface, this structural bond has to do with power and sexuality. In a patriarchal society, the traditional power distribution assigns the position of desire and wanting to women and the position of power and completeness to men. It is this power distribution that explains why hysteria is traditionally associated with women, although it is much more accurate to identify it with the demanding position in that role distribution. This becomes all the more obvious once we go beyond the surface, that is, beyond desire and jouissance.[1] On a deeper level, the hysterical structure has everything to do with knowledge and truth. Time and again, in his or her quest for an answer, the hysterical subject will expose the fallacy of the master's knowledge. At the end of the day, the truth is that every master is a desiring subject as well, subject to symbolic castration, like everyone else. And more often than not, this exposure takes place on stage, in front of a third party.[2]

The most well-known scene in that respect goes back to maître Charcot, demonstrating during his leçons du mardi (seminars on Tuesday) hysterical attacks and his power to direct his patients via hypnosis. The hysterical women seem to be puppets on his string, bowing, stretching, convulsing on stage before the eyes of a group of bewildered male spectators. The famous oil painting by Pierre-André Brouillet (Une leçon clinique du Dr. Charcot, 1887, Musée de Nice) shows the absence of women in the audience. A number of questions can be asked. Who is performing? The hysterical subject, showing her convulsions? Or the master, showing off his knowledge in front of the admiring audience? Secondly, who is demonstrating whom? Is it the doctor who demonstrates the patient? Or is it the patient who demonstrates the doctor? And finally, what is actually demonstrated? Does the scene testify to the knowledge and the power of the master? Or does it add the provocation that his knowledge and power are not strong enough? Let us not forget that Charcot, in spite of his fame, did not cure any of his hysterical patients. So where does his fame come from if he did not cure them?

At this point, we can discover a strange and, as we will argue, an essential feature of the structural relationship between the hysteric and the master. Charcot became a master, because his hysterical patients helped him to demonstrate that the then generally accepted knowledge did not work. That explains Freud's reaction, based on his thorough neurological knowledge, when he assisted to Charcot's presentations. Freud pointed out to Charcot that "these attacks are not possible; this does not follow the book." To which Charcot replied: "La théorie, c'est bon, mais cela n'empêche pas d'exister" (Theory is good, but does not keep things from existing) (Freud, 1893f, p.13). He could not have better articulated the result of the interaction between mastery and hysteria. The knowledge of the phallic master does not cover everything, on the contrary even. The irony of Charcot's answer to Freud is that it might very well be applied to Charcot's theory as well. Or to Freud's, for that matter, when he wrote his case study on Dora.

Surprising as it may sound, this brings us to the political dimension of hysteria. That is, to the matter of power and violence. Indeed, the repression or denial of the truth—that is, the inescapability of lack—results more often than not in violent power structures. Power is used to silence those who expose the master by telling the truth. The fact that Juliet Mitchell addressed this matter in her first book (1974!), combining her insights with those of Reich, Laing, and Lacan, and the fact that precisely this political dimension was largely ignored testifies to her foresight. As we will argue in the conclusion, our contemporary society has undergone a substantial change, obliging us to reconsider a number of things. And again, Juliet Mitchell's ideas correspond to the changes of our times. This new society is one of siblings run by Big Brother.

Hysteria and Politics

Ever since Michel Foucault's studies (1972, 1997), we are familiar with the idea that the history of psychiatry is a history of power and discipline, erecting reason as an ostensibly serene and neutral judge, while allowing it to comprise, and at the same time mask, multiple forms of subjugation. As such, and following Mitchell, we can regard hysteria is a political matter. As illustrations, we will provide the reader with three examples exposing a blend of politics and psychiatry.

The first example is almost completely forgotten. Madame Théroigne de Méricourt was one of the leading women during the French Revolution, fighting for female rights. After being warned several times by her male companions and revolutionaries, she was imprisoned in 1793 and the feminist women's meetings were banned. Instead of being guillotined, she was declared insane and remained detained for the rest of her life in La Salpétrière, where she died in 1817. The famous psychiatrist Esquirol, one of the founding fathers of French psychiatry, was her doctor. In his book *Des maladies mentales* (*On Mental Diseases*), he describes her as a monomaniac, meaning that she was beyond cure. After her death, he gave her body to Dr. Demoutier, his friend and colleague. In the phrenological tradition of the time, Demoutier measured her skull and concluded: "Although the intellectual faculties were clearly developed, they served only to accomplish deeds based on passion" (Allegaert, 2012, p. 55, 133). Obviously, passion is opposed to intellectual faculties.

Before introducing the contemporary version of Théroigne, let us look at a better-known couple: Sigmund Freud and Dora. Freud was a very ambitious man, and at the start of the previous century, he hoped to become famous with the publication of *The Interpretation of Dreams* (1900). His original intention was to use Dora's treatment in order to demonstrate the validity and the usefulness of his new method. He had already a title for the book: *Dreams and Hysteria*. But he had to change it into the more modest *Bruchstück einer Hysterie-Analyse* (*Fragment of an Analysis of a Case of Hysteria*). The case study shows that he had every reason to be modest. Dora's dreams are big question marks, as is literally mentioned in one of her dreams: "She asked about a hundred times." These questions concern her female identity, her sexuality, and the position assigned to her by the desire of a man (Freud, 1905e, p. 94). Instead of taking her question seriously, Freud steps into the shoes of the Oedipal master and produces knowledge. He explains her dreams and in the same movement, he tells her how she has to behave as a member of her sex. Instead of accepting his masterly explanations, she stops the treatment, after having made it clear that his explanations do not mean that much to her: "Why, has anything so very remarkable come out?" (Freud, 1905e, 105).

A contemporary version of Théroigne de Mericourt is Pussy Riot, that is, the women who provoked superphallic master Putin and as a result were convicted to three years of Siberian gulag.[3] What is less well known is that the judge declared them insane as well. In the verdict, they are diagnosed as suffering from a mixed-personality disorder, that is: "a condition that includes different combinations of a proactive approach to life, a drive for self-fulfilment, stubbornly defending their opinion, inflated self-esteem, inclination to oppositional behaviour, and propensity for protest reactions."[4] The message is clear: women who dare to challenge masculine power are insane, and the hysterical subject that challenges the phallic master has to pay the price.

The examples illustrate how an analogous structure works within, at first sight, quite different power relations: revolutionary, therapeutic, and political. Traditionally, this structure is simplified to a man–woman relation, in terms of sexual repression and resistance. In our opinion, this simplification has a defensive function, because a more fundamental discord of human nature is ignored. Lacan mentions this internal discord in his seminal paper on the mirror stage (1966, p. 96) and explains it later as the result of a primordial loss at the time of birth (1966, pp. 845–46). This marks the human being with a fundamental lack and a resulting desire to regain a lost plenitude. From early days onward, the responsibility both for the lack and the answer to it are projected on the other. This is Freud's reading of the Oedipus complex: the father has the penis, and he has to give it to me.

Lacan points to the radical nature of the loss and the impossibility to regain the original plenitude. This is structurally impossible because the subject tries to regain what is lost via the Symbolic order. As it is precisely the introduction into the Symbolic order that caused the loss, desire is eternal. The lack felt by the subject is the lack of the Symbolic, and hence, also a lack in knowledge and control. Based on Mitchell, we can say that the patriarchal processing of the original loss turns it into a much-discussed sexual lack for women (the phallus) and a neglected maternal lack for men (the womb). The result is a power play between men and women. Somebody must be blamed for the lack; somebody must have the Phallus. In this way, positions are distributed: the knowingly, almighty master, and his (or her) antithesis, the demanding other, with in between them the phallic signifier. The political world and gender relations are two fields illustrating the externalization of the originally internal discord.

Consider also the Enlightenment. At first sight, this period brings light into darkness and frees us from the dominance of religion. During the reign of religious discourse, male priests were the seat of knowledge. Women were considered to be the source of all evil, starting with Eve. Did the Enlightenment change this view? The weight on the spiritual was replaced by a weight on rationality. Psychiatric patients were considered as suffering from déraison, lack of reason (Foucault, 1972). The prohibition on the body was replaced by a prohibition on passion. It does not take much insight to recognize the same equation: rationality stands for masculinity, passion for femininity. Théroigne de Méricourt was not sinful, she was passionate and hence, mad. Today, this division between rationality and passion sounds obsolete. In the Western world, religion has lost much of its established significance and even ideologies have been declared dead. Does this mean that the underlying power structure has disappeared? Closer scrutiny unmasks the contemporary priests: they are the new (pseudo)scientists, promising total knowledge, based on cognitive brain studies. Their belief is that we are just one step away from total knowledge, the Grand Theory of Everything, thus becoming the (phallic) masters of the universe, in control of everything and everyone.

Hysterical Discourse and Discourse of the Master

If we study the history of religion, philosophy, and science, time and again, we can discover the same structure based on the same binary opposition (Verhaeghe, 2004). Soul versus body. Rationality versus passion. Cognitive versus affective. Man versus woman. Phallic plenitude versus not-All. Knowledge versus truth. This originally internal division, one that no subject can escape, reappears in typical social structures, as made evident by Lacan's theory on the hysterical discourse in its relation to the discourse of the master (see Figures 7.1–7.3 at the end of the chapter).

One of the advantages of this theory is that it does not start from gender, reifying hysteria as a feminine tendency and ignoring phenomena that speak of male hysteria. Another advantage is that it shows the interdependence of the hysteric and the master (Verhaeghe, 1999).[5]

Briefly summarized (see Figure 7.2), hysterical discourse stages the hysterical divided subject (noted as $) in the position of the agent, driven by its own truth (noted as object *a*). This truth is simple: every human being is marked by an ontological lack, based on a loss at birth; ever since, we are divided and looking for an answer. This is what drives us beyond knowledge (in matters of gender, life and death drives, there are no final answers). In order to get reassurance, the hysterical subject addresses the other as a master (noted as S1, the master signifier), obliging him to produce knowledge (noted as S2, the reunion of all signifiers). But this knowledge can never bridge (//) the gap toward the truth (Lacan, 1991).

The other formula shows us the discourse of the master (see Figure 7.3). The master figure (noted as S1), sitting on top of his own division (noted as $), projects his knowledge (noted as S2) on the other. The hoped-for result, that is, the other is satisfied and everything is under control, is not attained. On the contrary, the product of this discourse is precisely a renewed confrontation with the remainders, that is, what cannot be grasped by knowledge (noted as *a*) (Lacan, 1991).

The confrontation between the hysterical discourse and the discourse of the master leads inevitably to a spiral that endorses both parties in their respective positions. The hysterical subject is looking for answers, and provokes the master figure to demonstrate his power. The master tries to reassure the hysterical subject with his knowledge but soon enough, he will have to face his own failure. Whatever the quality of this knowledge, it can never adequately tell the truth about what drives the human subject. On the contrary, this knowledge is based on the Symbolic and denies its inherent lack, formulated by Lacan as symbolic castration. Acknowledging this castration would imply acknowledging *le pas-tout*, the not-All, and the failure of the master. Most masters are not willing to accept this failure. Often enough, the result is a violent reaction against the one, the hysterical subject, who threatens to expose their failure, their castration. This violence is then enacted in religious, political, or scientific-therapeutic terms. That is, in terms of their particular knowledge (S2). The other is characterized as sinful, dangerous, or disturbed.

A well-known feminist slogan tells us that the personal is the political. The internal discord mentioned above is present in every one of us, meaning that every one of us is marked by an original loss and divided between body and soul, between drive and mastery, between passion and rationality. This is the personal part. Every one of us tries to come to terms with this division. Education provides us a conventional way to handle this division. It provides us with the conventional answers. Here we find the Freudian Oedipus complex: the law of the father assigns boys and girls their "legitimate" places, phallic versus castrated. Now, the political part comes in view. Normally, says Freud, when we grow up, this complex should be destroyed, but this is never fully the case (see Verhaeghe, 2009). Religion, ideology, politics, and even science provide the different stages where this structural imbalance is continued.

Hysterical Structure and the Stage

Time and again, hysteria confronts us with the lack in the Symbolic order and hence, the lack of knowledge in relationship to the Real and the drive. The crucial elements are birth, death and sexuality, as they constitute the human condition. The hysterical demand for an answer defies conventional knowledge (Lacan, 1975). This defiance cannot be answered in the Symbolic as such, because it addresses the failure of the Symbolic order itself. Precisely this failure explains the structural link between hysteria and the theater. Hysteria needs a stage and every hysterical performance is an acting-out addressed to the Other. The divided subject brings something on stage that exposes the failure of the Master, while at the same time confirming the master in his position. At the end of the play, the failure is obvious, and results in the impossibility of full satisfaction. The impossibility is obvious if you look at the hysterical stage par excellence, namely Hollywood romantic dramas. At first instance, the (make-)belief is realized, because there is a male hero (occasionally a giant ape will do the job as well), who saves the female star. However, when everything is turning for the good, tragedy enters the scene. The boat sinks, the ape dies, the plane crashes, the loved one is killed, etcetera. The impossibility remains, and the desire is never satisfied.

Hence, hysteria is the term for a particular structure, in which master and divided subject play their part. For Lacan, hysterical subject and divided subject are synonymous (Lacan, 1991). As a structure, it can be filled by many contents. Therefore another classic hysterical feature appears: its chameleon-like nature. Mitchell understands this as the mimetic character of hysteria: if the other changes, the hysteric has a new model to identify with. The stage and the master change through time: priests, doctors, analysts, scientists, politicians...operating in church, hospital, consultation room, university, or courtroom. Each new master sets a new stage and presents the divided subject with new answers.

And each time, the hysteric identifies with these answers, thus taking another color, namely the color of the new master. So, a religious stage with religious masters produces religious hysteria. A medical stage with medical masters produces medical hysteria. A political stage with political masters produces political hysteria. On every stage, the interaction ends inevitably with an exposure of the master's failure. When Charcot's patients produced his hysterical attacks, they followed his suggestions, and hence, his desire. But in following them, they proved at the same time the failure of his medical approach. Obviously, the psychoanalytic scene is not free from this structure. For Lacan (2004) acting out is an appeal addressed to the Other and every hysterical symptom is a demand for interpretation, that is, a demand for a final answer. If an analyst believes that his answers are correct and absolute, he will share Freud's fate with respect to Dora. His interpretations will be refuted and refused. In that respect, a traditional analyst is not that different from Charcot as he might imagine.

This leads us to an important issue. It is said by conventional psychiatry that hysteria has disappeared. Contemporary psychiatry focuses on personality disorders, with the patient diagnosed with a "borderline personality disorder" on top of the list. The clinical examples in Juliet Mitchell's recent books do not look like the classic hysterical patients. Why should they? The stage has changed, so must have hysteria. With a slight exaggeration we can state that the well-behaved hysteric of the late nineteenth century, who, due to an unresolved Oedipal problem fantasizes about forbidden sexual acts and who out of sheer feelings of guilt develops phobic or conversion symptoms within a largely imaginary mental world, is threatened by extinction. Today we are dealing with a promiscuous, aggressive, and/or self-mutilating "borderline" patient with a complex traumatic history, who may nourish an addiction and/or an eating disorders. What social changes have elicited this symptomatology? A Belgian psychiatrist applied the DSM IV-R criteria for borderline personality disorder to our contemporary society. His conclusion is that the borderline personality has become the norm, not the exception (De Wachter, 2012). To be sure: "borderline personality disorder" is not a Lacanian category. In our opinion, and building from Mitchell's (2003, pp. 20–21) account of the relationship between hysteria and borderline personality, we perceive the latter condition as the actual pathological position of hysteria, reformed as a response to the contemporary situation (Verhaeghe, 2014b). No less than their nineteenth-century forebears, the contemporary hysterical subject is based on a common identification with the desire of the contemporary Other. But whose desire are they identifying with? Who is the master of the contemporary hysterical subject? And what is their stage? The answers to these questions lead us to the political field and to an unexpected extension of Juliet Mitchell's theory on siblings.

Perverse Society and the Postmodern Superego: Enjoy!

Traditional hysteria was embedded in a traditional patriarchal society. Although the patriarch might take different forms (a religious father is not the same as a scientific father) the basic Oedipal structure remained the same. A typical role assignment was installed time and again. Power and knowledge resided with the man/father, while desire and lack resided with the woman/mother. Answers were expected from the father, the main one being a prohibition on Oedipal desire. The conventional Oedipal reading declares that women are castrated, and that men are phallic heroes. In real life, it is the other way around, as explained by Lacan in his famous chapter seven on love in seminar XX. Women escape the phallic reduction, and men are the phallic misfits. Every man acquires his inscription in the Symbolic through the phallic signifier, but it is only the primal father (the exception) who is supposed to have the phallus. A normal man never meets the phallic standard. In contrast, a woman—not The Woman—may define herself in relationship to the not-All, instead of alienating herself to the phallic signifier. The hysterical subject, whether a man or a woman, remains within the phallic logic, meaning that he or she expects the phallus from the master and in doing so, demonstrates his failure to deliver.

A patriarchal society is a typically neurotic society. The primal father is installed based on repression and on the installation of the patriarchal law. This law installs the phallic principle as the basis for the symbolic order. Every lack is explained in terms of castration, meaning that in this imaginary world everything can be fully understood as long as you address the phallic father, the one who knows. Underneath lies the object of primary repression, meaning that part of the Real that escapes this phallic order, something we are not very willing to confront, because it provokes anxiety. Reducing women to a category of castrated and hence lesser beings is a reassuring strategy. But time and again, the phallic patriarch is confronted with the limits of this strategy. This explains the two forms of neurosis in patriarchal society, with their typical gender distribution: obsessional neurosis for men, hysteria for women. The obsessional tries desperately to safeguard the Oedipal law and the rules; the hysteric challenges them by demanding answers. Both of them have to construct symptoms, in order to cope with their anxiety. If they enter analysis, they will have to come to terms with what lies beyond this law, instead of defending or fighting it. This "beyond" is exactly what cannot be understood in the Symbolic, hence Lacan's denominations: the not-All, the lack of the Other, S (A) with a slash over the A. Traditional patriarchal society is based on repression and the accompanying return of the repressed. Primarily, that which is repressed is the failure of the system, meaning the fact that the symbolic order is not able to cover fully the Real of the drive. Birth, death and sexuality escape the phallic order. Via the Oedipal structure, the subject is taught to handle the lack in phallic terms (big, bigger, biggest). There is no room for femininity beyond the phallic enjoyment. The cornerstone of this system is primary repression.

Today, classic hysteria and obsessional neurosis seem to have disappeared, in spite of the "obsessive/compulsive" character of the widely used DSM. This coincides with the decline of patriarchal society in its traditional form. We got rid of the patriarchs of former times, the primal fathers who used to run everything. This is in several respects a cultural progress, and the problems that we are facing in our contemporary society should not be used to plead for a return to the supposedly good old times. It is much more interesting to ask ourselves how we can understand this contemporary society from a psychoanalytic perspective and where hysteria fits in it. Our thesis is that the former patriarchal society with its neurotic structure has been replaced by a Big Brother society that has a perverse structure. If this is the case, how can this be argued, and what are the effects for the hysterical subject and its need for a stage? The short answer is that the whole world has been turned into a stage and that the hysteric has exchanged castration anxiety for *invidia*, envy.

In our opinion, our contemporary society has become a perverse one, because it is based on a primary *disavowal*, not only of castration, but even a disavowal of lack as such. The prohibiting father and his laws are discarded. In this respect, we don't share Mitchell's idea that the contemporary annihilation of the father results in a psychotic structure (Mitchell, 2003, p.175).[6] In the world of the perverse Other, nothing is lacking and total enjoyment is not only a possibility, it is even a moral obligation. The command of the new superego is simply: "Enjoy!" and anyone who fails to do so has to be ashamed of himself. In the absence of the father, enjoyment and perfection have become the new norms. This is the desire of the perverse Other. The underlying message is that there is no structural lack and that everything is within reach. Big (Br)Other preaches his message of obligatory enjoyment 3,000 times a day (the average number of advertisements an American is exposed to per day). In the words of Michael Foley (2010): "The Ad drives the Id."

Applied to sexuality, this means that the former prohibition is replaced by an obligation. Equals, siblings, can agree and sign a contract or even an informed consent. Everything is allowed, as long as the participants agree. We call this perverse, because as a strategy it contains the same manipulation as the sexual pervert uses. In the work by Marquis de Sade, the victim is seduced with the promise of an ultimate enjoyment—ultimate meaning: beyond the always limited phallic pleasure—but this promise is never held, much the contrary. The only thing the perverse other is interested in is total control. The contemporary advertisements create the impression that they really care, that they want to provide the public with perfect products leading to full enjoyment. Obviously, the only thing they really care about is to be in control of the money.

Depressive Hedonia

Both the neurotic and the perverse society create their own myth in order to cover up the underlying truth about the lack in the symbolic order. The neurotic society burdens us with the myth of the perfect couple and eternal love: find the right (phallic) partner, and you will be happy forever. The underlying truth is that the perfect partner turns out to be castrated. The net result is feelings of guilt ("I don't have the phallus") or disappointment ("S/he did not have the phallus, after all"). The contemporary myth tells us that if we buy the right stuff, do the right exercises, and work hard enough, we will have a perfect enjoyment. "Happiness is a choice." The underlying and disavowed truth is that total jouissance is impossible. The new myth has a very important side effect as it is based on the illusion of voluntarism. Everything is stripped down to a matter of decision and personal effort. This implies that if you do not take that decision, and do not work hard enough, it is your mistake and your fault. As a result, Victorian guilt and neurosis are replaced by postmodern shame and depression: if we do not enjoy, we are losers who have failed our duty.

This idea of voluntarism is indicative for a new belief, namely total controllability and manageability, based on our personal effort. As there is no castration and even no lack, every one of us can and must have a perfect body, a perfect relationship, perfect sex, perfect children, and stay young forever. If that is not the case, the sole explanations are that you did not put enough effort in it or made the wrong choices. Juli Zeh has depicted this world in her novel *Corpus delicti*, where, what she describes as The Method, obliges every one of us to be perfectly healthy. This reminds me of the perverse command by Marquis de Sade in *La Philosophie dans le Boudoir*: "Français, encore un effort!" ("French citizens, yet another effort!"). What is less clear in Zeh's novel is that this perfect body is obliged to enjoy. The effect of such an obligatory enjoyment is painfully shown in the movie *Shame*, directed by Steve McQueen, where the main character is permanently fooling around without actually enjoying himself, and more recently in Lars von Trier's *Nymphomaniac*. Mark Fisher (2009, p. 21) has coined an apt phrase for this state: depressive hedonia. Sadly, this is the paradox of a new superego obligation: the more we have to enjoy, the lesser satisfaction we experience, and the more we end with what Lacan terms a *plus-de-jouir*. This Lacanian expression contains a duplicity that is hard to translate. The ever higher levels of enjoyment, plus meaning more, lead to a loss of satisfaction ("plus de" is a negation) that borders with anxiety. It is the same anxiety that Freud discovered beyond the pleasure principle and that Lacan tried to grasp with his very last thoughts on jouissance.

The World as a Stage: Big Brother Is Watching You

The duplicity of the perverse system is that it creates the illusion of personal freedom while control is literally in the air and omnipresent (Bauman and Lyon, 2013). Flat screens have replaced the stringent stare of the Holy Father (remember the old-fashioned paintings with a holy Eye framed in a triangle). CCTV and other surveillance apparatus have their eyes on everyone. From a traditional point of view, one would expect a central controlling father figure in this contemporary version of Bentham's Panopticon. It is exactly the opposite: the tower is empty; the only thing in there is a powerful computer server, permitting everyone to watch and control everyone else, all the time. In such a social formation, *siblings* are running the very show that controls them. This becomes clear if one considers the most important contemporary surveillance apparatus, that is, the so-called social media, LinkedIn, Facebook, Twitter, Instagram, and the like. The postmodern human being exposes himself constantly to the controlling gaze of what he or she thinks are peers. What are we controlled for and what is its effect? The moral obligation is perfection and enjoyment. In absence of the father, the standard against which we assess ourselves is the mirror stage other who mirrors completeness without lack (e.g., posting success after success for others to see). For lack of a differentiating criterion, all siblings want to be more equal to their equal's completeness than the other. Freud talked jokingly about the "the narcissism of the minor differences," while Lacan describes the aggression at the base of the mirror stage.

The obligatory identification with the mirror stage other has serious effects on the relationship between subject, gender, and authority. Patriarchal society installed a phallic gender differentiation, with clear-cut gender roles, together with a clear differentiation between the generations, children versus parents. The perverse society does not acknowledge the lack and disavows castration; therefore the traditional gender differentiation becomes blurred. It is our contention that the contemporary man is quite feminine by Victorian standards, the contemporary woman might be quite masculine against the same criteria, and possibility of a transgender subject illustrates the interstitial spaces opened by the decline of gender differentiation through repression. At the same time, the perverse society does not acknowledge the law of the father; therefore the differentiation between the generations becomes blurred as well. Mother and daughter are presented as two sisters, and fathers are competing with their sons, especially as the father has lost his position of authority. Big Brother has replaced the authoritarian father of the Victorian era. His most prominent characteristic, besides the fact that he is watching all the time, is that he is an anonymous peer. It is impossible to get hold of this ghost, which means that it is impossible to knock him off his pedestal and kill him.

"Big Brother is watching you" might very well become the iconic formula of our times. George Orwell would be amazed to see how his expression fits more and more a paradoxical reality. The paradox resides in the fact that our reality needs endorsement from the virtual world via the Internet and the social media. The fact that we are dealing with a virtual world does not make it less real, on the contrary. Life is increasingly experienced as one big reality show where something is only real on condition that it appears on the screen and is "liked" by others; if not, it does not exist. As a result, the world is increasingly experienced as one big stage with an omnipresent, anonymous, and watchful eye, covering the scene nonstop. Our body has to be perfect, our smile has to be genuine, and our enjoyment has to be total.[7]

The disavowal of lack leads to a divergence between the texture of our everyday lives and the conviction that everything is under control and perfectly manageable. If not, it must be that some individual made a mistake, because there is no structural lack; someone has to be blamed. Many documentaries on science suggest that total knowledge is almost there. In the meantime, this conviction has taken hilarious and painful proportions. If the weather forecast is wrong, the weatherman has to apologize. A painful example is the conviction of six Italian scientists, because they failed to predict the 2009 earthquake in L'Aquila. Here as well, failure has become a question of personal responsibility.

Hysteria Facing Big Brother

What are the effects for the hysterical subject? The world has been turned into one big stage, where everyone is constantly performing. This is good news; the hysterical subject does not have to look for a theatre any longer. The bad news is that the master has become invisible, and that it is very hard to challenge Big Brother. He is hiding behind the screen and does not pretend to be a master anymore. As a result, the theatre has lost its traditional function for hysteria. Exposing the failure of the patriarchally determined gender roles is almost impossible, because the roles have become blurred. Defying the sexual prohibition is superfluous, now that enjoyment is obligatory. And lastly, provoking the master is hard, because he is invisible.

The only thing left for the hysterical subject is to challenge the idea of total enjoyment by exposing the real of the body. Self-mutilation in some borderline personality patients mirrors performance art, thus setting a painful new scene. For example, the performance artist Marina Abramovic knives her fingers, sits in a heap of bones, and convinces at least a part of the audience to manipulate her body with a variety of pointy objects. She is literally the incarnation of the contemporary hysteria, challenging enjoyment as demanded by the perverse (br)Other. Another example is performance artist Orlan, developing her Carnal art project. She undergoes a process of continuous plastic surgery, transforming herself into a variety of elements, as seen in famous paintings and sculptures of women. On the surface, Orlan's goal, using plastic surgery in order to achieve it, matches the classic hysterical one, namely the acquirement of the phallic ideal of female beauty as depicted by male artists. But her own words tell us something different: "I can observe my own body cut open, without suffering...I see myself all the way down to my entrails; a new mirror stage...I can see to the heart of my lover."[8]

In clinical terms, more often than not, this confronts us with the new form hysteria has taken, that is, the so-called borderline personality disorder. Borderline patients experience an unstable self-image and self-direction as a product of labile identifications, and oscillate between overinvolvement and underinvolvement in relationships conceived of either as perfect or as devalued. These subjects do not have the luxury of a patriarchal master against whom they can revolt; they have to defend themselves against an imposed jouissance as the demand for enjoyment without lack. One way to revolt is to cut and burn or starve their own body and expose their wounded or emaciated flesh to the world. At the same time, they expose the failure of a Big Brother society, just like postmodern artists do on the art scene.

Siblings and Subjectivity

It is our thesis that patriarchal society is shifting toward a society of siblings, where the horizontal level is far more important than the vertical one. At this point, Juliet Mitchell's theory might prove to be even more revolutionary than she thought herself. Her theory is first of all new because she addresses the importance of siblings in a more or less traditional society—hence her references to the Freudian case studies. At the same time, she indicates in her book a more fundamental change, the one that we interpret as a shift to a Big Brother society. This shift has changed the traditional question about subjectivity. Instead of the classic hysterical worry ("Am I a man or a woman in relation to the Other?"), the contemporary "borderline" subject faces a far more fundamental question: "Do I or don't I exist, in relation to the Big (br)Other?" As Mitchell puts it: "The crucial absence here, then, is not the absent phallus (the castration complex) but the absent self" (Mitchell, 2003, p. 29).

How to think subjectivity if there is no lack, if castration is disavowed and the not-All is denied and instead of that completeness is expected from everyone? Gender implies difference and a symbolic lack; Big Brother siblings imply similarity and imaginary completeness. Under a functioning Oedipal regime, a child could compete with his siblings for the love of his mother and father, thus acquiring a unique position instead of uniqueness. Juliet Mitchell introduces "the law of the mother," permitting the child to be different from the other children, while the law of the father reunites them in one category, based on the incest prohibition. The two laws are both instrumental in the becoming of a subject; in their necessary combination they provided the foundation of the Oedipal structure. The irony is that Mitchell corrects both Freud's (the passive mother) and Lacan's (the devouring crocodile mother) theory of the Oedipal complex at a time when the Oedipal structure is disappearing. In our opinion, Mitchell's theory convincingly demonstrates the necessary combination of the two laws. The implication is that the contemporary disappearance of the law of the father implies at the same time the loss of the law of the mother. Our era is already living the results of this disappearance. The lack of distance makes it hard to have a clear view on these effects. We do know that we need recognition by the Other. If the Other is the one of the mirror stage, this need for recognition turns into an endless mirror fight: either me or the other, with a deadly dimension. What Mitchell (2003, p.43) described as something temporary—"the realization that one is not unique, that someone stands exactly in the same place as oneself and that though one has found a friend, this loss of uniqueness is, at least temporarily, equivalent to annihilation"—runs the risk of becoming something enduring, a loss of a sense of self based upon an existential anxiety: Who am I?

The inevitable conclusion is that we need to rethink our theory and our practice. At this time, it is not yet clear in which direction this will develop. We are convinced that a central focus should be on authority, as essentially different from power. The trouble is not that we have become a fatherless society—many contemporary fathers are much more into fatherhood than their own fathers ever were. The trouble is that authority, as a symbolic function attached to a position, has disappeared. The challenge is to develop difference and subjectivity on a horizontal level, as vertical differentiation (based on traditional authority) is disappearing. Instead of focussing on the dangers of a world reduced to the mirror stage, we should ask ourselves how a leaderless society may function (Ross, 2012).

And what about our clinical practice? Does a perverse society with an obligation to enjoy ask for a different analyst compared to a patriarchal society with a prohibition on desire? If we follow the classic Oedipal solution, the subject is duped by the primal father. If we enter the postmodern perverse scene, the subject is duped by Big Brother. The net result is that we are duped anyway, meaning that there is no argument whatsoever for a return to patriarchy. The question to be asked is how this shift will mark the subject, and how analysis might respond to it.

A number of changes have already taken place. Our psychoanalytic practice is based on transference and especially on the analysis of transference. A patriarchal neurotic society installs a different transference compared to a Big Brother perverse society. We experience this with our "borderline" patients who are not addressing us in a vertical way. The analyst is losing his traditionally parental transference position, and we are already reinventing our clinical practice, with a shift toward a group approach, be it institutional psychotherapy, self-help groups, or mentalization-based therapy. We will need to rethink our theories as well—the Oedipal theory simply does not fit any more. At this point, Juliet Mitchell's work might provide an important inspiration. Her early focus on the political just as her latest work on siblings testifies how she feels the pulse of the time.

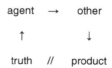

Figure 7.1

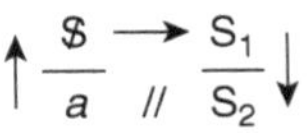

$$\uparrow \frac{\$}{a} \;\;//\;\; \xrightarrow{} \frac{S_1}{S_2} \downarrow$$

Figure 7.2

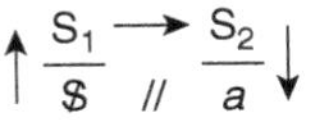

$$\uparrow \frac{S_1}{\$} \;\;//\;\; \xrightarrow{} \frac{S_2}{a} \downarrow$$

Explanation of symbols:

S1   master signifier

S2   knowledge

$ the ever divided subject

a   that what escapes every form of symbolisation

Figure 7.3

Notes

1. Jouissance is one of Lacan's most notoriously difficult concepts, especially as it evolved during the development of his theory. It indicates the limit between a pleasure arising from the drive that can be controlled and one that cannot, thus threatening the subject with death. It is Lacan's understanding of Freud's death drive (see Verhaeghe, 2009).
2. Indeed, the symbolic order requires a threefold structure, otherwise it is impossible to introduce difference. To give you an idea: indicating the left- and right-hand side of a room (two elements) requires a third element (in most cases: our own position), otherwise differentiation is impossible.
3. See http://en.wikipedia.org/wiki/Pussy_Riot.
4. See *The New Yorker*: http://www.newyorker.com/online/blogs /newsdesk/2012/08/the-pussy-riot-verdict.html.
5. For a didactic explanation of Lacan's discourse theory, see Verhaeghe, P. (1995). Papers by the authors can be downloaded from http:// www.psychoanalysis.ugent.be.
6. The Lacanian structural reading of psychosis is different from the Anglo-Saxon perspective (see Vanheule, 2011).
7. The circle, as described by Dave Eggers (2013), is more real than we imagine.
8. Extract from the Carnal art manifesto. See http://orlan.eu/adriensina /manifeste/carnal.html.

References

Allegaert, P. and Brokken, Ann. eds., 2012. *Nerveuze vrouwen. Twee eeuwen vrouwen en hun psychiaters*. (Trans.: Two Centuries of Women and Their Psychiatrists). Museum Dr. Guislain, Gent: Lannoo.

Bauman, Z. and Lyon, D. 2013. *Liquid Surveillance*. Cambridge: Polity Press.

De Wachter, D. 2012. *Borderline Times*. Gent: Lannoo.

Eggers, D. 2013. *The Circle*, London: Vintage Books.

Fisher, M. 2009. *Capitalist Realism. Is There No Alternative?* Winchester & Washington: Zero Books.

Foley, M. 2010. *The Age of Absurdity. Why Modern Life Makes It Hard to be Happy.* London: Simon & Schuster.

Foucault, M. 1972. *Histoire de la folie à l'âge classique*. Paris: Gallimard.

Foucault, M. 1997. *The Birth of the Clinic. An Archaeology of Medical Perception.* Translated by A. Sheridan. London: Routledge.

Freud, S. 1978 [1893]. Charcot. *The Standard Edition of the Complete Psychological Works of Sigmund Freud*, 9–23. London: The Hogarth Press.

Freud, S. 1978 [1905e]. Fragment of an Analysis of a Case of Hysteria. *The Standard Edition of the Complete Psychological Works of Sigmund Freud, Vol. 7*, 1–122. London: The Hogarth Press.

Freud, S. 1978 [1927]. Fetishism, *The Standard Edition of the Complete Psychological Works of Sigmund Freud, Vol. 21*, 149–158. London: The Hogarth Press.

Israël, L. 1984. *Hysterie, sekse en de geneesheer.* Leuven/Amersfoort: Acco. (Original French: L'hystérique, le sexe et le médecin).

Lacan, J. 1966. Le Stade du miroir comme formateur de la fonction du Je. In *Ecrits*, pp. 93–100. Paris: Seuil.

Lacan, J. 1966. Position de l'inconscient. In *Ecrits*, 829–850. Paris: Seuil.

Lacan, J. 1975 [1972–73]. *Le Séminaire, livre XX: Encore* Edited by J.-A. Miller. Paris: Seuil.

Lacan, J. 1990 [1974]. *Television: a Challenge to the Psychoanalytic Establishment.* Translated by D. Hollier. New York: Norton.

Lacan, J. 1991 [1969–70]. *Le Séminaire, livre XVII, L'Envers de la psychanalyse.* Edited by J. A. Miller. Paris: Seuil.

Lacan, J. 2004 [1962–63]. Le Séminaire, livre X, L'angoisse Edited by J.-A. Miller. Paris: Seuil.

Mitchell, J. 2000. *Madmen and Medusas: Reclaiming Hysteria.* New York: Basic Books.

Mitchell, J. 2003 [1974]. *Psychoanalysis and Feminism.* New York: Basic Books.

Mitchell, J. 2003. *Siblings: Sex and Violence.* Cambridge: Polity Press.

Ross, C. 2012. *The Leaderless Revolution: How Ordinary People Will Take Power and Change Politics in the Twenty-First Century.* New York: Blue Rider Press.

Vanheule, S. 2011. *The Subject of Psychosis: A Lacanian Perspective.* London and New York: Palgrave Macmillan.

Verhaeghe, P. 1995. "From Impossibility to Inability: Lacan's Theory of the Four Discourses." *The Letter*, 3: 76–100. (Digital version on http://www.psychoanalysis.ugent.be).

Verhaeghe, P. ([1987] 1999). *Does the Woman Exist? From Freud's Hysteric to Lacan's Feminine.* New York: The Other Press.

Verhaeghe, P. 2009. *New Studies of Old Villains. A Radical Reconsideration of the Oedipus Complex*. (Foreword by Juliet Mitchell.) New York: Other Press.

Verhaeghe, P. 2001. "Mind Your Body & Lacan's Answer to a Classical Deadlock." In: *Beyond Gender. From Subject to Drive*. Edited by P. Verhaeghe, pp. 99–132, New York: Other Press. (Digital version on http://www.psychoanalysis.ugent.be).

Verhaeghe, P. 2004. "Phallacies of Binary Reasoning: Drive beyond Gender." In: *Dialogues on Sexuality, Gender and Psychoanalysis*. Edited by I. Matthis, 53–66. London: Karnac (Digital version on http://www.psychoanalysis.ugent.be).

Verhaeghe, P. 2014a. *What about Me?* Brunswick: Scribe Publications.

Verhaeghe, P. 2014b Today's Madness Does Not Make Sense. In *Lacan on Madness: Madness, Yes You Can't*. Edited by P. Gherovici and M. Steinkoler London: Routledge, Taylor & Francis Group.

Zeh, J. 2012. *The Method*. Londen: Harvill Secker.

Chapter 8

Reframing Obsessional Neurosis: The Rat Man's Siblings

Robbie Duschinsky and Rachel Leigh

In *Siblings* (2003, 19), Mitchell suggests that "the introduction of a lateral paradigm reframes the classical neuroses." The truth of this claim has been well demonstrated by Mitchell's work on hysteria. However, the advance represented by the introduction of the lateral axis has yet to be applied to obsessional neurosis. At the level of the relationship between the ego and the drive, both hysteria and obsessional neuroses are constellations of defences against the Oedipus complex. Freud ([1896a] 2001, 146) was the first to declare the need to "set alongside of hysteria the obsessional neurosis as a self-sufficient and independent disorder." Yet he also at points treated obsessional neurosis as if it were a branch of hysteria, and throughout his writings he would observe important parallels as well as contrasts between the two disorders. If, indeed, "the language of an obsessional neurosis—the means by which it expresses its secret thoughts—is, as it were, only a dialect of the language of hysteria" ([1909a] 2001, 196–7), then insights from Mitchell's analysis of the latter neurosis may well help shed light on the former.

The central site in his corpus at which Freud elaborates his theory of obsessional neurosis is the "Notes upon a Case of Obsessional Neurosis," which details the case of Ernst Lanzer. Lanzer entered treatment with Freud in 1907. His personal and professional life had come to an impasse in the face of inhibitions and compulsive thoughts. Freud called Lanzer "the Rat Man" in his published "Notes upon a Case of Obsessional Neurosis," since many of these compulsions were organized by the theme of rats. While lateral relations are not highlighted in the published text, the significance of Lorenz's siblings to his neurosis is evident in Freud's case notes. It was Freud's practice to make written notes on his cases "on the evening of the day of treatment" ([1909a] 2001, 159). Usually these were destroyed. However, the first four months of case notes on the Rat Man were found among Freud's papers in London upon his death.

Freud publicly presented the Lanzer case no less than five times to the Vienna Psychoanalytic Society between October 30, 1907, and April 8, 1908, and also as the opening five-hour presentation at the first Congress of the International Psychoanalytic Association on April 27, 1908 (Jones 1955, II, 49). Given that Freud was able to report that "the patient's mental health was restored to him by the analysis," this repetition appears to have been both a mark of confidence in the capacity of the case to illustrate obsessional neurosis and its analysis ([1909a] 2001, 249). Since Lanzer had previously been treated without effect by the renowned psychiatrist Wagner-Jauregg, Freud's success appeared all the more remarkable. As Beigler (1975, 276) describes, Freud was here "fashioning a cure for the previously incurable. To have had so brilliant a result with so difficult a patient in only eleven months was no small achievement." Perhaps, however, the repetition in Freud's presentation of the case together with the survival of the case notes can also be thought of as the marks of something left troublingly unresolved and unbound. Describing his feelings during the composition of the published text in a letter to Jung, Freud wrote: "It just pours out of me, and even so it's inadequate" ([1909b] 1979, 116). Even many years later, Freud would suggest that "obsessional neurosis is unquestionably the most interesting and repaying subject of analytic research. But as a problem it has not yet been mastered" ([1926] 2001, 113). Anna Freud (1966, 116) reports a remark from her father that, in the study of obsessional neurosis, perhaps "a group of people may succeed where the single individual fails." Turning this remark at a right-angle, this chapter will explore the possibility that it is precisely attention to group—lateral—process which can help further advance our understanding of the Rat Man case and of obsessional phenomena.

Unlike the Wolf Man case study in which siblings appear clearly in the manifest content of the published text and therefore have been the subject of ongoing discussion (e.g., Oliver 2009), the latent status of Freud's thoughts on the Rat Man's sibling relationships has meant that their significance has been little discussed. Indeed, it has not been uncommon for commentators on the case to offer specific repudiations that the sibling relationships have significance; perhaps the most stark is Veszy-Wagner (1967, 602), who states that "Rat Man had three sisters who, besides possible sexual games in childhood, later played no role." In reframing the "Notes upon a Case of Obsessional Neurosis," the chapter will shed new light on the significance of siblings to the Rat Man case study, and through this lay the groundwork for future reflections on the role of the lateral axis in obsessional neurosis.

The Rat Man's Father

Two chief symptoms brought Ernst Lanzer, a graduate law student, to analysis with Freud. First, Lanzer experienced prohibitions regarding seemingly inconsequential actions. Second, he also experienced inner voices, which commanded him to behave in ways he found bizarre and at odds with his conscious desires, such as to kill himself by cutting his throat with a razor or to exhibit his penis to the ghost of his dead father. Lanzer "had wasted years, he told me, in fighting against these ideas of his" (Freud [1909a] 2001, 158). Freud's published study focuses on an incident early in the analysis. Lanzer was on military maneuvers when he lost a pair of glasses and ordered a new pair in the mail. He was told by the Captain that he owed Lieutenant A, who had advanced the money at the post office for the new pair. This was a mistake, however, and the money was actually owed to the young woman at the post office, who had advanced him the money herself. Lanzer, who knew this, nonetheless found himself making a vow to pay back Lieutenant A. This motivated him to take a train journey to Lieutenant A, but which actually brought him to Freud's door. Freud interpreted Lanzer's actions as precipitated by the constellation of relations from his family history. In finding himself in a "sequel" to his father's marriage dilemma, Lanzer experienced obsessive symptoms relating to the repayment of a military debt—which it would be impossible to repay to Lieutenant A because it was never owed to him, but to the lady at the post office. Lanzer described fears that if he did not obey the compulsion, then his beloved and his father would be subject to an awful torture. The torture, which he had heard about from a military colleague, was that a pot [*Topf*] containing starving rats would be placed on the buttocks of the victim; the rats would be tormented with a hot poker so that, looking for escape, they would bore with teeth and claws into the anus. Freud was surprised to learn, however, that Lanzer's father had died a few years earlier, and that the punishments would not solely take place "not only to our present life but also to eternity—to the next world" ([1909a] 2001, 169).

Speaking at the Vienna Psychoanalytic Society on April 8, 1908 (Nunberg and Federn 1962: I, 370–1), Freud reported that the obsessive symptoms were hinged together by three words related to *Ratten* [rats]. A first related word was *Spielratte* [an irresponsible gambler], which characterized Lanzer's father, who gambled away the regiment's money during his time in the army and when helped out by a friend, never repaid the debt. Rats represented his father, payment, and this unpaid debt. The second related term was *Heiraten* [getting married]. Whereas his mother wanted him to marry a wealthy young woman, Lanzer chose his infertile cousin, Gisela, as his love-object. This choice stood in contrast to his father, who Lanzer perceived as having married his mother rather than a poorer woman, with whom he was in love. Third, Lanzer reported to Freud that in his speech he elided the difference between *Ratten* and *raten* [to guess]. Freud interpreted that rats represented the patient's experience of powerful doubt in relation to his love objects, since this love was continually felt to be disrupted and contaminated by unintegrated rage. Rats thus articulated Lanzer's relationship with his father and money, his mother and love, and ambivalence; they also hinged Lanzer's life and wishes with the actions of his father.

Freud deciphers the episode of the attempt to pay back the lieutenant for the glasses as an expression of ambivalence, caused primarily by the conflict between a conscious love for the father and unconscious feelings of rage toward him. The obsessional neurosis was understood as a two-fold defence against these feelings of rage. First, the reproach toward the paternal object to which it had originally been directed was displaced as unbound libido onto thought. Thoughts themselves were invested with the quality of erotic objects, from which the obsessional would expect pleasure and for which they would experience self-reproach. The result is obsessive thoughts, obsessive doubts, and anxieties. Second, the rivalry with the father at the genital level was circumvented by a displacement onto anal material: in "obsessional neurotics—we can observe the result of a regressive debasement of the genital organisation. This is expressed in the fact that every phantasy originally conceived on the genital level is transposed to the anal level—the penis being replaced by the fecal mass and the vagina by the rectum" ([1917] 2001, 131). Freud's interpretation in the published case study emphasized the significance of the relationship with the father for Lanzer's symptoms. On Freud's interpretation, Lanzer's conflicts about erotic desire and marriage were redirected via the father's history into an anal concern about paying a debt (through the money=feces equation); the threat of the rat torture to his father and Gisela if the debt was not paid manifested Lanzer's ambivalence between conscious love for his father, and unconscious hate for his father's refusal to support his marriage to Gisela.

The Rat Man's Mother

Yet even while the analysis was still taking place, this interpretation was subject to criticism. Speaking at the Vienna Psychoanalytic Society on the occasion of one of Freud's presentations of the "Rat Man" in 1908, Otto Rank objected that "all factors clearly point to the patient's love for his mother, even though there has not yet been any direct reference to this in the analytic material." Freud replied that "Rank will probably prove to be right in his assumption that incestuous wishes for the mother play a role, though the relationship is complicated by the presence of four sisters" (Nunberg and Federn [1908] 1962: 1, 233). This is an extraordinary statement: Freud is explaining that his focus on the unconscious hatred of the father in the Rat Man case study is caused by the fact that too much sibling material obscured his view of the mother! In the published case study, perhaps responding to Rank's concern, Freud justified his focus on the father in the published case study on the basis that "the theme of the rats has lacked any element directed towards his mother, evidently because there is very strong resistance in relation to her" ([1909a] 2001, 293).

Examining the case notes, it does indeed seem to be true that the figure of the mother is overshadowed by the extensive notes on Lanzer's sibling relationships. However, this has not stopped later analysts contesting Freud's account of the case, and arguing—in line with a broader rise in attention to the mother in psychoanalytic theory in the generation after Freud—for the significance of the patient's mother in this paradigmatic case of obsessional neurosis (Künstlicher 1998; Mahoney 2007). Offering a good example of how attention beyond the father can help sharpen our understanding of the case, Bass has astutely observed that Freud's focus on the father means that he does not consider the psychical meaning of the young lady at the post office. Lanzer incurs a real debt for the glasses to this woman, and which his obsession with paying Lieutenant A meant that he was set to exploit her by not reimbursing her payment.

Arguments for the missed importance of the mother have often drawn upon a comparison of the published case with the unpublished notes for deepening our understanding of the Lanzer case, and through it of obsessional neurosis. For example, commenting on Lanzer's first analytic session with Freud, Crockatt (2013) has observed that "Freud published his initial consultation almost verbatim with one significant omission: 'After I had told him my terms, he said he must consult his mother.' The patient, it will be recalled, was 29 years old at that time." From this analysis Crockatt is able to deftly draw out the significance of themes of differentiation and undifferentiation in Lanzer's symptoms: the issue of merger or submergence into the mother is managed in part through the way in which Lanzer dealt with and agonised over money. This conclusion agrees with that of Verhaeghe (2001, 161), who argues that "in the case of obsessional neurosis, the underlying anxiety is much greater than in the case of hysteria. Traditionally, Freud ascribes this anxiety to the father figure, thus making his traditional mistake…the fear of the obsessional concerns the first Other, the mother, whose demanding is interpreted as an attempt to incorporate the subject." The December analytical sessions in the case notes particularly address this threat of incorporation, framed as a need to avoid relationship with the mother in order to avoid contamination. "His mother suffered from an abdominal affection and now has a bad smell from her genitals, which makes him very angry. She herself says that she stinks unless she has frequent baths, but that she cannot afford it, and this appals him" ([1909] 2001, 296). Both to escape from the need to engage in a permeable relationship with his mother and as a reaction formation against his disgust, Lanzer "hands over all his money to his mother because he does not want to have anything from her" ([1909a] 2001, 297). Transposed onto an anal register, the prohibition on desire for the mother becomes disgust for her genitals and for monetary interaction with her.

Lanzer's Siblings

In line with such reflections, Freud observes that the patient's "sexual desires for his mother and sister and his sister's premature death were linked up with the young hero's chastisement at his father's hand" ([1909a] 2001, 207). He goes on to clarify that "the death of an elder sister, which took place when he was between three and four years old, played a great part in his phantasies, and was brought into intimate connection with his childish misdemeanours during the same period" ([1909] 2001, 235). However, this "great part" and "intimate connection" are left unexplored. Besides these remarks, in the rest of Freud's published case ambivalence toward the father is shorn of its "link up" with siblings, and ambivalence toward the father is examined alone as the central etiological factor in the obsessional neurosis.

Attention to the significance of Lanzer's mother in Freud's notes on the case has also led commentators at points to note the importance of the patient's siblings to his history and development. Much of this analysis, while helpful and perceptive (e.g., Mahoney 1986), has attended to siblings within a frame that privileges their significance primarily in terms of the meanings for Lanzer of his mother's reproductive capabilities. However, two texts stand out as presenting sustained attention to sibling dynamics in the case notes. One is Billig (1999), who draws attention to a passage in the case notes which begins: "He is cheerful, untrammelled and active, and is behaving aggressively to a girl, a dressmaker" ([1909a] 2001, 278). Billig states that "behaving aggressively" means to sexually pursue, and proposes that this is supported by the fact that the next reference to the dressmaker describes Lanzer's intercourse with her. After mention of pursuing the dressmaker:

> Confessions followed about his relations to his sisters. He made, so he said, repeated attacks on his next younger sister, Julie, after his father's death [when he is around 20]; and these—he had once actually assaulted her—must have been the explanation of his pathological changes. He once had a dream of copulating with Julie. He was overcome with remorse and fear at having broken his vow to keep away from her. He woke up and was delighted to find it was only a dream. He then went into her bedroom and smacked her bottom under the bedclothes...From this we conclude that his being chastised by his father was related to assaulting his sisters. But how? Purely sadistically or already in a clearly sexual way? His elder or his younger sisters? Julie is three years his junior, and as the scenes we are in search of must have been when he was three or four, she can scarcely be the one. Katherine, his sister who died? ([1909a] 2001: 278).

Billig draws attention to the fact that Freud here associates Lanzer's "pathological changes" with his possible incest with his sister. He reads Freud's indefinite description as an obfuscation of definite sibling incest. "Consequently," Billig (1999, 152) concludes, "readers of the case history are not informed that changes in Lorenz's condition may be connected with such incest." In support for his contention, Billig notes Lanzer's remark to Julie's husband that: "If Julie has a baby in 9 months' time, you needn't think I am its father; I am innocent" ([1909a] 2001, 314). He also compares the case notes with the published version of the fifth analytic session, observing that they are identical besides the last few lines: Freud expunged his patient's statement that his compulsions were figured by a sense of guilt for memories of having already committed the most despicable deed.

In contrast to Billig's perspective stands Zetzel's 1965 International Psycho-analytical Congress paper. Since it was Zetzel who first introduced the equalizing concept of "therapeutic alliance" between analyst and patient into the psychoanalytic lexicon, it is perhaps unsurprising that she would be an exception to the neglect of Freud's quite extensive remarks on lateral dynamics in the Rat Man case notes.[1] Zetzel's analysis, when considered carefully, can stand as a useful corrective to Billig's insightful but limited account of the sibling material. Zetzel (1966, 125) uses the evidence of the case notes to observe that an important scene in which Lanzer flew into a rage with his father coincided with the death of his sister: "His famous—but not subjectively remembered—outburst of rage almost certainly occurred during the course of Katherine's fatal illness. In this affective storm the little boy attacked his father." This is the only time, Lanzer states, he was beaten by his father. Whereas the overall arc of Freud's interpretation had situated Lanzer's rage with his father as an effect of a perceived threat of death if he continued to masturbate and retain Oedipal aspirations, Zetzel emphasizes that the threat of castration would have been indelibly marked and sharpened the trauma of his sister's passing. This ambivalence and confusion regarding the meaning of his sister's death in the context of his father's prohibition would have predisposed him to the obsessive symptoms which began from his father's death, and intensified on the death of his aunt (his father's sister).

Zetzel hypothesizes that the traumas of the castration complex and the sister's death became confused for the patient. Whereas most interpretations of the "opposition between the two objects of his love, his father and the 'lady'" ([1909a], 179) following Freud have viewed this as reflecting Lanzer's castration complex, Zetzel's interpretation refines and redefines this account. *Love/hate* would not only be tied to *sexuality/prohibition*, but also to *life/death* and *vertical/lateral*. In support of Zetzel's reading of the case notes, there is a footnote to the published case in which Freud states that "his sexual desires for his mother and sister and his sister's premature death were linked up with the young hero's chastisement at his father's hand" ([1909a] 2001, 207). Freud also states that "I traced a connection with death from his having been threatened with death at a prehistoric period if he touched himself and brought about an erection of his penis, and suggested that he attributed his sister's death to masturbating" ([1909a] 2001, 309). In further support for the way that the meanings of sex, sisters, and death are woven together in the Lanzer household, it can be noted that the patient's parents had children every two years until Katherine's death in 1881—and then it is nearly five years before Julie was born in 1886 (Mahoney 1986, 65).

Zetzel's reflections suggest that Lanzer's unconscious reproach toward the father would have included and been sustained by an irreducibly sibling component. This component would also have played a determinative role in his love-interest in his cousin:

> This, I believe, also determined his attachment in adult life to a young woman, Gisela, in whom he found a suitable replacement for his dead sister. From the published notes and daily record we get a picture of Gisela as (i) a first cousin; (ii) possibly too old for him (her age is not mentioned); (iii) almost certainly sterile, a fact which made her resemble a prepuberty little girl; and (iv) a woman who was subject to frequent serious and disabling periods of ill health. In addition, the

fact that this cousin who was herself highly ambivalent may also have been abused by her stepfather, and was at least as disturbed in respect of her psychosexual life as the patient, suggests that her own personality loaned itself to a relationship characterized by many infantile features. There is a wealth of material in the original notes to support the hypothesis that the Rat Man's persistent attachment to his ailing cousin represented an over-determined, necessarily ambivalent effort to revive his sister as he last recalled her, namely, as an increasingly tired little girl who was finally carried away to the room in which she was to die (Zetzel 1966, 126).

As we have seen, Billig's interest is to downplay the significance of unconscious reproach toward either the dead older sister or the father, in favor of preconscious or conscious guilt regarding Lanzer's actual incest with his younger sister. By contrast, Zetzel offers the more acute analysis in connecting Lanzer's desire for his cousin to his unconscious feelings toward his older sister Katherine, and Lanzer's unconscious hatred of his father to a prohibition on sexuality that had been tangled up with death. A cousin, as Mitchell (1974, 373) observed in *Psychoanalysis and Feminism*, is structurally the nearest person to a sibling. Mitchell suggests that romance with a cousin can serve as a defence against the threat of sibling incest between brother and sister and an effective sublimation for it. Likewise, marriage with a cousin accepts the authority of the father to forbid violent competition for the family's women, while at the same time supplanting the father at the closest possible remove through identification with his role. Indeed, Freud notes that Lanzer's "father was first cousin of his mother" ([1909a] 2001, 287), making both the cousins yet closer to siblings and the identification with the father even more intense.

Furthermore, whereas Billig interprets the patient's relation to his sister as solely sexual and references to aggression as mere euphemism, Zetzel's remarks encompass the lack of clean differentiation between aggression and sexuality in the clinical material. This weave between aggression and sexuality is, as Mitchell (2003) observes, characteristic in particular of dynamics along the lateral axis. Zetzel's account agrees with Freud who, as we have seen in the passage from the case notes cited by Billig, leaves open two riddles for the interpretation of the patient's guilt for assaulting a sister: "Purely sadistically or already in a clearly sexual way? His elder or his younger sisters?" Her interpretation also agrees with Mitchell (2003), who sees the extent of a lack of differentiation between sex and violence as an index of uncontained lateral trauma. Rather than following Billig in sheering sexuality from aggression, and Lanzer's behavior as an adult toward his younger sister from infantile material, it seems more plausible to follow Zetzel and interpret Lanzer's behavior toward Julie as occurring on the horizon of the relation with the dead older sister and of his castration complex.

To demonstrate the value of this approach, let us take the two symptoms that dominate Freud's recounting of the case: the vow to pay back the money to the lieutenant, and the fear of rat punishment for his cousin Gisela and (dead) father if he does not. Freud states that the patient's compulsions are the product of "oaths that he has forgotten" ([1909a] 2001: 260). Vows and vowing appear in four places in Freud's recounting of the case. One is in the text cited by Billig: because of his sexual/aggressive acts/wishes toward Julie, Lanzer feels "fear at having broken his vow to keep away from her." Billig's interpretation directs us to the fact that the money Lanzer vowed to give the lieutenant was actually owed to the nice lady at the post office. The patient travels all over Austria trying to pay the lieutenant and not pay the lieutenant, until he arrives at Freud's door and receives analysis. Then, calmer, he can simply post the money owed to the lady. Billig's interpretation would suggest that the lady could not be repaid because of the "vow to keep away from her" originally directed at Julie. However three other vows mentioned in the text can deepen our understanding of what it means to the patient when he vows. Besides the repayment vow, and the vow to keep away from Julie, a third vow in the case material is the formula used by the patient to forbid himself masturbation: "I swear on my blessed soul to abandon it." Lanzer had anxiety that if he broke this vow, and masturbated, then "his father would be bound to die" ([1909a] 2001: 165). When asked about his formula to prevent masturbation, Lanzer made an association with the words used by his mother to forbid his seeing Gisela: "On my soul, you will not go" ([1909] 200,: 262). Given the word-for-word fit in formulation, it is implausible to see the meaning of the vow not to approach Julie outside of the repeated vows made by Lanzer to prohibit himself masturbation, in the context of Oedipal and castration anxieties.

Yet if "I swear on my soul to abandon it" resonates with his mother's words, it also echoes with much earlier words heard by the patient. Lanzer reports three memories of his elder sister Katherine before she died. A first memory is a love-vow made by Katherine that "On my soul, if you die I shall kill myself" ([1909] 2001, 264). A second memory is of Katherine "being carried to bed" and then, sometime later, of "his asking 'Where is Katherine?' and going into the room and finding his father sitting in an arm-chair and crying." In light of Zetzel's interpretation, the act of vowing can be viewed as invested and complicated by confusion and ambivalence over the role of love and of his father in his sister's death. Furthermore, Lanzer's third memory of his older sister helps make further sense of Lanzer's vow to repay the lieutenant. The vow is made because Lanzer feels that if he does not repay the lieutenant then a pot [*Topf*] containing starving rats would be placed on the buttocks of his cousin and (dead) father. This strange fear becomes rather more explicable in light of Lanzer's early memory that "he first noticed the difference between the sexes when he saw his deceased sister Katherine (five years his senior) sitting on the pot" [*Topf*] ([1909] 2001, 276). Indeed, Lanzer himself appears to testify in favor of such an interpretation. He tells Freud that "when his sister asked him what it was that he liked about his cousin he replied jokingly 'her behind'" ([1909] 2001, 277). Lanzer's obsessional neurosis can then be regarded as a flight from a genital sexuality, in which the stakes are reproductive difference and annihilation, into obsessive thoughts in an anal register. His confusion of love and hate for his dead sister and father remain unconscious—not only avoided but forgotten. Yet the conflict between these feelings and those of his conscious experience in adulthood animate obsessive symptoms directed toward his beloved cousin, his younger sister Julie, and a wish to exhibit his penis to the ghost of his dead father.

As well as a metaphor for the ambivalence of Oedipal wishes and anxieties, the rat who threatens to bore with teeth and claws into the anus of Lanzer's cousin and (dead) father can also therefore be recognized as a metonymically displaced signifier for the figure of the younger sibling and of reproductive difference. The patient reported to Freud that "he used to *creep away* [*verkroch*] and hide, filled with terror and indignation, when one of his brothers or sisters was beaten" ([1909] 2001, 206). As Freud ([1897a] 1986,219; [1919] 2001) remarks elsewhere, there may be pleasure as well as pain in both observing the beating of a sibling, and in the phantasy that one is receiving pain/love in their place. Furthermore, the beating of a sibling in the Lanzer household appears to have been a moment when their genitals were visible. Fear and indignation toward pain and sadomasochistic pleasure, precisely in the link-up between the castration and sibling complexes, reappears in the threat of the rat punishment to his father and cousin. The threat of "rats *creeping into* [*Hineinkriechen*] the rectum" is interpreted by Freud as a reversal of the theme of creeping out from, which he suggests symbolizes a wish "that men can have babies just as well as women" ([1909a] 2001, 220). Mitchell (2003) identifies that the wish to have a child through anal childbirth represents a foreclosure of reproductive difference. For the hysteric, this fantasy emerges because reproductive difference represents the threat of a displaced self. By contrast, for Lanzer, reproductive difference is implicated in the traumatic articulation of Katherine's death with punishment by his father ([1909a] 2001, 265).

Support for this conclusion lies in Lanzer's report to Freud that both part of his desire for his cousin Gisela, and part of his indecision over whether to marry her, lay in her infertility. He begrudges his sister her capacity for reproduction, a rebuke which is folded within an obsessional prohibition on his own sexual wishes:

> The patient had a charming little niece of whom he was very fond. One day this idea came into his head: "If you indulge in intercourse, something will happen to Ella" (i.e. she will die). When the omissions have been made good, we have: "Every time you copulate, even with a stranger, you will not be able to avoid the reflection that in your married life sexual intercourse can never bring you a child (on account of the lady's sterility). This will grieve you so much that you will become envious of your sister on account of little Ella, and you will grudge her the child. These envious impulses will inevitably lead to the child's death" ([1909] 2001, 226–7).

The patient also had several tooth-related dreams in which sisters, pain, and birth were drawn together. With teeth, we remain firmly in the orbit of rodents here (rodent, from the Latin *rodere*: to gnaw). Two such dreams were related by the patient on January 6 and 7, 1908:

> He dreamt that he went to the dentist to have a bad tooth pulled out. He pulled one out, but it was not the right one, but the one next to it which only had something slightly wrong with it. When it came out he was astonished by its size.
>
> He had a carious tooth; it did not ache, however, but was only slightly tender, sometimes. He went to the dentist once to have it filled. The dentist, however, said there was nothing to be done except to extract it. He was not usually a coward, but he was kept back by the idea that somehow or other his pain would damage his cousin, and he refused to have it done ([1909a] 2001, 315).

Freud tells Lanzer confidently that these dreams are about castration, and that the big tooth is his father's penis, which he wants to cut off in retaliation for prohibiting his incestuous desires. However in the process notes he expresses concern and confusion: "what could be the meaning of its not having been the right tooth?" ([1909a] 2001, 316). Lanzer's own interpretation of the dreams is significant: they are about the death of a relative. It might be wondered whether the incorrect excision of the big tooth in the series of teeth might relate to a wish/fear that death/ the father had extracted *him* from the series of siblings and put him into the deathbed, rather than his sister who only had something slightly wrong with her (castration), which should not warrant death. The pain of a further extraction in the second dream would hurt his cousin because, as Freud later realized and added as a footnote to *The Interpretation of Dreams*, the extraction of a tooth does not simply represent castration but also childbirth since "in both cases (castration and birth) what is in question is the separation of a part of the body from the whole" ([1900] 2001, 387–8). In Lanzer's mind, his sexual desire is firmly bound up with the threat of pain to those he loves: the danger of castration posed by masturbation from the father becomes the same thought as the threat to his sister if he desires her.

Freud's/Lanzer's Siblings

Much of the preceding analysis merely fleshes out, using material from the case notes, Freud's terse remark that the patient's "sexual desires for his mother and sister and his sister's premature death were linked up with the young hero's chastisement at his father's hand" ([1909a] 2001, 207). Why were siblings left to the side in the published case, producing such disparity between the detailed material on the importance of Lanzer's siblings for his symptoms in the unpublished notes, and their relegation to minor figures in published case? The reason can be found explicitly stated in Freud's the case notes. Freud writes that there was material presented by Lanzer, which he found himself so resistant to include in his interpretations that he had "forgotten owing to complexes of my own" ([1909a] 2001, 264). This material, precisely, was the heart of the link between the sibling and castration complexes: memories of Katherine's vow that "On my soul, if you die I shall kill myself" and of Katherine being taken to bed to die in the next room and of their father crying. Freud observes that "in both cases it was a question of his sister's death," which was "the consideration which I had forgotten" ([1909a] 2001, 264).

It seems probable that among the complexes that Freud perceives blocked attention to Katherine in his interpretations was the death of his little brother during his childhood. Writing to Fliess, Freud ([1897b] 1986: 268) recalls that "I greeted my one-year-younger brother (who died after a few months) with adverse wishes and genuine childhood jealousy; and that his death left the germ of [self-]reproaches in me." Considering Freud's writings specifically and thus the subsequent history of psychoanalytic theory as a palimpsest on the surface produced by these writings, Mitchell (2000, 239) has observed that "this unacknowledged dead brother can be said to have 'possessed' the theory of psychoanalysis, ever present in the accounts but completely unintegrated into the theory or practice." In the case of the Rat Man, Stroeken (2007) has identified several reasons for identification between analyst and analysand, among them the fact that both Lanzer and Freud came from a family of seven children: two boys and five girls.

Yet Freud's remark regarding "complexes of my own" in the plural suggests that the dead younger brother may not have been the only factor in play: a second childhood constellation may also have been relevant in limiting Freud's attention to siblings in the published case of the Rat Man. In the same letter to Fliess cited above, Freud relates that, together with his nephew who was the same age as him, when he was three he had "behaved cruelly to my niece, who was a year younger." Highlighting the significance of his guilt for his brother's death and his memory of sadistic collusion with his nephew against his niece, Freud concludes his recollections by stating that "this nephew and this younger brother have determined, then, what is neurotic, but also what is intense, in all my friendships." The content of the cruel behavior toward the niece is not identified in the letter to Fliess. It is, however, identified in Freud's paper on screen memories: he and his nephew threw his niece down in a meadow in Freiburg and snatched the dandelions she was holding. Anzieu (1986, 285) has situated this story as a screen memory for Freud's "sexual play" as a child with his sisters and niece, undifferentiated between sexuality and aggression. Certainly in favor of such an interpretation are Freud's associations to the memory, which are of "some pictures that I once saw at a burlesque exhibition" and that "taking flowers from a girl means to deflower her" ([1899] 2001, 312, 316).

Freud proposes that part of the salience of the meadow memory lies in the fact that the next time he saw this niece and nephew in Freiburg, he was 17 and fell in love with a young girl called Gisela Fluss (whose dress reminded Freud of his niece's flowers). During this time, however, Freud notes that his family had the idea for him to "marry my cousin" ([1899] 2001, 314). In the event, neither marriage with the cousin nor with Gisela Fluss came to anything. Yet her name appears again 35 years later, followed by three exclamation marks, in Freud's process notes to the session with Lanzer of November 18 in which he accidently writes the name "Gisela Fluss" instead of the name of Lanzer's fiancé and cousin ([1909a] 2001, 280). This is evidence for the role of material from Freud's past in shaping his attention predominantly to Lanzer's father rather than infantile sibling experiences of love, hate, and death in interpreting the patient's ambivalent love for his cousin. The weave between love/hate would therefore only be tied by Freud to sexuality/prohibition in the published case—leaving the threads of life/death and vertical/lateral dangling and unelaborated.[2]

Obsessional Neurosis and Hysteria

Glover (1935, 131) makes the general point that "the real significance of obsessions cannot be appreciated until the relations of the disease...to hysteria...have been established." Having examined the role of the lateral axis in the Rat Man case study, we now are in a better position to analyze the relevance of Mitchell's account of the role of the lateral axis in hysteria for reconsidering obsessional neurosis. Let us start by considering the common ground between the two neuroses. For Freud the figure of Oedipus in Sophocles was such a good paradigm of neurosis because, as well as revealing the structure of hysteria, "the original Oedipus was himself a case of obsessional neurosis—the riddle of the sphinx" (Freud [1907] 1974, 33). For Freud, "the riddle of the sphinx" was "the question of where babies come from" (Freud [1924] 2001, 37). Hysteria and obsessional neurosis are circumventions of the answer to this question, and of the dissolution of the Oedipus complex in the experience of castration and/or deferral that it implies. Instead of accepting the loss of the object, both neuroses retain the object in the form of symptoms, which serve as "compromises," supported from both sides by the forbidden drive and its censorship ([1916] 2001, 359). Such compromises permit the subject a sense of themselves that excludes the conflicts raised by the sphinx's riddle: "Hysteria and obsessional neurosis are, from this perspective, pathologies of individuation. The boundaries of the 'I' have been drawn so as to alienate the drives. The cost is that they become aliens pounding at the gates" (Lear 1990, 176).

In situating both hysteria and obsessional neurosis as defences against disturbing psychical material, Freud observes that "up to this point the processes in hysteria, and in phobias and obsessions are the same; from now on their paths diverge. In hysteria, the incompatible idea is rendered innocuous by its sum of excitation being transformed into something somatic. For this I should like to propose the name of conversion" ([1894] 2001, 48). Thus in hysteria, the emotion associated with the object becomes partly separated from the representation to which it is attached. The emotion is then converted into unfulfillable wants, while the repressed idea is localized within a particular activity or part of the body which serves as a symbol, producing conversion symptoms on the body. This split between emotion and representation is sustained by an ongoing series of identifications, in which the hysteric attempts to escape from conflict by blurring his or her own identity with that of the object, only to be disappointed and move on.

In obsessional neurosis, Freud observes that affect has likewise been partly separated from a repressed reproach. He identifies that among "the most important characteristics of obsessional neurosis" is an inexorable either-or split between love and hate. Freud ([1909a] 2001: 239) identifies that in such cases "love has not succeeded in extinguishing the hatred but only in driving it down into the unconscious; and in the unconscious the hatred, safe from the danger of being destroyed by the operations of consciousness, is able to persist." Winnicott ([1953] 1965, 19) glosses the process with characteristic crispness and tenderness: "every attempt is made to annul one idea by another, but nothing succeeds. Behind the whole process is a confusion, and no amount of tidying that the patient can do alters this confusion, because it is maintained; it is unconsciously maintained in order to hide something very simple; namely, the fact that, in some specific setting of which the patient is unaware, hate is more powerful than love." The affect associated with the reproach is displaced on to another contiguous but ostensibly unrelated idea, producing a sexualization of thought with anal-erotic content. In short, "thoughts are constructed to defend the subject against what he might feel" (de Georges 2009, 55). The result is a super-ego punitively concerned to pin down and punish the ego for the cascade of associatively linked thoughts through which the unconscious reproach, in conflict with conscious love, finds expression ([1916] 2001, 182). Indeed, at a topographical level, it has been suggested that the unconscious hate is to some degree incorporated by the super-ego, and reproach toward the object for its imperfections becomes pervasive accusations of the ego's unworthiness and guilt by the super-ego (e.g. Deutsch 1932; Lacan [1958] 2002, Seminar June 4).

Freud observes that "every obsessional neurosis seems to have a substratum of hysterical symptoms that have been formed at a very early stage. But it is subsequently shaped along quite different lines" ([1925] 2001, 113). The hysterical core is that both neuroses are attempts to circumvent the loss of the object which is implied by what Freud calls "the riddle of the sphinx": where do babies come from? Their difference lies in the mechanism of defence: whereas in hysteria repression is effected through amnesia and the return of the repressed in the form of conversion symptoms and resentful wanting, in obsessional neurosis the affect is severed from the particular reproach that elicited it and is instead transferred along lines of contiguity to associated ideas.

As Mitchell demonstrates, the hysteric fights an emptiness left by the displacement of their existence by the possibility of the other. "It is," she remarks in *Mad Men and Medusas* (2000, 20), "the catastrophic awareness that one is not unique which triggers the onset of hysteria." Hysterical symptoms form because the question of "where do babies come from?" produces a traumatic threat of substitutability that threatens the subject's sense of self. Yet part of the process through which this trauma is repressed means that the subject mistakes the existential threat of substitutability for a matter of someone preventing them from getting what they want. In this context, "the desperate, exuberant protests, the labile identifications and demonstrative sexualising" of the hysteric "are a way of asserting an existence that has gone missing" (2000, 107). The obsessional neurotic also faces the riddle of the sphinx, which raises the issues of life and of genitality. The riddle is dealt with in a different way to the hysteric, however.

The hysteric protests the displacement of a singular existence through a repression that transposes the question into the anxious and exuberant domain of sexuality, wanting, and embodiment. The obsessional neurotic, by contrast, transposes the riddle to the domain of thought, in an anal-sadistic register. In this domain, the issue is raised of the relationship between *polar opposites*. This relationship is framed by doubt and encroachment—as the displaced affect is transferred between contiguous ideas in order to maintain a polarized boundary separating it from the idea or experience to which it belonged. For example, "defence against the obsessional ideas may be effected by a forcible diversion on to other thoughts with a content as contrary as possible. This is why obsessional brooding, if it succeeds, regularly deals with abstract and suprasensual things; because the ideas that have been repressed are always concerned with sensuality" ([1896b] 2001, 172). If the Rat Man were to become aware of the hate for his father, it would contaminate his consciously held image of love.

Yet the movement of the transfer of the displaced affect between different thoughts produces a labile sense of doubt. This doubt protects the boundaries that sustain the subject's sense of self, holding in place the constellation of defences and anxieties. At the same time, however, this doubt about what the subject feels and thinks is the product of and further contributes to an unsteadiness that threatens to topple the self by contaminating the totalizing experience that organizes and defines it: of love without encroachment by hate. For instance, in the Rat Man case, Lanzer reports having been "angry this morning when Constanze [his eldest sister] had invited him to go to the play with her. He promptly wished her the rats and then began to have doubts as to whether he should go or not and as to which of the two decisions would be giving way to a compulsion. Her invitation had upset a rendezvous with the dressmaker and a visit to this cousin, who is ill...While he was wishing Constanze the rats he felt a rat gnawing at his own anus and had a visual image of it" ([1909a] 2001, 308).

The potential contamination of associating thoughts, as this example shows, produces seemingly irrational anxiety and self-reproaches, and is fought through two forms of symptoms. On the one hand, there are prohibitions that keep the subject from actions or topics that have been invested with the displaced affect. Included here are linguistic prohibitions, in which particular bits of language must be kept separate from others (Holland 1975). The other symptoms formed in this context, and a product of the first, are compulsions: "The compulsion on the other hand is an attempt at a compensation for the doubt and at a correction of the intolerable conditions of inhibition to which the doubt bears witness. If the patient, by the help of displacement, succeeds at last in bringing one of his inhibited intentions to a decision, then the intention *must* be carried out. It is true that this intention is not his original one, but the energy dammed up in the latter cannot let slip the opportunity of finding an outlet" ([1909a] 2001, 243–4). Yet, as the prohibitions and compulsions become associated with the transferred affect, they themselves become unsettling and potentially contaminating. The subject feels at once impervious (since the conflict between conscious love and unconscious reproach has been displaced onto the domain of thought) and terribly vulnerable (as association continually threatens to undo the severance of the terms of this conflict).

The importance of the lateral axis for hysteria lies in the fact that the possibility of siblings necessarily and irreducibly raises the question of the sphinx in its hysteric form by highlighting substitutability. The Rat Man case shows us how the vertical and lateral can intersect in the paradigmatic case of obsessional neurosis, as the loss of the older sister became fused in thought with the father's threat of castration. Reflection on this case suggests that siblings can raise two, related issues: polarized opposition between self and other, and the threat of encroachment. These two themes are suggested by Freud's comment that the birth of a new sibling is experienced as an "*egoistic* sense of injury," and "gives grounds for receiving the new brothers or sisters with *repugnance*" ([1916] 2001, 334). More precisely, as Mitchell has theorized, the plenitude the subject imagines themselves to have as the property of their place in the family is necessarily threatened or haunted by the potential of substitutability. Mitchell argues that the "primary identifications made with parents are subject to trauma (you think you are like your parents or one of your parents but you are not – at least, not yet)," and as such are organized around themes of "negation" (2003, 14, likely following Green 1999). By contrast, Mitchell argues that "the primary identification with the peer group is positive and subject not to negation but to differentiation: you are like the others but with differences" (2003: 14). Whereas the vertical axis is negotiated in terms of negation, the child is confronted with the difference of the sibling or potential sibling. One way of avoiding a substantial engagement with this difference, and in fact foreclosing it, is to reduce the difference between siblings to that of a polar opposition; within this constellation, the subject can retain their plenitude in the face of the other, who is figured as merely a disturbing negative or shadow.

As we have seen in the case of the Rat Man, the ambivalence between love and hate for the patient's dead sister became fused with ambivalence toward the father, provoking a retreat of libido onto the domain of thought. There the sibling or potential peer is, on the register of anal-erotic relations, reframed in terms of the possibility of contamination. To some degree this retreat is normative: Siblings often argue over which one has exclusive possession of particular objects or spaces, for example experiencing clothes as contaminated if handed down from older siblings. The clothes function here as a symbol of the potential encroachment of the sibling on the existential place the subject is trying to carve out for themselves, and the uniqueness that they fear may be required in order to warrant love. However, the threat of the sibling can also produce more pathological behaviors, as in the case of the Rat Man where lateral differentiation became confused with vertical negation.

Here, then, we may find a reason for Freud's ([1896b] 2001) observation that women are more subject to hysteria because they are inclined to "passivity" and men to obsessional neurosis because they are inclined to "activity," which would later be echoed by later analysts (e.g. Ferenczi [1908] 1927, 25). While some have alleged that this is yet another case of Freud's gender essentialism, Verhaeghe (2004, 386) counterargues that "the coupling of the neuroses with a specific gender is only indirect and has to do with historical artefacts . . . patriarchal society almost exclusively assigns the active position to men, hence the gender associations." The association between hysteria and femininity has been deftly situated by Mitchell (2000, 324–5):

> The idea that there are psychical consequences to anatomical differences, while probably correct, is also unnecessary. It is redundant as an explanation. It is the kinship displacement of the girl, rather than her socially inscribed definition of anatomical inferiority that renders her more subject to the more visible dimensions of hysteria—it is this which sets up a social relationship between femininity and hysteria which is then wrongly read as necessary. There is no difference between male and female hysteria. However, the girl may be more often or more seriously displaced.

When Freud ([1914] 2001, 90–1) states that the parent's investment in their child is "a revival and reproduction of their own narcissism, which they have long since overvalued," the child more likely to receive this overvaluation is male in our culture. Whilst girls might be enjoined to the fantasy of being a princess, this discourse is marked by the signs of play and fantasy, and contains within it full awareness of the disappointments of reality for young female subjects (Walkerdine 1997). Not so perhaps for boys, for whom masculinity as plenitude is enjoined without qualifying markers: become the phallus. As a result, the boy may be more likely to be pinioned by the contradiction between absolutes of presence and negation, rather than grieved and identity made a matter of differentiation. In the case of the Rat Man, the threat of childhood castration and the injunction to become the phallus as an adult had been confused with the process of lateral differentiation, so that the patient was forced to continually displace into symptoms the unbearable matrix of affects around sexuality/prohibition, life/death, and father/sister.

The ego-ideal is the part of the super-ego that soaks up all the cultural and parental expectations felt by the subject, and then holds the ego to account for distance or proximity to these expectations. Despite advances made thanks to feminist efforts, this process in our culture remains differentiated by sex. Her position within cultural and familial relations of power mean that a girl is, cumulatively and continually, disillusioned regarding the possibility of plenitude. By contrast, the boy is not only enjoined to a greater investment in the illusion of perfection, but this narcissistic investment is one which is tied to his genital organ by virtue of the way in which his family and society respond to a subject with a penis. When the contradiction between the disappointments of reality and inherited, ungrieved-for plenitude becomes too great, obsessional neurosis becomes more likely. The magnitude of disappointments, pulverizing too severely any taste or dream of plenitude, may be one reason for the finding that the social class of the subjects with clinically significant obsessional symptoms is "significantly lower, 74% being in the lower social classes" (Heyman 2001, 327). If it is the case that "it is not at all rare for both of the two children to fall ill later on of a defence neurosis—the brother with obsessions and the sister with hysteria" (Freud [1896b] 2001, 164), an explanation for this may be proposed in the organization of patriarchal cultural and familial relations. The same cultural and familial forms that give the sister no recognized place and thereby predispose her to hysteria encourage her brother to dream of absolutes opposed in relations of incompatible negation rather than differentiation, and so predispose him to obsessional neurosis.

Concluding Reflections

Freud observed that "obsessional neurosis is unquestionably the most interesting and repaying subject of analytic research. But as a problem it has not yet been mastered" ([1925] 2001, 113). Drawing on Mitchell's work, it has been argued here that sibling relationships or the possibility of sibling relationships can play a significant role in the predisposition to obsessional neurosis. Attention to the role of the lateral axis in obsessional neurosis raises a curious question, which has been strangely ignored by psychoanalytic theory, and on which this chapter will close. Freud states clearly that the riddle of the Sphinx is the question: "where do babies come from?" Yet on the surface he has no historico-textual support for this statement. In the play by Sophocles, no mention is made of the content of the Sphinx's riddle. The conventional interpretation, in a tradition following from Apollodorus (1976, 145), has the Sphinx ask "which creature has one voice and yet becomes four-footed and two-footed and three-footed?" to which Oedipus answers "Man." This addresses the intersection of human beings and time in the form of generations, spotlighting Oedipus himself in the weave of his embodiment as exposed child, as king, and as blinded old man. Nonetheless it decidedly does not address the issue of where babies come from. Freud's citation of the riddle as the question "where do babies come from?" might then, perhaps, be read as an interpretation, highlighting the reversibility of generation in the unconscious where there is no linear time.

Yet there is a less well-known tradition, attributed to Theodectas of Phaselis by Athenaeus in Book 10 of the *Deipnosophistae*, which does provide a textual basis for Freud's claim regarding the Sphinx's riddle. In this tradition, the sphinx ask two, linked riddles. Good evidence for Freud's acquaintance with this tradition is provided by a bookplate he designed in 1910, which describes Oedipus as the one who "knew the famous riddles," plural (Armstrong 2005, 54). Athenaeus states that the second riddle is: "There are two sisters: one gives birth to the other and she, in turn, gives birth to the first. Who are the two sisters?" (d'Huy 2012). The correct answer, given by Oedipus to the Sphinx, is that the siblings are "day and night." Here we do have the question of where babies come from, a textual basis for Freud's claim. Moreover, it is a question that is only likely to be solved by someone like Oedipus who is, as Freud states, both a hysteric and an obsessional neurotic, disposed to answer the question of birth with an answer focused on the issues of singularity and generation (hysteria) and doubt between encroaching opposites (obsessional neurosis), both raised by the figure of the sibling.

Notes

1. Unfortunately, her paper is generally misread as suggesting merely that the patient's remarks that evoke his older sister's death were a metaphor for or instance in troubled relations with his father and mother (e.g., Myerson 1966; Solano-Suarez 2009). As Daru Huppert observes, there has been no place provided by theory to "put" sustained analysis of sibling relationships.
2. The moments in the Rat Man case study in which Freud identifies the significance of clinical material relating to death, as a result, are cut off from their sibling context. In an interpretation made possible by this severance, Lacan ([1956] 1991: 181) would later join together these passages into an account of obsessional neurosis in general as an attempt to grapple with the question "Am I alive or dead?" No mention is made of the patent's lost sister.

References

Anzieu, D. 1986. *Freud's Self-Analysis*. New York: International Universities Press.

Apollodorus 1976. *Gods and Heroes of the Greeks*, translated by Michael Simpson, Amherst, MA: University of Massachusetts Press.

Armstrong, R. H. 2005. *Freud and the Ancient World*, New York: Cornell University Press.

Athenaeus 1930. *Deipnosophistae*, translated. Loeb Classical Library, London: William Heinemann.

Beigler, J. S. 1975. "A Commentary on Freud's Treatment of the Rat Man," *Annual of Psychoanalysis*, 3: 271–285.

Billig, M. "Freud's Response to Reported Incest: The Case of Paul Lorenz, the 'Rat Man.'" *Psychoanalytic Studies* 1.2 (1999): 145–158.

Crockatt, P. 2013. "A View of 'The Rat Man,'" unpublished manuscript.

De Georges, P. 2009. "A Thought that Burdens the Soul," *Psychoanalytic Notebooks*, 18: 55–65.

Deutsch, H. 1932. "Obsessional Ceremonial and Obsessional Acts," in *Psycho-Analysis of the Neuroses*, translated by W. D. Robson-Scott, 175–197. London: Hogarth Press.

D'Huy, J. 2012. "Aquitaine on the Road of Oedipus? The Sphinx as a Prehistoric Story," *Société d'études et de recherches préhistoriques des Eyzies*, 61: 15–21.

Ferenczi, S. [1908] 1925. "Analytic Conception of Psycho-Neuroses." In *Further Contributions to the Theory and Technique of Psycho-analysis*, London: Karnac.

Freud, A. 1966. "Obsessional Neurosis: A Summary of Psycho-Analytic Views as Presented at the Congress." *International Journal of Psychoanalysis*, 47: 116–122.

Freud, S. [1894] 2001. "The Neuro-psychoses of Defence." In *The Standard Edition of the Complete Psychological Works of Sigmund Freud Vol. 3*, translated by James Strachey, 41–61. Hogarth Press, London.

Freud, S. [1896a] 2001. "Heredity and the Aetiology of the Neuroses." *SE 3*, 141–158.

Freud, S. [1896b] 2001. "Further Remarks on the Neuropsychoses of Defence." *SE 3*, 159–188.

Freud, S. [1897a] 1998. "Letter from Freud to Fliess, January 3rd 1897." *The Complete Letters of Sigmund Freud to Wilhelm Fliess, 1887–1904*, edited by Jeffrey Masson, 219–221. Cambridge, MA: Harvard University Press.

Freud, S. [1897b] 1986. "Letter from Freud to Fliess, October 3rd 1897," *The Complete Letters of Sigmund Freud to Wilhelm Fliess, 1887–1904*, edited by Jeffrey Masson, 267–270. Cambridge, MA: Harvard University Press.

Freud, S. [1899] 2001. "Screen Memories." *SE3*, 303–322.

Freud, S. [1907] 2001. "Obsessive Actions and Religious Practices." *SE 9*, 115–128.

Freud, S. [1907] 1976. "Letter from Freud to Jung, April 14th 1907," *The Freud/Jung Letters*, edited by William McGuire, 33–4. New York: Picador.

Freud, S. [1909a] 2001. "Notes upon a Case of Obsessional Neurosis." *Standard Edition*, Volume 10, edited by James Strachey, 153–318. London: Vintage.

Freud, S. [1909b] 1976. "149F: Letter from Freud to Jung, 30th June 1909," *The Freud/Jung Letters*, edited by William McGuire, 116–7. New York: Picador.

Freud, S. [1914] 2001. "On Narcissism." *SE 14*, 73–104.

Freud, S. [1916] 2001. "Introductory Lectures." *SE 15–16*, 1–463.

Freud, S. [1917] 2001. "On Transformations of Instinct as Exemplified in Anal Eroticism." *SE 17*, 127–133.

Freud, S. [1919] 2001. "A Child is Being Beaten." *SE 17*, 179–204.

Freud, S. [1923] 2001. "The Ego and the Id." *SE 19*, 12–68.

Freud, S. [1924] 2001. "An Autobiographical Study." *SE 20*, 7–76.

Freud, S. [1925] 2001. "Inhibitions, Symptoms and Anxiety." *SE 20*, 87–178.

Glover, E. 1935. "A Developmental Study of the Obsessional Neurosis." *The International Journal of Psychoanalysis*, 16, 131–144.

Green, A. 1999. *The Work of the Negative*, translated by Andrew Weller, NY: Free Association Books.

Heyman, I., Fombonne, E., Simmons, H., Ford, T., Meltzer, H., and Goodman, R. 2001. "Prevalence of Obsessive-Compulsive Disorder in the British Nationwide Survey of Child Mental Health," *The British Journal of Psychiatry* 179: 324–329.

Holland, N. 1975. "An Identity for the Rat-Man." *International Review of Psycho-Analysis*, 2: 157–169.

Jones, E. 1955. *The Life and Work of Sigmund Freud*, New York: Basic Books.

Künstlicher, R. 1998. "Horror at Pleasure of His Own of which He Himself is Not Aware: The Case of the Rat Man." In *On Freud's Couch*, edited by I. Matthis and I. Szecsödy, 127–162. Northvale, NJ: Jason Aronson.

Lacan, J. [1956] 1991. *The Seminar of Jacques Lacan III: The Psychoses 1955–56*, edited by John Forrester, New York: Norton.

Lacan, J. [1958] 2002. *The Seminar of Jacques Lacan V: The Formations of the Unconscious*, translated by Cormac Gallagher, London: Karnac.

Lear, J. 1990. *Love and Its Place in Nature*, London: Faber.

Mahoney, P. 1986. *Freud and the Rat Man*, New Haven, CT: Yale University Press.

Mahoney, P. 2007. "Reading the Notes on the Rat Man Case." *Canadian Journal of Psychoanalysis* 15(1): 93–117.

Mitchell, J. 1974. *Psychoanalysis and Feminism*, New York: Basic Books.

Mitchell, J. 2000. *Mad Men and Medusas*, London: Penguin.

Mitchell, J. 2003. *Siblings: Sex and Violence*, Cambridge: Polity.

Myerson, P. G. 1966. "Comment on Dr Zetzel's Paper." *International Journal of Psycho-analysis* 47: 139–142.

Nunberg, H. and Federn, E., editors. 1962. *Minutes of the Vienna Psychanalytic Society*, Volume 1. New York: International Universities Press.

Oliver, K. 2009. *Animal Lessons*. New York: Columbia University Press.

Solono-Suarez, E. (2009) "Learning to Read Obsessional Neurosis." *Psychoanalytic Notebooks*, 18: 29–42.

Stroeken, H. P. 2007. "Note on the Extraordinary Similarity Between the Worlds of Freud and of the Ratman." *International Forum of Psychoanalysis*, 16: 100–102.

Verhaeghe, P. 2001. *Beyond Gender*, New York: Other Press.

Verhaeghe, P. 2004. *On Being Normal and Other Disorders*, London: Karnac.

Veszy-Wagner, L. 1967. "Zwangsneurose und latent Homosexualitat" *Psyche* 21: 295–615.

Walkerdine, V. 1997. *Daddy's Girl*, Cambridge, MA: Harvard University Press.

Winnicott, D. [1953] 1965. "Psycho-Analysis and the Sense of Guilt." In *The Maturational Processes and the Facilitating Environment: Studies in the Theory of Emotional Development*, London: Tavistock.

Zetzel, E. R. 1966. "1965: Additional Notes Upon a Case of Obsessional Neurosis: Freud 1909." *International Journal of Psychoanalysis*, 47: 123–129.

Chapter 9

Minimal Difference: On Siblings, Sex, and Violence

Mignon Nixon

Since Freud, Juliet Mitchell observes, psychoanalysis has been trapped in an Oedipal paradigm. And if psychoanalysis itself suffers from what might be deemed an Oedipal obsession, privileging parent–child relationships to the detriment of sibling dynamics, the humanities are also dominated by Oedipal thinking. Despite the efforts of psychoanalytic feminism to expose the patriarchal hierarchies underpinning Oedipal models of discipleship, influence, legacy, and genealogy, the humanities still reflexively ascribe generative and destructive power principally to the passions that cross generations, attending to relationships of descent and difference while neglecting those of alliance and affinity, to borrow Mitchell's terms. In her book *Siblings: Sex and Violence*, Mitchell reflects upon this lack.

There is a certain irony here, of course. A cardinal attraction of psychoanalysis for feminism has been its critique of "vertical paradigms." The disavowal of authority and un-mastering of knowledge in Lacan's reading of Freud enabled psychoanalytic feminism to contest, precisely, Oedipal thinking. The insight that descent and difference overshadow alliance and affinity in the patriarchal cultural hierarchy that psychoanalysis analyzes, but is also bound up with, is integral to the discourse of psychoanalytic feminism. Mitchell's own ground-breaking study *Psychoanalysis and Feminism* (1974) established the significance of psychoanalysis for analyzing the structures of patriarchal oppression, laying the theoretical ground for efforts to break with an exclusively Oedipal model of the family. With her work on siblings, Mitchell however intervenes in an evolving discourse on the family and the group that has turned sharply away from psychoanalysis. In *Siblings: Sex and Violence* (2003), she argues, as she did 30 years earlier in *Psychoanalysis and Feminism*, that we abandon psychoanalysis at our peril.

Mitchell's starting point is that psychoanalysis must be held to account intellectually for its own failure to "think siblings." For while psychoanalysis has been trapped in a vertical, Oedipal paradigm, thinking on alliance and affinity—same-sex relationships and groups—has been formulated as gender theory, a discourse with an increasingly strained allegiance to psychoanalysis and feminism. From Mitchell's perspective, the divergence of psychoanalysis and gender theory is damaging to both. The failure to think laterally about the social imaginary has vitiated psychoanalysis in the humanities at a pivotal moment in the history of gender. The disavowal of psychoanalysis by gender theory meanwhile estranges "the social" from "the psychical" at a time of war, when such splitting is particularly dangerous, and vulnerable to exploitation by militarist culture. For Mitchell, the obligation of psychoanalysis is not to continue to coexist with gender theory in awkward political alliance but to grapple with the failure of psychoanalysis to theorize gender.

"As psychoanalysis stands," writes Mitchell, "the concept of 'gender' cannot properly be made to fit into it"(Mitchell 2003, 111). In *Siblings*, Mitchell provides a critical revision of the theory of psychoanalysis such that gender not only fits in, but finds an "autonomous place." This autonomous place is a lateral axis of gender that complements the vertical line of sexual difference. The preeminence that psychoanalysis has historically accorded the parent–child dynamic and its attendant fantasies, has, Mitchell argues, led it to conceive of difference only as maximal difference: generational difference and sexual difference. Gender, she maintains, requires a theory of minimal difference. In psychoanalysis, sexual difference—either/or—overshadows sibling or gender difference—the same, but different.

Thinking siblings entails a radical revision of psychoanalysis. For if siblings are only added to the existing theory, Mitchell argues, they will be subsumed in the same old Oedipal plot. In psychoanalysis, particularly as concerns sexuality, "we no longer have a theory that goes against the grain of ideology," Mitchell writes, "and once this happens, its progress tends to be additive rather than creative, its prescriptions remedial, rather than radical" (Mitchell 2003, 114). As with Lacan's re-reading of Freud, or Klein's, psychoanalysis renews itself only by returning to its theoretical roots. Mitchell's ambition is to extend psychoanalysis, and by implication, the humanities' recourse to psychoanalytic theory, to the nexus of lateral social relationships and intra-generational groups, and to accord these, in her phrase, "a lateral autonomous place" in theory and in praxis.

In the humanities, too, psychoanalytic theory suffers from its perceived preoccupation with the individual and the Oedipal family to the exclusion of the social group. This is partly because psychoanalysis remains in thrall to Oedipal thinking, as Mitchell maintains, but is also symptomatic of a broader rejection of theories of subjectivity by the technologized humanities on a war footing (Nixon 2014). Pressured into conformity with a militarist research culture suspicious of subjectivity, but also estranged from a left political culture that considers subjectivity antithetical to politics, psychoanalysis finds itself in the untenable position of being both an orthodoxy—a theory that does not go against the grain of ideology—and an orphan—a theory of subjectivity deemed superfluous by a culture that, like most war cultures, disavows subjectivity itself.

It may be useful briefly to recollect how we arrived at this place. I will do so from the perspective of my own field of study, art informed by feminism. Partly as an effect of Mitchell's own *Psychoanalysis and Feminism*, psychoanalysis was once recognized as an evolving theory of subjectivity in which the trends of individual and social experience were closely intertwined. Mary Kelly's *Post-Partum Document* (1973–1979) exemplifies this position. Conceived in tandem with Mitchell's *Psychoanalysis and Feminism* while both Kelly and Mitchell were participants in the History Group, a feminist reading group in London, Kelly's now-iconic work of Conceptual art charts the relationship of the artist and her infant son from the child's birth to the age of six. Confronting the elision of maternal subjectivity in cultural representation, including psychoanalysis (but also sociology, medicine, anthropology, and linguistics), Kelly documents the maternal–infantile relationship as a mutual (re-) negotiation of the Oedipal complex. Produced in the same moment of psychoanalytic feminism that also gave rise to Laura Mulvey and Peter Wollen's film *Riddles of the Sphinx* (1977), Kelly's *Post-Partum Document* and Mitchell's *Psychoanalysis and Feminism* attest to a dynamic relay between feminism, psychoanalysis, and art in which questions of subjectivity and politics overlapped, and in which psychoanalytic theory did go against the grain of patriarchal ideology and did seem to hold a radical potential.

Now, partly as an effect of the failure of psychoanalysis to engage creatively with gender discourse, the individual and the group are increasingly perceived as divergent, if not incompatible, modes of subjectivity. The psychical, it is often assumed, belongs to individual subjectivity and the family, while the political is assigned to the social group. Again, there is a certain irony in this. The work of critical postmodernism, informed by feminism and psychoanalysis, was to trouble this rigid patriarchal divide, bringing subjectivity to bear on politics (Owens 1983). At stake in this was an understanding of subjectivity as social in itself. Hence, Kelly described the *Post-Partum Document* as "an ongoing process of analysis and visualization of the mother-child relationship," refusing the cultural designation of childbirth and parenting as quintessentially private family matters while also claiming authority for the individual subject to "analyse and visualize" this dynamic (Kelly 1983, xv). Postmodernism continued to pursue this path, contending, as in the indelible 1980s montages of Barbara Kruger, that subjectivity was constructed in and through—but potentially also in resistance to—the coercive social rhetoric of the mass-cultural image. For Kruger, we make ourselves up, invent ourselves as subjects, in a relay of images that psychoanalysis, as a theory of patriarchy, can help equip us to analyze and to critique, exposing, for example, the fantasy structures of militarization promulgated at the height of the Cold War and the ways that war fantasies are underpinned by the same gender stereotypes advertising persistently repeats. For Kelly and Kruger among many others working at this time, psychoanalytic theory was political.

The later gradual rejection of psychoanalysis was also on political grounds. Two trends of that rejection are most significant for Mitchell's *Siblings*. First, psychoanalysis, or more specifically psychoanalytic feminism, failed to respond to the intellectual and political demand to theorize gender and account for its omission as an autonomous problem in psychoanalysis (Butler 1990). (Psychoanalysis itself, institutional psychoanalysis, seems not even to have registered this demand.) Where *Psychoanalysis and Feminism* countered an earlier feminist repudiation of psychoanalysis as sexist, if not misogynistic, and complicit with patriarchy, no such systematic defence or revision of the theory appeared in response to this subsequent critique of psychoanalysis as "heteronormative," conventionalizing, and oppressive. *Siblings* can be seen as that belated response.

The second basis for the rejection of psychoanalysis is more recent and is bound up with a broad renunciation of theoretical feminism in the politics of war. The crisis mentality of war has militated against theoretical reflection on subjectivity, another manifestation of the splitting of the psychic and the social that our militarist culture encourages and our left politics mimics. *Siblings*, published in 2003, anticipates many of the political implications of this disavowal, in particular our collective inability to make sense of the abuses of Abu Ghraib, a fresh instance of the sexualized violence, endemic to all war, that Mitchell calls violence-perversion.[1] And so, the very horrors that precipitated a political climate of urgency in which psychoanalysis was dismissed also called out for psychoanalytically informed responses to a war culture of sexualized, and strangely subjectivized, atrocity.

It is sometimes overlooked that psychoanalysis is a war discourse, many of its classic texts having been produced in wartime, by the agents and victims of war. Writing in 1915, amid the epic destruction of the First World War, Freud opened this discourse with an observation that resonates powerfully with the appearance of the first photographs of Abu Ghraib:

> The individual citizen can with horror convince himself in this war of what would occasionally cross his mind in peace-time—that the state has forbidden to the individual the practice of wrong-doing, not because it desires to abolish it, but because it desires to monopolize it....A belligerent state permits itself every such misdeed, every such act of violence, as would disgrace the individual. (Freud 1915, 279)

For Freud, the subjectivity of the belligerent state—its desire—is all but unfathomable. He writes on behalf of the citizen left "bewildered" by total war. For Mitchell, war is, as it was for the Italian psychoanalyst Franco Fornari, a social institution (Fornari 1975). It is susceptible to analysis, but that analysis, she maintains, requires siblings. Psychoanalysis needs siblings to think about war because war is waged at the sibling level. "We defeat, kill and rape our peers" (Mitchell 2003, xv). The origins of the destructiveness we bring to bear in war summons hatred of our first and most intimate enemy. To this extent, war is a problem of lateral relations and requires a theory specific to that condition:

> In discussions of "otherness," whether of gender, race, class, or ethnicity, hatred of the other is explained by the obvious fact that the "other" is different. Sibling experience displays the contrary: the position that is occupied by the sibling is first experienced as "the same"— hatred is for one who is the same: it is this hatred for a sameness that displaces which then generates the category of "other" as a protection. (Mitchell, 2003, 48)

The timing of the publication of *Siblings* was fortuitous for any citizen of the so-called war on terror. Written before the invasion of Afghanistan and Iraq, *Siblings* nevertheless anticipated its disturbing conjunctures of sexuality and violence. Such anticipation was possible, of course, because the sexual atrocities that rapidly became the hallmark of the occupation repeated a pattern of wars past, most conspicuously, in United States history, the American war in Vietnam, in which rape and torture were routine entries in the lexicon of atrocity. "How do we account for the rampant sexuality of war"—for the fact that "sexual violence seems to 'automatically' accompany war violence?" Mitchell has asked (Mitchell 2000, 129). These questions were both prescient and belated.

Forty years earlier, in response to the American war in Vietnam, a war of apocalyptic, genocidal violence and extravagant atrocity, the artist Nancy Spero had also posed them. Spero's *War Series* (1966–1970) took the form of gouache and ink drawings on thin poster-sized sheets of paper depicting a phantasmagoria of sexualized violence. "I started working rapidly on paper," Spero recalled, producing "angry works, scatological, manifestos against a senseless obscene war" (Spero, cited in Nixon 2008, 30). "Male bombs" with cartoon erections, grotesquely extended, ejaculate in murderous ecstasy. Female bombs rain blood. Bombs shit infant heads. In one drawing, *Fuck* (1966), seven silver jets trace a frenzied spiral in the sky, bearing on their wings the insignia not of U.S.A. but of F.U.C.K. Tiny, helpless, naked bodies in the throes of death are the quarry dangling from every fiery mouth—the nose of every plane transformed to a serpent's maw—in a gruesome exhibition of blood lust. Mercilessly entangling sex and violence, Spero's *War Series* portrays the machinery of war as obscene. The destruction wreaked on the war victim, the death act that haunts the sex act, takes on a distinctly and disturbingly perverse inflection. Here, sexual violence is a defining condition of war. Exhibited almost exclusively in antiwar shows, Spero's *War Series* eluded critical responses at the time. This critical silence testifies to the neglect that attends representations of war sexuality, as if that annexation of sexuality to war, which formed the focus of Spero's response to the American war in Vietnam, could only surface into discourse in 2003, with the invasion of Iraq, when the *War Series* emerged like a return of the repressed in exhibitions and criticism. Spero's *War Series* is indignant in its condemnation of the obscenities of war, which renders sexuality so virulently destructive, but it is also insistent in its demand for the perversities of war violence to be incorporated in the discourse of war, to be thought.

Mitchell answers this demand by stating that "war is a de-repression." In war, she observes, the desire to kill is no longer unconscious but can be acted upon. Killing may take the form of a "violence perversion, which is psychically structured like a sexual perversion." Pointing out that if "a sexual perversion is a failure of repression" and "we are all considered sexually polymorphously perverse in infancy," there is reason to consider that we are also violently polymorphously perverse, that "as a species we are at least as violence promiscuous as we are sexual promiscuous" (Mitchell, 2003, 36). In the de-repression of war, murderousness and the polymorphous perversity of infancy both come into the ascendant in a situation of extreme paranoid anxiety. Violence is sexualized, and the repressed violence of sexuality becomes manifest in rape, torture, and sexualized killing.

Published in 2003, *Siblings* coincided with the abuses of Abu Ghraib and the clandestine horrors of rendition, torture, and secret prisons. The appearance of photographs of sexual abuse and torture staged and actively traded by soldiers made it undeniable that the war's violence had assumed a perverse form. We were witnessing, in effect, a martial code of violence perversion. Disturbing as this revelation was, its only innovation may have been the wide dissemination of the images. In Vietnam, atrocity was rife but was rhetorically controlled, as it would later be in Afghanistan and Iraq, by a telling term, aberration. Military authorities declared individual acts of atrocity—displays of "violence perversion," conducted in the context of a military strategy so annihilative that it was itself, in the eyes of many, an atrocity writ large—aberrant.[2] Yet, the pervasiveness and sexualized brutality of such actions begged a question. Was the aberrant act enunciative of an individual perversion or a social one? To understand how individual and social violence are articulated in perversion requires, as Mitchell would later point out, a theory of sex and violence at the level of the social. And that theory, for her, finds its origin in hatred toward the sibling, the intimate stranger who is the ur-enemy. Sibling violence is common, universal as fantasy, but culturally deemed aberrant and therefore denied. In war, Mitchell speculates, the desire to kill the sibling who poses an existential threat to oneself returns with a vengeance. The act of atrocity, as a display of violence perversity, restages the aberrant act, or fantasy, of torturing or murdering the sibling.[3] To begin to comprehend the perversity of war atrocity, Mitchell suggests, it is necessary not only to grasp its origins in infantile fantasies of destructiveness—our violence perversity—but also to take account of hatred of the original enemy, the sibling.

Hatred toward the other arises, Mitchell contends, through hatred of the same: "it is this hatred for a sameness that displaces which then generates the category of 'other' as a protection" (Mitchell, 2003, 48). The arrival of the sibling is traumatic, "the trauma of being annihilated by one who stands in one's place" (Mitchell 2003, 10). Displacement by a sibling, whether actual or only feared in fantasy, arouses hatred and murderousness, a trend that psychoanalysis subsumes in the castration complex, or in Mitchell's terms, verticalizes. Effaced from the case histories of psychoanalysis, siblings and their surrogates come to the fore in Mitchell's account as figures that precipitate the trauma of annihilation but also instigate social subjectivity. Mitchell terms this social subjectivity seriality.

"Representing seriality is crucial," Mitchell observes, because the serial subject is able "to turn the sense of the death of itself into a mourning process for its unique self so that it can be re-created as one among others—a part of a series" (Mitchell 2003, 29).[4] This perception of oneself as part of a series implies a social subject position that is distinct from the fantasy of uniqueness on the one hand and of mass unity on the other. In the situation of war, serial subjectivity enables what Mitchell calls "lateral authority," a constraining of violence among peers. War, Mitchell claims, brings lateral relations to the fore. In war we kill and rape our peers, she observes, but "ironically, it is in societies based on the social contract of brotherhood that these activities are not laterally controlled. Our social imaginary can envisage only vertical authority" (Mitchell 2003, xv). We kill and rape our peers with our peers, but we rely on the hierarchical authority of the state, which instigates this violence, to control it. Looking cross-culturally to kinship and social orders in which lateral relations are more complexly articulated, Mitchell argues that our subservience to vertical authority in war is culturally specific, and potentially subject to change.

In her classic essay "On Violence," Hannah Arendt argued that "the first generation to grow up under the shadow of the atom bomb" (Arendt 1970, 116) rebelled against patriarchal (vertical) authority to resist the war in Vietnam, a development she described as belonging "among the totally unexpected events of this century" (Arendt 1970, 130). As evidence of the latent potential of the exercise of what Mitchell would call lateral control, Arendt cites the example of the People's Park protest in Berkeley, California, where heavily armed police and the National Guard were called upon to attack unarmed student protesters. "Some Guardsmen fraternized openly with their 'enemies' and one of them threw down his arms and shouted: 'I can't stand this anymore,'" she relates (Arendt 1970, 131). Such "fraternizing with the enemy" (in the context of a conflict that was taking on the character of a civil war) brings home the reality of sameness, of being laterally aligned, and precipitates a spontaneous refusal to exercise violence on behalf of the state. By contrast, in the infamous massacre and maiming of student protesters at Kent State University in Ohio, members of the National Guard who fired on unarmed demonstrators displayed their rigid adherence to, and identification with, vertical authority, in an event that galvanized protests across the world, including a little-noticed performance by the American dancer, choreographer, and filmmaker, Yvonne Rainer.

In art, a serial logic emerged in the 1960s, roughly contemporaneously with the war in Vietnam and the antiwar movement, in which many artists associated with Minimalism, including Rainer, took an active part (see Bryan-Wilson 2009). From the early to the mid-1960s, Rainer choreographed and danced with a contingent of artists—a sibling group, as it were—loosely affiliated under the name Judson Dance Theatre, derived from the activist Judson Memorial Church in Greenwich Village, New York, where they performed. Inspired by John Cage, the kind of movement Judson choreographers pioneered is often described as task-based performance, subjecting ordinary, pedestrian actions such as walking, running, or manipulating objects, to the discipline of dance. One aim of Judson was to subvert the dynamic of mastery in classical dance by replacing virtuosic movement, solo performance, and the charisma of the lead dancer, with nonhierarchical, inclusive procedures, incorporating untrained performers and laying particular emphasis on the contingency of the event. Judson Dance was not an explicitly political practice, but its social dynamics were predicated on a rejection of mastery and hierarchy and an embrace of what has been described as an egalitarian ethos (Bane 1980). To situate this history in Mitchell's terms, the Judson choreographers were working on the lateral axis of a cultural form that seemed "trapped in the vertical."

Street Action is not a work of Judson Dance Theatre, and is not exactly a work of art at all. It is a protest work, perhaps, or an artistic response to a political crisis, namely, the revelation on April 30, 1970, of the American invasion of Cambodia, followed on May 4 by the attack of the National Guard on protesting students at Kent State, a massacre in which four students were shot to death and another nine wounded, including one who was paralyzed. Timed to coincide with a weekend arts festival in Lower Manhattan, *Street Action* brought together some 40 students, friends, and acquaintances of Rainer, who arranged the group in a three-column formation, led by herself and two other dancers, Douglas Dunn and Sara Rudner. Very slowly, the group began to move down the middle of the street, reproducing a gait, the M-walk, devised by Rainer for a dance work entitled *The Mind is a Muscle*, and adapted from the mechanized movement of workers in Fritz Lang's 1927 film *Metropolis*. Here, however, the participants linked arms, "transforming the movement," as the art historian Carrie Lambert-Beatty has noted, "from drone-like submission to mournful solidarity" (Lambert-Beatty 2008, 239). The route traced by the phalanx marked off a single block in a then newly defined artistic district of SoHo. By Rainer's recollection, that trip around the block took an hour, and by the end of it, the group had dwindled to five. For untrained performers, the physical discipline of the swaying lockstep motion on straight legs, its slowness, and the requirement that the participants keep their eyes lowered and averted, was oppressively difficult to sustain.

Describing the performance as a minimal march, Lambert-Beatty points to the contrast between the physical restraint of the M-Walk and the prevailing culture of protest. "The three front figures seem to stand solidly on their feet, almost as if, rather than leading a forward surge, they were trying to restrain one," she remarks (ibid., 238). *Street Action* defied the rhetoric of antiwar demonstrations. It did not attempt to draw a crowd. Bystanders were not encouraged to join the procession. By refusing to make eye contact with passers-by, the performers, as in Rainer's dance work, declined to engage in false unities. Rather than swelling in size, the procession dwindled as it went, dramatizing the difficulty of collective action, and perhaps more particularly, the obstacles to the type of action that would result in an expansion of the social imaginary to encompass a "lateral control" on violence. The ambition of *Street Action* is, in the words of participants and critics, minimal—a minimal march, "a minimal mortification" (ibid., 238). These formulations echo the critical vocabulary of Minimalism, or course, and invoke Rainer's own influential writing on that term as deployed in dance (Rainer 1966). What is notable in the context of *Siblings*, however, is that the term minimal seems to encompass both a sense of minimal difference and minimal affect. The almost uniform postures that the participants' bodies are constrained to adopt and to maintain construct the body politic as, in Mitchell's terms, a sibling group, composed of figures that are "the same but different," subject to the serial logic of lateral rather than vertical authority and assimilation. By discouraging mass identification and by enacting a ritual of mourning in which individual actors are engaged as part of a series, *Street Action* reflects upon the dynamic of group resistance to war. Its extreme restraint also, crucially, counters the hystericization of political protest by the state, a maneuvre by which the state stigmatizes protest as impotent and consolidates its authority over war. Imagining the body politic as a sibling group, *Street Action* is composed of peers, individual actors who with deliberate restraint resist rather than protest the authority of the state.

In *Street Action*, individuals moved together as a body, intimately linked, but with evident strain, their eyes turned downward in attitudes of mournful reflection. What the sibling matrix offers, above all perhaps, is a mediating term between the restrictive implications of psychic subjectivity, understood as individual, introverted, and fragmentary, and the totalizing implications of a social economy defined as anti-subjective, extroverted, and unified. As an enactment of serial subjectivity, *Street Action* articulated individual reflection and social responsibility through a choreographed performance of "same but different" individual agents. In so doing, it called upon principles of seriality derived not from psychoanalysis, but from art.

In art, "representing seriality" became crucial in the so-called Minimalism, or Serial Art, of the 1960s and was bound up with the shift from an expressive model of subjectivity, centered on the sovereign self (as in Abstract Expressionism), to a model of social subjectivity predicated on what Mitchell would later call minimal difference. Psychoanalysis has rarely been brought to bear on seriality in art.[5] For as long as lateral relations were perceived to fall outside the perspective of psychoanalysis, seriality was construed as anti-subjective. One implication of psychoanalysis being "trapped in the vertical" therefore has been that its exclusions have extended to other discourses in which the social imaginary is also at stake. Critical interpretations of seriality in art, therefore, have tended to assert its renunciation of subjectivity on the tacit authority of psychoanalysis itself. From this perspective, the psychic structure of seriality does not exist—in theory. Rather, seriality is emblematic of a turn away from subjective expression toward anti-subjective sociality (Krauss 1977). By offering a specifically psychoanalytic account of lateral social relationships, Mitchell's theoretical intervention therefore returns to critical discourse a set of terms she has, albeit unintentionally, adapted from it. For seriality is a term of art, a term used to disavow subjectivity in its individualist sense, but also to articulate "lateral relations" in a social as well as a formal sense. This term appears at a pivotal moment in the history of gender, on the cusp of the feminist movement and in a time of war that would expose "siblings, sex, and violence" as a dynamic "in love and sexuality" and "in hate and war." In a corollary to the opening up of an autonomous place for gender in psychoanalysis, seriality "fits into" psychoanalytic theory and is only extra-psychoanalytic to the extent that psychoanalysis is constrained by its own omissions. Mitchell's theory of siblings broaches the possibility of restoring subjectivity to seriality through a rigorous reconsideration of subjectivity itself.

A decade after the publication of *Siblings: Sex and Violence*, its radical re-thinking of psychoanalysis reverberates in the humanities, and perhaps particularly in art, which has embraced "thinking siblings" as a means of working against the grain of hierarchy and gender ideology. As generative as the model has proven, its first principle, that we abandon psychoanalysis at our peril, can sometimes be overlooked. To substitute the lateral axis of gender for the vertical axis of difference, and particularly to assign destructiveness and oppression exclusively to the line of descent are critical reflexes to resist. For Mitchell, the sibling, far from benign, represents an existential threat, one to which we respond with all the destructiveness that is in us. "Minimal difference" signifies a mitigation of the catastrophe of psychic annihilation, a return from the dead. Only with the most painful difficulty do we sublimate hatred of the same into love. In war, Mitchell reminds us, we exploit our hatred of the same to "generate the category of 'other.'" Thinking siblings is not a refuge from our badness, only a theory that, like psychoanalysis itself, may help us to grapple with it. Seriality is hard won.

Notes

1. Two compelling responses to the abuses of Abu Ghraib and the psychic dynamics of the war on terror are by contributors to this volume: Judith Butler, *Frames of War: When Is Live Grievable?* (London: Verso, 2009) and Jacqueline Rose, *The Last Resistance* (London: Verso, 2007).
2. On the extent of atrocities conducted by the American military in Vietnam, and the deceptive characterization of them as aberrations, see Nick Turse, *Kill Anything That Moves: The Real American War in Vietnam* (New York: Metropolitan Books, 2013).
3. The truism of war, "kill or be killed," governs the distinction between so-called legitimate killing and murder. That distinction breaks down in many forms of modern warfare, not least bombing, but it is a crucial line for Mitchell's theory.
4. Seriality is also crucially significant as "the symbolization of the repetition of trauma." See Tamar Garb and Mignon Nixon, "A Conversation with Juliet Mitchell," *October* 113 (Summer 2005), p. 20.
5. Important exceptions are Hal Foster, *The Return of the Real* (Cambridge, MA: MIT Press/October Books, 1996) and Briony Fer, *The Infinite Line* (New Haven and London: Yale University Press).

References

Arendt, Hannah. 1970. *On Violence*. Houghton Mifflin Harcourt.

Bane, Sally. 1980/1993. *Democracy's Body: Judson Dance Theatre 1962–1964*. Duke University Press.

Bryan-Wilson, Julia. 2009. *Art Workers: Radical Practice in the Vietnam War Era*. Berkeley: University of California.

Butler, Judith. 1990. *Gender Trouble: Feminism and the Subversion of Identity*. New York: Routledge.

Fornari, Franco. 1975. *The Psychoanalysis of War*. Bloomington: Indiana University Press.

Freud, S. 1915. "Thoughts for the Times on War and Death," In *Standard Edition of the Complete Psychological Works of Sigmund Freud. Vol. 14*, translated by James Strachey, London: Hogarth.

Kelly, Mary, 1983. "Preface," *Post-Partum Document*, xv. London: Routledge.

Krauss, Rosalind. 1977. *Passages in Modern Sculpture*. Cambridge, MA: MIT Press.

Lambert-Beatty, Carrie. 2008. *Being Watched: Yvonne Rainer and the 1960s* Cambridge, MA: MIT Press/October Books.

Mitchell, Juliet. 2000. *Mad Men and Medusas: Reclaiming Hysteria and the Effect of Sibling Relationships on the Human Condition*. London: Allen Lane.

Nixon, M. 2008. "Book of Tongues." In Nancy Spero: *Dissidances*, 30. Barcelona and Madrid: Museu d'Art Contemporani de Barcelona and Museo Nacional Centro de Art Reina Sofia.

Nixon, M. 2014. "Louise Lawler: No Drones," *October* 147 (Winter 2014).

Owens, Craig. 1983. "The Discourse of Others: Feminists and Postmodernism." In *Beyond Recognition: Representation, Power, and Culture*. Berkeley: University of California Press.

Rainer, Yvonne. 1966. "A Quasi Survey of Some 'Minimalist' Tendencies in the Quantitatively Minimal Dance Activity Midst the Plethora, or an Analysis of Trio A." In Yvonne Rainer. 1974. *Work 1961–73*. Halifax: Press of the Nova Scotia College of Art and Design.

Chapter 10

Crimes of Identity

Gayatri Chakravorty Spivak

I was honored to have been asked to deliver the 2014 Juliet Mitchell capstone lecture at Cambridge. I was in awe of Juliet Mitchell before I met her—I believe in 1993, with Michael Riffaterre at the School of Criticism and Theory—and have retained that feeling. I taught her iconic *Psychoanalysis and Feminism* again and again after the mid-1970s, in the obligatory feminist theory class that I had begun to teach from the end of the 1960s.[1]

In my prepared speech, I had made two points:

One, that having a certain kind of "identity" allows groups with preferred "identities" to initiate and sustain policy that, although legal, may be construed as "criminal" by natural law, if it were humane in the colloquial sense. In the workshop following the talk, I was asked why these would not be called "crimes of capital." The answer was that capital, the abstract as such, is not susceptible to behavioral diagnosis. As one of the participants remarked: "whether crimes of capital would have been possible at all if there wasn't a certain logic of identity in place. I am not sure whether crimes of capital would have been possible if it wasn't for a certain logic of gendered identity, a certain logic of class identity that has been inscribed in the bodies of those men who have committed these suicides." In terms of conjuncture discourse, managing gender and class by race-ideology, I was shifting the field of identity from capitalism-mobilized *claims* to capitalism-accusing *crimes*. To invoke "crimes of capital" is incorrect. To invoke "crimes of capitalism" is banal in Hannah Arendt's sense, and plagued by the usual rentier bad faith within academic leftism, engaged in a perennial small-stakes effort to secure a place within capitalist globalization, unable to acknowledge complicity.[2] "Capital" or "capitalism" are faceless structural enemies. I wanted to bring the scenario into the field of identity precisely because it is more personalized. It inhabits the "human" in the humanities. It profits from the equally ambiguous but important contribution of dominant feminism: "the personal is political."

The second point is theoretical. Working within the German classical tradition, we are aware that "origins" of philosophical discourse cannot be accessed. Kant thought of the synthetic a priori and made it accessible only by transcendental deduction. Derrida rewrote it as the indefinite story of differance, perhaps resonating the Lacanian insight of the "Discourse of Rome: The Function and Field of Speech and Language in Psychoanalysis."[3] In the powerful and influential piece "The Force of Law," this inaccessible "origin" is described as "the metaphysical origins of law."[4] In Derrida, there was also the idea of the relationship without relationship between gift and responsibility, justice and law, writing in the general and narrow senses. Barthes understood this as the relationship (without relationship) between the writable and the readable.[5] And so on.

Within this tradition, that inaccessibility is always given a benign name—transcendental, differential, metaphysical, "sophistical" in the positive sense etc. My own thinking of planetarity—and Laurie Anderson's—is harsher: ""planetary" is bigger than "geological," where random means nothing, which no thought can weigh." Fiction makes us experience this impossible by dropping into geology: Mahasweta's pterodactyl, Morrison's request not to pass on her story of a mother's child sacrifice as "just weather," not geography or history, geology.[6] This unsentimentalized thinking of the human in the planet made me suspect that the "human"-izing of the human by way of the synthetic a priori etc., given that it is inextricably connected with the violence of the Anthropocene, should perhaps be understood by way of the concept-metaphor of rape, rather than the Law of the Father, the incest taboo alone, which seemed to me, after generalized rape, its naturalization. Later, I connected this to Juliet Mitchell's statement in the new introduction to the second edition of *Psychoanalysis and Feminism*: "While it is true that women may be socialised into assuming the position of the second sex, this conscious deliberate socialisation is inadequate to explain the structure of sexual difference and inequalities that always arise from it. Despite the fact that there is enormous diversity in social practice."[7] I explain this structure as the "human"-izing of the animal/natural: Rape. We are—male and female—raped into humanity and don't mind it: do we put on its knowledge with its power? Nancy Fraser reminded us in the next day's workshop of "one standard feminist line that rape is not an act of sex but an act of power." Power, force, the force of law may be though as rape in the general sense. Here we can use Juliet Mitchell's sentence: "Rape is not sexuality that is violent but violence that has been sexualized," and write: "Rape is the coveted agency of that which must be transcendentally deduced become sexualized. That agency would be to control inaccessible origins: sperm fantasy."[8]

For the moment, let us not resist the counterintuitive by the self-congratulation of a common sense.

The problem with this is paleonymy: as "rape" proceeded in the English language from the general sense of "theft" into sexual violence, there is no way that this word could be understood extra-morally. This is in fact the problem with all of the words for the inaccessibility of the origin. "Transcendental" is understood as the supernatural, difference as antiracist/sexist and so on. They are supposedly unconditional, but unconditionality is always contaminated by conditions.

I warned about this in the extemporized introduction to my prepared paper: perhaps you should think about rape and the way in which Foucault talked about power, I said. As a name. But of course many of us complained about the fact that power was also in the language—and rape is more than in the language—so that power had a paleonymy and therefore one was responsible for choosing just that word. Remember that, so am I. Responsible.

Derrida's general philosophy may be vulgarized as follows: theory is a practice. The theorizer does not cling to concept-metaphors and establish them as master-concepts. Derrida more or less stays with this in his writings, though not invariably. It is a difficult thing to keep up. And so, with embracing the violence of rape as the correct description of the violation of the animal by the making-human, I tried to take on this challenge and suggest that this concept-metaphor should not be used again, should be seen as universalizable, not universalized; that it should not be naturalized. And of course, I failed.[9] Can the reader walk with me on this one? Can humanism itself be understood as the child of rape? And thus put us in the double bind, since you do not throw the child out with the possibility of rape.

In response to Nancy's vigorous reminder of the dangers of my claim, I wanted to write a piece that was going to act out all the warnings, knowing, of course, that I should not have ventured up to the perilous point where it became a necessity.

Time to open the prepared paper and see if it can be revised to be safe:

The most significant crimes in our world today are committed on the issue of identity. Identity is defined by and predicated on collective legitimate birth. The great Dalit thinker, Bhimrao Ramji Ambedkar, suggested in 1916 that caste—and this was unusual for a man who had suffered severe caste prejudice—as a general rule of group formation could be defined by and predicated on the difference in the use of surplus women and surplus men in every society. This relates to the sentence I quoted from Juliet Mitchell. Socialization into sex is different for different societies. But it happens in all societies. The caste system in its wretchedness is not like any other system of group formation. Nonetheless Ambedkar says it is a general rule.

Group formation is a way of establishing identity. How shall we think Babasaheb Ambedkar's insight?

We needed a reality check: to think the unconditional ethical before good feelings about sexual preference—as you know, Levinas's missionary position sex establishes the human as human.[10] Good feelings!

In 1990, thinking about identity, I looked up a dictionary and I wrote—this is a translation from my Bengali

> that the source of the word "identity" was given as Latin *idem* or Sanskrit *idam* and both were cited as meaning "same." Now the meaning of the Latin word *idem* is not exactly "same" in the sense of "one," but rather "same" in the sense of multitudes or repetitions. That which is primordial [*anadi*] and unique [*ekamevadvitiam*] is not *idem*, it is rather that which can be cited through many re-citations. To make these two meanings one is a clandestine patching up of a loose part of the text-ile fabric of conceptuality. At least from the outside it seems that in our solemn recitation of *Hindutva* [Hinduness, a key word of Hindu nationalism] this clan-destiny or ruse is at work. The little Sanskrit that I learned under the able guidance of Miss Nilima Pyne at the Diocesan School in Calcutta allowed me to suspect that the Sanskrit *idam* is also not the undiminishing singly manifest [*akshaya ekarupa*]. Then I looked at the Sanskrit dictionary. *Idam* is not only not the undiminishing selfsame, as a pronoun it does not have the dignity of a noun, is always enclitic or inclined towards the noun, always dependent upon the proximity of a particular self, and must always therefore remain monstrative, indexed. All over the world today, "identity politics" (that is to say a separation in the name of the undifferentiated identity of religion, nation, or subnation) is big news and almost everywhere bad news.[11] The unremarkable and unremarked ruse in the United States students' dictionary [Merriam-Webster's college edition, I think] makes visible the fraud at the heart of identity politics. As a memorial to that publication I submit this outlandish deconstructed translation [I submitted on that occasion, and later I will connect it to my use of "rape" in the current essay] of "identity," only for that occasion—not *ahamvada* [ego-ism as ipseism] but *idamvada*. If our thinking shakes the stakes of the spirit's *ahamvada* to show *idamvada* [shaking up autonormativity to show heteronormativity]—we do not want to know it, and therefore we protect ourselves in the name of a specific national identity.[12]

Crimes of identity are always collective, although individuals suffer grotesquely. At the benevolent end, good works become "criminal" in effect; in effect because the benefactors forget that history is larger than personal goodwill. Laws are fought for, sometimes passed, litigations are undertaken and the emphasis remains on enforcement. Thought this way, "crime" expands, often inhabiting an imaginary natural law—this is how it was in nature—including but overflowing the boundaries of positive law. "Rape" is the only word I can use to indicate a certain harsh unconditionality initiating all human beings before the altogether conditioned notion of consent and nature. If Babasaheb Ambedkar is right, we are looking at what German classical philosophy would call transcendental intuition, where transcendental has nothing to do with the supernatural. English words, where words fail us; crime, rape, transcendental. Such a situation is possible in all the languages of the world.

In India, we are currently deeply concerned with rape because it was brought to public attention by a most grotesquely violent occurrence of it in the capital city, toward an educated woman and her educated partner. I want to begin my presentation in that concern.

I have often argued that gender in the general sense is our first instrument of abstraction. It is the tacit collective globalizer long before cartographers could think the globe, mapping negotiations between the sacred and the profane and the relationship between the sexes, with sexual difference unevenly abstracted into gender/gendering as the chief semiotic instrument of negotiation. Nationalism and religion come into play here. Yet this unconditional producer of the socius, conditioning the proper, remains ungeneralizable. It holds the possibility of defining the female identity as potential surplus object of a pleasure that is in excess of, yet defining, sexuality. The exemplary instance of this surplus pleasure is rape as the fruit of victory in war, itself a crime of identity.[13]

On the occasion of borders, I have discussed Lacan's invocation of drives grasping on to borders of the body and related it to the sense of borders that must be protected as war.[14]

I want to invoke this here, as Lacan's imagining of the contaminating relationship between the unspeculable work of the drives—unspeculable because you cannot produce its reflection since the subject has not been started yet—and the normative deviation of fantasy. I do not wish to write of perversions, Lacan writes in effect, I would rather deal with fantasy.[15] The normative deviation of fantasy sets the norm by mistakenly establishing the unspeculable as specular and the result of that speculation as a repetition of the same; it is the realm of desire. Of course, the normative definition which will redress this grounding error, within that ground, will set in place the asymmetry of the Law of the Father alone.

In the field of positive law, we are still fighting this one in the question of gay marriage.

Forgive me for going through this fable so fast. Please keep in mind the broad outlines: the unspeculable turned into the specular by normative deviation, the imaginary; the specular turned into the limited asymmetry of speculation. This asymmetry is only limited because, although the asymmetry of the Father alone oversees this move, it is in the interests of guarding the infinitely repeatable as the same: the absolute symmetry of the Idea; the patronymic; the seamless signifying system of the symbolic.

I am more interested in Lacan's narrativization of the unconditional unspeculable. Lacan describes the presubjective drive falling upon the "anatomical trace of a margin or border;"—every word here is full of meaning—"lips, enclosure of the teeth, rim of the anus, penile fissure, vagina, fissure of eyelid, indeed hollow of the ear.... Respiratory erogeneity... comes into play through spasms." In other words, border-thinking is an undecided and primary constituent of our perception of reality itself, where reason is fashioned out of what precedes it. It is of no interest to me if this account is correct and therefore an instrument of cure. The literary critic learns from the singular and unverifiable. What is of interest to me is that here in the place before the speculations of the subject Lacan places the extra-moral possibility of the infinite extension of rape; borders, holes in the body. In the narrative itself, classic psychoanalysis cannot distinguish between seduction and rape and the distinction between truth and exactitude becomes patriarchially counterproductive. French Freud has not considered this particular problem significant. Juliet Mitchell's tremendous intervention in *Psychoanalysis and Feminism* does not specifically thematize rape. What I am speaking of today thematizes her bold parenthesis; the only mention of rape in that early book ("That rape does indeed occur is only an indirectly related issue"). This is the relentlessness of the unconditional.[16] I am focused on that indirection, the refraction of the transcendental. Indeed, apart from Jeffrey Moussaief Masson's *The Assault on Truth*, which treats seduction and rape together and points at the disavowal of real sexual abuse in Freudian psychoanalysis, rape is not necessarily a concern for those who wish to bring feminism and psychoanalysis together. Rape in the narrow sense is neither seduction nor incest. Where incest is supposed to distinguish the human from nature and seduction is morally ambiguous after the law, rape in the narrow sense makes it hard to determine the border of the human and the upper primates.

If Jacques Lacan, the master imaginer, implies rape as a potential before subject signifier and ego, I attend to that imagining and suggest that redress for rape cannot be in the sphere of unconditional ethics but firmly in the field of agency, where the intending subject is accountable to what Kant would call "mere reason." There we require an epistemological performance which cannot always be expected of what we have now come to designate as "activism." It is an imaginative training that rape in the narrow sense, if such a thing can be thought, still extends all the way from the most public to the most private, from war crime to domestic violence. But this is "after," this is in the field of agency, intervention; activism. Sexual violence without consent, coercive. And the unconditional possibility of rape in the general sense as the unaccountable origin of the human should at least be thinkable during the time of the reading of this chapter.

No modern European thinker of the subject is free of German classical philosophy. The Cartesian line is more historical, the invocation of Christianity wittingly or unwittingly reactive. Within the main tradition, the common element is the break between the transcendental and the phenomenal. Kant keeps the break alive; Hegel narrativizes it, staging the break repeatedly, in various ways. Kant keeps the rupture between (the unconditionality of) pure reason and understanding blank, although contaminated into a textual blank, with the understanding presumably philosophizing on the analogy of the sense perceptible manifold. Many years ago, Rosalind Coward and John Ellis showed that Lacan had read Hegel.[17] And indeed, Lacan speaks of Descartes and Hegel as being metonymic of psychoanalysis, unearthing part of it and disclosing it as the whole. Here we can tabulate Lacan's bond to Kant as well as Hegel, as he narrativizes the unconditional and programmed material transcendental by way of a manifold—the body's borders—that will become sense-perceptible by way of the grounding error of signifier/fantasy—leading to the subject/ego site of conflict, secured by the specular/discursive access provided for analysis. A complex trajectory, but the Kantian imprint is determining—the necessary intuition of the drives remaining unspeculable (though compromised here by narrativization): rape in the general sense. Kant's warning to Locke: the necessity of the synthetic a priori cannot be proved, only demonstrated.

Rape in the general sense is not susceptible to proof. Its demonstrability cannot be argued, although Andrea Dworkin did make a heroic attempt, creating a clearly excessive binary opposition. At the other extreme, such a binary opposition is legitimized by reversal because of the incalculability of gendering—into a straightforward relationship between desire and violence: "she, or indeed he, asked for it."

Remaining within psychoanalysis, Mitchell moves from "killing is raping and raping is killing" to "a suggestion of death and sex drives being constituted in the same moment."[18] Perhaps death and sex are somewhat naturalized here? Freud and Lacan have always found in fiction the experience of the impossible. Reversing the situation and reading the literary in Freud, let me propose that the ripple in the pervasive ocean of thanatos that is the normative deviation of the emergence of life (an unbalanced psychic machine) shares a structure with rape, if rape is understood as generalized "objectlessness" (no individual is the object of the "planetary" or the synthetic a priori).

The character Lucy in J. M. Coetzee's novel *Disgrace*, pregnant after being raped, gives us a sense of the "objectlessness" of rape by refusing to be interpellated as victim:

> [She] cast[s] aside...the affective value system attached to reproductive heteronormativity as it is accepted as the currency to measure human dignity. [I was comparing this to Cordelia's speech in *Lear*.] I do not think this is an acceptance of rape, but a refusal to be raped by instrumentalising reproduction. Coetzee's Lucy is made to make clear that the "nothing" is not to be itself measured as the absence of "everything" by the old epistemico-affective value form; the system of knowing-loving.[19]

Let me point out that Coetzee, in his usual manner, is not only mingling race, class, and gender but also, given contemporary South Africa, the idea of the new nation as well. Nationalism, starting from group formations preceding the formation of nation states by far, sanctions crimes of group identity.

Disgrace's twist, the situation of the white creole in the postcolonial nation, could not be imagined by Kant. The best he can do is to make a gesture toward the colonized:

> The country whose inhabitants are citizens of one and the same Commonwealth (by birth) is called the *fatherland;* those where they live without this condition is a *foreign country;* and these, if they are part of a wider landownership, are called *provinces* (in the meaning given by the Romans), which, while not integrated into an empire as a place of fellow-citizens, but is only a possession as a subordinate position, must respect the ground of the ruling state as a *motherland.*[20]

Freud is able to perceive nationalism as part of fetishism, but he, too, cannot ask that specific question.[21] Lacan is altogether less political but, as I have suggested elsewhere, the transcendental border-perception, made specular, can also determine the tremendous identitarian pull of nationalism, legitimizing birth, disavowing rape in general, as if an origin can be accessed. In *Nationalism and Imagination* I have suggested that full-blown nationalism conjures with something as private as a simple comfort in one's space and is not therefore amenable to the public use of reason.[22]

Edward W. Said cited Erich Auerbach citing Hugo of St Victor, the immensely learned twelfth-century cleric, who was both a rationalist and a mystic: "The man who finds his homeland sweet is still a tender beginner; he to whom every soil is as his native one is already strong; but he is perfect to whom the entire world is as a foreign land."[23] I have elsewhere written that these impressive words, from an exceptional intellectual with no family obligations, should be tempered with a thinking of the wife in exogamy—rather than the agents of the Alexandria codex—as the type case of the diasporic, as the word is now used.[24] I will not revisit that argument here but rather submit that the cleric's statement was a disavowal of the discursive potential of rape in general. In order to so do, I must remind you of the implications of the conviction—that gender is our first instrument of abstraction—with which I started my remarks.

I repeat, this unconditional producer of the socius, condition proper, remains ungeneralizable. Exogamous wives outside of the romantic view of marriage are different in different social formations, capable of desiring violence. The unconditional producer of the socius holds the possibility of defining female identity as potential surplus object of a pleasure that is in excess of, yet defining, sexuality. The exemplary instance of this surplus pleasure is rape as the fruit of victory in war, itself a crime of identity.

Coetzee's Lucy, a character in fiction, is staged as undoing rape by perhaps recognizing the access to humanity as rape in the general sense. In terms of this experience of the impossible, I will spend some time with rape in the narrow sense.

Open any day's newspaper and you will see accounts of brutal and terrifying rape cases, almost invariably of women by men. This morning, I read of a mullah raping a beautiful minor girl so brutally that the area between her vagina and anus suffered dreadful wounds and she almost bled to death. I hear that her family wants to kill her and the mullah will go scot-free. There is an item also of the brutal gang rape of Thangjam Manorama, her vagina area bullet-ridden to destroy evidence, because she was a political radical, fighting for tribal independence.[25] Visit a prison, and you will hear of cases of male rapes just as brutal. The theorizing about is rape sex or violence goes on, the terrifying work of keeping and enforcing the law goes on. I take my cues from Farida Akhter, Flavia Agnes, Catharine MacKinnon; and many other sisters.[26] What I am saying today is that this is the human condition. It is a scandalous thing to say because for some reason we have sentimentalized the concept of the human, with underived universal rights and so on, in the last few centuries. I think, if we can acknowledge that real education de-humanizes so that we can promote social justice, an endeavor that turns rape around and makes it productive, as in the fictive example of *Disgrace*'s Lucy, we would be better off. I have often connected rape-culture and bribe-culture—thinking of both as "normal"—rape as the extra in gender and bribe in the economic. Just as rape does not look like rape if there is sex in it, so bribe disappears if it is simply capitalist expression of "normal" human greed, perfectly practicable if you have received institutional education, seen today in the resumption of subprime lending in the automobile industry, no lesson learnt after 2007. My citing these examples will I hope assure you that I am not interested in speaking in generalized abstractions; these examples are class marked. Therefore, not only am I not "turning reality into nothing but abstractions" but, I am asking us to acknowledge that in many very different kinds of areas, the structure of a sudden and unaccountable entry into humanity—and indeed the originary move for every possibility of being-human shares very much more in common with the structure that I can only call rape. If we accept this, then we are complicit with rape, we do not try to redress what can be called rape only by making and enforcing laws in the name of humanity; but, more practically, we act toward the artificiality of, in the name of a forever thwarted social justice as a result of a certain kind of education which effectively de-humanizes, if the human is understood as not necessarily anodyne and benign as most people of our class and our education tend to do. This is how I understand MacKinnon's placing of the *prakrit* (natural) before the *Sanskrit* (repaired): "The analysis is structured to treat law as first substantive then abstract on the view that, in this sphere and perhaps others, law is interpreted and practiced on the basis of substantive experiences and material commitments, from which doctrinal and formal positions inevitably derive" (p.v). Recently, sitting at a table with an altogether accomplished art historian who suggested that most people would like to do good to others, I had to say the entire world does not resemble you and she later confided to her husband that I intimidated her. This idea, of a welcome de-humanizing kept up with difficulty, should not intimidate—but simply allow us not to claim post-humanism when it is convenient to do so, and become aware that the anthropocene is not just climate change, not just the bad human; it is the double bind of the human as such.

In the discussion of gender as our first instrument of abstraction, I have previously made three further suggestions: that this use of reproductive heteronormativity includes everything that emerges from the difference between how much we need and how much we can make; that the autonormativity of the Idea—infinite repeatability of the same—disavows this; and finally, that in the field of sexual reproduction as the most generalizable clue to heteronormativity, the queer use of its affective and legal resources is "extra-moral" in the Nietzschean sense, as far as possible. Now I am ready to take reproductive heteronormativity—provoked by the passage in Mitchell that I have already quoted—as the social account of the transcendental and unconditional discursivity of rape in the general sense. This indeconstructible unconditionality, like Marx's realm of freedom, is not susceptible to social engineering. Therefore the redress of rape in the narrow sense, as nonconsensual sexual violence, is only possible through agential work in three ways: (a) interventionist enforcement of the law, (b) juridico-legal constitutionality in the making of the law; and (c) undoing class apartheid in education and making room for long-term imaginative training for epistemological performance—producing problem solvers rather than enforcing solutions to problems.

I take them up briefly and in sequence.

(a) Interventionist involvement on a worldwide scale, undertaken by what is now called the International Civil Society, must use the tremendous generalizing resources of the digital. Digital redress cannot recognize the contingent. You can programme for all kinds of mistakes and compensations etc. but the contingent as such will always escape. You can even plan for many contingencies that you can imagine but the contingent as such you cannot imagine; it must be neutralized. Not only can digital redress not recognize the contingent but it must resist all thought of the unconditional as impractical. It must generalize in order to redress what it perceives as gender inequality, and believe me I am not against this. Yet it must also be recognized that the unconditional is in unavoidable tension with this generalization that produces platforms of action for international civil society, one size fits all gender toolkits for field workers from urban to rural. Gendered microcredit sees income production as such as unquestioned good. We cannot get around this if we must solve gender problems, ranging from homophobic laws through domestic violence, pharmaceutical dumping, absence of reproductive rights, unequal pay, dowry trafficking, HIV-AIDS, war rape, casual rape, genital mutilation and the like. Yet, this generalized redress produces problem solving that cannot last, for three reasons at least: the tremendous counterforce of sustainable underdevelopment, the *longue durée* of internalized gendering and class apartheid in education. Short-term problem solving must continue indefinitely, resources must be sought and deployed. Since, however, the sources are largely corporate, their ties with the presuppositions and values of sustainable underdevelopment are strong. Therefore, even to the generally impatient members of the Human Rights lobby I would make the hopeless request that internalized gendering be approached through patience and respect and that the protocols of the epistemological machine of the victims be learned with critical intimacy. Only then can dominant feminism—with no social contract—try to rearrange desires; ours as well as theirs. Ignorance of language and historical detail are the main problems here and this is an ongoing process of decline.

(b) I began this talk in the memory of Jyoti Singh, gang-raped savagely in Delhi on December 16, 2012. Apart from protests, the consequences have been juridico-legal. The extreme limit of the crime of identity—a crime predicated on the "identity" of the victim—war rape, is susceptible to international criminal law, with limits to enforceability. By and large, however, we are still speaking of the juridico-legal nation-state constitutionality. When we think of the enforcers of the law we realize that, in the paradigm of agential redress, the problem is not confined to gender but to worldwide class apartheid in education, which allows me to segue to its undoing.

(c) As long as education below a certain class line remains the memorizing of generally uncomprehended rote answers to set questions, and teachers (among others) can bribe their way into employment, the enforcers of the law, the street police and the rural police, assume rape-culture and bribe-culture to be normal. Here we speak of rape, once again, as violent and brutal sexual practice as pleasure in excess, which relates to the generalized rape toward which Ambedkar pointed so long ago. The redress here is attention to quality—top, bottom, and middle. Attention to first language education in combination with global languages. Absence of this is why, the assumption, of even so heroic a figure as Catharine MacKinnon, that

> by providing a critical grasp of the legal tools of the field, [her book can] aspire to narrow the gap between the law's promise and performance in [the] domain [of "social inequality between and among women and men, legal sex equality guarantees, and the present and possible relation between the two"] by promoting change toward equality goals

will have too restricted a field.[27] Massively important work such as hers must be persistently supplemented by expanding the readership for her book. (She knows this in her earlier, less legal book, which "engages sexual politics on the level of epistemology.") The expansion of epistemological training can only happen in the language the student "feels," even as he or she learns English for the big world. Otherwise, rape/ bribe (*kamini/kanchan*) will work as normal, rape as bribe will work as normal.

Attention to first language education in combination with global languages is called for. The strength of gender education should be interwoven into classroom practice, rather than depend on consciousness raising at the very start. Things must change as we go up the education ladder, of course. Here, too, class and the historical *longue durée* must be learnt through direct unconditional contact. Learned accounts must be judiciously consulted as secondary, because most learned accounts do not go below this radar.

Knowledge management—group learning with charts or cards—and toolkits, cannot cross epistemological divides. Although structured evaluation is certainly needed for a sense of progress in both participant and funder, we must learn to rely on the unexpected or on contingent results.

In this limited but crucial enclosure of redress, this last item—education, creating a general will for social justice in all children—is not far from Freud's liberal revision of the Kantian sublime into sublimation, or from Lacan's straightforward account of the ethics of psychoanalysis, or yet Derrida's call for a new Enlightenment. Freud was perhaps only a European liberal. Yet in this era of leadership talk, role model talk, empowerment talk, the trashing of democracy as voting bloc politics talk, self-interested, often gender-compromised culturalisms, disguising the profound aporia between unconditional liberty understood as autonomy, and the conditions of equality for others who do not resemble us—we should pay attention again to Freud's discourse of collective identification through leader-identification, of the emergence of the ego ideal rather than the super-ego. *Massenpsychologie und Ich-Analyse* (Mass Psychology and I-analysis), risibly translated as "Group Psychology and the Analysis of the Ego," still holds lessons that, in spite of Reich's smart and superficial work, remains to be unpacked in the context of what I am calling rape in the general sense and its agential redress in the narrow sense.

About creating a general will for social justice I said at the University of Utrecht on the 300th anniversary of the Peace of Utrecht

Israel is described times without number as "the only democracy in the Middle East," although it plays the retaliation game energetically, basing it on a "faith-based"—the word fills me with horror—narrative, quite opposed to the promise of democracy. Democracy is now equated with an operating civil structure, the functioning of a hierarchized bureaucracy, and "clean" elections.' We have plenty of examples around the world, that unrelenting state violence on the model of revenge and retaliation can co-exist with so-called democracy. Revenge is indeed a kind of wild justice that proves that no retribution is just to the outlines of the tribute. It has nothing, however, to do with a vision of social justice which builds itself on its own indefinite continuation.

It is this agential indefinite that we work at for the abridgement of the culture of rape, after the indeconstructible, unconditionality of rape in the general sense, which opens the human.

I have been asking for an affirmative sabotage of the Enlightenment wished upon us by colonialism. I have often used the metaphor of the children of rape to support this. Today the distinction between metaphor and concept is undone for me in an intuition of unconditionality. Kant did indeed inaugurate modernity by binding free will, rewriting fatalism by a rearrangement of the desire for philosophy, which desired the danger of the entire mistake, declaring free will by determined necessity, leaving fatalism unguarded in the *longue durée* of history. That counterintuitive mark of the modern largely misfired. What took its place was the race-class-determined binary opposition of free will and fatalism that runs our world today, with the so-called abstract workings of capital running a deconstruction. For the rest, the task is for the readers of the future. The Christo-Leninist alternative offered by Badiou-Negri-Zizek is an historical symptom.

In conclusion, then. The horrors of rape continue unabated and are on the increase. It is a crime of identity where you are punished because you are female or feminized. I have suggested all through this chapter that you cannot redress rape in this narrow sense by an appeal to our humanity. The imposition of the human upon the animate can itself be described as rape, absolute contingency. I invoked the synthetic a priori, but in fact all mythology contains images of divine violence upon the phenomenal woman. Therefore rape in the narrow sense has to be fought in the sphere of agency, with something as institutionalized as education, preparing the subject for connecting with something as institutional as the law in a mode other than its enforcement alone. We must de-humanize ourselves to combat rape in the narrow sense, as we must to combat the Anthropocene. Rape in the narrow sense is indeed power more than sex, the only unearned and narrow example being the one you earn by being by identity male or masculized. If I have been able to make any inroads at all please "read" the items offered below—pointing to crimes of identity that cannot be punished—according to the suggestions made in the chapter. I would ask you also please to remember that these are one-time only suggestions, that any attempt to make of rape in the general sense a universal concept-metaphor of making human will be visited by vigorous opposition and would undo the difference between the victim and the perpetrator. That very danger might warn us that this transient argument might harbor dark truths best kept transcendentalized.

First a crime of national/global identity—European agribusiness, which has invaded an old rural development organization in the area where I work, whose members cannot understand that they are being invaded, as it is done cunningly through Bangladesh, remotely diasporic Bangladeshi Germans. I wish I had the time to speak of Antonio Gramsci's brilliant anticipation of this.

And next, three icons, where we see three women, pictured metonymically because their appropriable—rapable—general identity can be used to depict crimes of ostensibly other sorts of politico-economic identity. That general identity—woman as such—does not need to be investigated in its gendering.

I had designed the following paragraphs of this chapter as a teaching moment—asking the readers to "read" three photographs according to the notions of "identity" and "crime" that I had laid out in the body of the chapter. Ut pictura poesis. I could not get permission to include the photographs.

The first one was the picture of an Indian peasant woman being held up by relatives, screaming with pain because of the suicide of her husband. This accompanies a sympathetic article by Ellen Barry, "After Farmers Commit Suicide, Debts Fall on Families in India" (*The New York Times*, February 22, 2014) where she correctly describes what I am calling a "crime of identity," calling it "global competition" rather than simply "globalization," the insertion of small farming into the circuit of (global) capital, today's financialized agribusiness of which I speak above. This and her veering off into examples of local cruelty, visibly horrible, does not make her general sense of things negligible:

> India's small farmers, once the country's economic backbone and most reliable vote bank, are increasingly being left behind. With global competition and rising costs cutting into their lean profits, their ranks are dwindling, as is their contribution to the gross domestic product. If rural voters once made their plight into front-page news around election time, this year the large parties are jockeying for the votes of the urban middle class, and the farmers' voices are all but silent.

From my equally general position of tempered sympathy with Barry, I was asking the reader to ask the question of the use of the elaborately mourning non-Euro woman as an "illustration" of arguments that must be put aside in the interest of human interest. I was not accusing the author or the photographer of anything. I was asking the reader to imagine the woman, whose name is given: Anitha Amgoth, because women holding certain identities are easy examples where the actual "crime" is not analyzed in any depth, only mentioned as human interest. In view of the inevitable shift into human interest proving the personal corruption of the global South (as opposed, I suppose to the clean "rule of law" practices of neoliberal capitalism), I had indeed also asked why Anitha's face is used to illustrate this crime, which is not a crime, global capital destroying primary production in the global South—against people identified in that specific subalternity—in the name of "development," aka insertion into the circuit of capital?[28] I am still not quite sure as to why I was denied access to this. I felt it as the impossibility of imaginative activism under the neoliberal "rule of law" approach. I also felt that academic freedom was here confronting an absurd version of "intellectual property." This too is a "crime of identity" in my sense against the teacherly, if you wish, spelling out the impossibility of teaching.

The second photograph was a beautifully focused image, with the light falling on the face of a young Afghan girl holding a book, reading. Who can deny that the very fact of an Afghan girl reading today is a heartwarming one. In my book *Other Asias*, I have discussed the attempts by Amir Abd-ur-Rahman Khan—the "Iron Amir"—to bring Afghanistan into state civility in the nineteenth century.[29] It is also well known by left and right alike (see Gregory Massell, *The Surrogate Proletariat*) that women in Soviet Afghanistan had access to education and were in public life.[30] Those were not the facts I was concentrating on as I offered this picture as a teaching text: I asked the question "does anybody ask a question (rather than provide a yes-no question for agreement) about her internalized gendering and is anyone engaged in remotely approaching the quality of education?" I have been for 30 years involved in the training of subaltern children, and holding a book unfortunately means nothing in terms of producing a will to social justice.

The last picture was one many of you have seen, which apparently is no longer being used by Care.org, the picture of a very beautiful African woman, dressed in cloth, with the caption "I am powerful." There my question was "does anyone ask what the word 'power,' kernel of the absurd word 'empowerment,' signifies—or, the relationship between any partner and this woman?" In other words, what do these women consider normal, can we enter their world, learning how not to construct them as forgettable items of news for public awareness or human rights work, or nongovernmental organization (NGO) gendering work, or public interest litigation or constitutional engagement? Professionals busy with these activities cannot, but we teachers of the humanities can, unless contemptuously dismissed, as I was by the pointperson at the photo company.

In addition to the question of permission to cite there was a question of permission from the individuals photographed. Here we are entering into the realm of absurdity.

For example, I may still receive permission to show the last photograph. Care.org does not use it any more, although it is still "trademarked." We are inquiring if the requirement for the permission may be waived, since she is a refugee and cannot be located. She may be adrift in the world, but her case is still a carapace of "the rule of law" where intellect is property. Her representation demands nonexclusive permission for this and future editions of the book, in all formats and in all languages for distribution throughout the world, and to include excerpts from the book that might appear in advertising, publicity, and promotional materials for the book, for example Amazon's Search Inside the Book.

I have recently argued that development is the insertion into the circuit of capital, without developing the subject of its ethical, or even appropriate social, use. This was hailed as an interesting contribution by my colleagues Ann Stoler and Akeel Bilgrami. That piece will be published into an academic collection edited by them. No pictures, no permissions. But that particular lesson, valued by my colleagues, is of course completely ignored by this absurd (for the spirit, not the letter, of the law) request. I want to cite Kant here—writing about "Cosmopolitan [read "global"] Right"—because he is always brought forward as the great-grandfather of questions of "academic freedom." Global right can be rationally if not amicably practiced between "all those of the earth's peoples who can enter into active relations [he uses the philosophical word *Verhältnis* rather than the more colloquial *Beziehung*] with one another [and it] is not something philanthropic (ethical), but a *rights*-related principle."[31]

The operative phrase in this passage is "active relations," *wirksam* in the original, which reminds the reader of the more common word *wirklich*—real. There is no real continuity between the subjects of the three photographs and my Cambridge audience, the readership of this collection, or the people in charge of the "rule of law" in neoliberalism, from whom I had to tolerate a good deal of bluntness in the last week.

Even as Kant makes clear that European settlers' rights only work if it is at a good distance from where pastoral folks lead their lives, he speaks, as he always does, for commerce. But the old man is conscientious although, as my exchange proves in a relatively micrological context, his lessons did not stick. (The macrology is historically, the United States, and today Israel.) For Kant goes on to write "settlements should...be established...only by treaty." Fair enough, get the permission of the person in the image. But he goes on further to write: "there must be no attempt to exploit the unknowingness of the natives."

The present case is not exactly similar. No one is establishing settlements on land; the property for settlement is intellectual. But as such, Kant's admonition bears on the lack of continuity where the "unknowingness" is a result of class apartheid in education. It is to bring about such continuity that some of us not only work, but toil. To have this request for permission from the subjects thrown at me in tones of righteous indignation in terms of fear of litigation, rather than the protection of the specific subjects, taught me why it is not possible to toil as a globally activist teacher. It was not my intention simply to criticize everyone, a pastime of the academic left. I was hoping that there would be some gain in looking at these faces of women in a different way, so that "the accumulation of knowledge whose methodological modernity...[has an] allegiance to the age of European world-taking [would not be so] plain for all to see."[32]

But perhaps it's just as well. After all, I was asking you to forget this lesson. So, why try to conserve something seen, when the society we live in proves its decrepitude by gated journalism, gated publishing, protected by high walls. Absolutely forget, even the lesson that the literary-ethical suspension in the space of the other is to de-humanize, if humanization from the animal is by way of rape in general, unless we want to mooch over being-human in the face of the Anthropocene.

Notes

1. Juliet Mitchell, *Psychoanalysis and Feminism. A Radical Reassessesment of Freudian Psychoanalysis* (New York: Basic Books, 1974).
2. Hannah Arendt, *Eichmann in Jerusalem: A Report on the Banality of Evil* (New York: Viking Press, 1963).
3. Jacques Lacan, "The Function and Field of Speech and Language in Psychoanalysis," in *Ecrits: A Selection*, tr. Alan Sheridan (New York & London: Norton, 1977), pp. 30–113.
4. Jacques Derrida, "Force de loi: le 'fondement mystique de l'autorité/ Force of Law: The 'Mystical Foundation of Authority,'" *Cardozo Law Review* 11 (1990), pp. 920–1046.
5. Roland Barthes, *S/Z. An Essay*, tr. Richard Miller (New York: The Noonday Press, 1974).
6. Mahasweta Devi, *Imaginary Maps: Three Stories*, tr. Gayatri Chakravorty Spivak (New York: Routledge, 1995); Toni Morrison, *Beloved* (New York: Knopf, 1987).
7. Mitchell, *Psychoanalysis*, p. xvii.
8. Mitchell, *Mad Men and Medusas: Reclaiming Hysteria* (New York: Basic Books, 2000), p. 256. Recently, in an interesting film by

Aleksander Motturi of Clandestino, the subaltern chosen, who had been tortured and jailed and undoubtedly wins our admiration, speaks his philosophy, because Aleksander wants to give him something more than just to be the example of refugee dumping: "The survival of the fittest as exemplified by the sperm managing to climb to the egg and going upward on the human line while the woman remains 'natural' and has to do nothing but wait for the child to be born." Rape can be this will to power sexualized.

9. I had tried this in 1990 with the translation of the word "identity" into a very strange Bengali, *idambad*. (I discuss this word in the text.) The word does not exist. I said there, "I want this word to exist only for the time that I give this talk." Indeed, no one has ever picked it up. I did another such transient translation of catachresis, which was *otikkhoy*, and I said that this translation is not going to survive beyond one hour in this room. That is just what happened. Can we, for an hour, think the terrible thought that the transcendental deduction of what we must think as rational subjects is akin to the contingent violence of rape?

10. For rather a long time, the early work of Emmanuel Levinas continued to influence many of us, so that we could write innocent sentences such as "to be human is to be born angled toward the other." What guaranteed this? A picture of access to humanship built on a nuclear heterosexual middle-class marriage. For a good comment on this, see Luce Irigaray," The Phenomenology of Eros," in *An Ethics of Sexual Difference*, tr. Carolyn Burke and Gillian C. Gill (London & New York: Continuum, 2004), p. 154–179. Levinas moved on to a more powerful position: "in the relationship in which the other is the one next to me [*le prochain*]...for reasons not at all transcendental but purely logical, the object-man must figure at the beginning of all knowing" (Emmanuel Levinas, *Otherwise than Being*, tr. Alphonso Lingis (Pittsburgh: Duquesne Univ. Press, 1999, pp. 58–59). But this too was secured by an embarrassingly inaccurate description of the woman in gestation and, on quite another front, remained consistent with support for legitimized violence of the state of Israel.

11. I will, later in the paper, disassociate myself from the view that US multiculturalism is, according to Arthur M. Schlesinger, "The disuniting of America" (Arthur M. Schlesinger, *The Disuniting of America,* New York: Norton, 1992). In the Indian context, however, I felt that I must speak out against separatism. I am not a situational relativist. One must take account of situations because one acts according to situational imperatives.

12. "Pro-pose" takes me back to an earlier discussion in my paper of the famous line of Nagarjuna: *Nasti ca mama kacana* pratijna [roughly, My proposition is not at all there]. Incidentally, my description of deconstruction work here found a nice bit of vindication. In the last chapter of Peggy Kamuf tr., *Specters of Marx: the State of the Debt, the*

Work of Mourning and the New International (New York: Routledge, 1994), Derrida shook the stakes of *ahamvada* in Marx to release the multitudinous iterations of an *idamvada*. Mechanical Marxists will not want to know it.

13. The collective rape of women in Tahrir Square as men celebrated the victory of Mr. Sisi as prime minister of Egypt sees so-called democracy as a fight.

14. Jacques Lacan, "Subversion of the Subject and the Dialectics of Desire in the Freudian Unconscious," in *Écrits*, tr. Bruce Fink (New York: Norton, 2007), p. 692; translation modified.

15. Fink, 691.

16. *Psychoanalysis*, p. 353.

17. Rosalind Coward and John Ellis, *Language and Materialism: Developments in Semiology and the Theory of the Subject* (Boston: Routledge, 1977).

18. Mitchell, *Mad Men*, p. 139.

19. Spivak, *An Aesthetic Education in the Era of Globalization* (Cambridge, MA and London: Harvard University Press, 2012), p. 322.

20. Kant, *Political Writings*, tr. H. B. Nisbet (Cambridge: Cambridge University Press, 1991), p. 160; translation modified.

21. Sigmund Freud, "Fetishism," in *Standard Edition of the Psychological Works*, tr. James Strachey et al. (New York: Norton, 1961), vol. XXI, p. 152.

22. Spivak, *Nationalism and the Imagination* (Kolkata: Seagull Books, 2010).

23. Said, *Orientalism* (New York: Vintage Books, 1994), p. 259.

24. Spivak, "Outside in the Metropolis: Diasporics?," reprinted in German translation in Isolde Charim and Gertraud Auer Borea, eds. *Lebensmodell Diaspora: über moderne Nomaden* (Bielefeld: Transcript, 2012), pp. 65–73.

25. Both items from *The New York Times*, July 20, 2014.

26. Farida Akhter is to be found at www.ubinig.org. Her real text is her untiring work for social justice, but one might read her classic *Depopulating Bangladesh: the Politics of Fertility* (Dhaka: Narigrantha, 1992); Flavia Agnes is a fierce feminist lawyer. Her group is majlis-law@gmail.com. The most recent piece is "The Making of a High Profile Rape Case" (*Economic and Political Weekly* 49.xxix; June 19, 2014).

27. MacKinnon, *Sex Equality*, p. v.

28. MacKinnon makes the connection with rape. "Under law, rape is a sex crime that is not regarded as a crime when it looks like sex" (*Feminist Theory of the State*, p. 172. Under law, crimes toward specific groups' livelihood ("crimes of identity") are not recognized as crimes when it looks like "development." MacKinnon is probably thinking also of Blackstone's definition of marriage as a unique contract: "By marriage, the husband and wife are one person in

law: that is, the very being or legal existence of the woman is suspended during the marriage, or at least is incorporated and consolidated into that of the husband: under whose wing, protection, and cover, she performs everything."

29. Spivak, "Foucault and Najibullah," *Other Asias* (Boston: Wiley Blackwell, 2007), pp. 132–160.

30. Gregory Massell, *The Surrogate Proletariat Moslem Women and Revolutionary Strategies in Soviet Central Asia, 1919–1929* (Princeton: Princeton University Press, 1974).

31. Immanuel Kant, *Political Writings*, p. 172; translation modified. The next passage quoted is from p. 173. It is important to keep in mind that, in *Rogues: Two Essays on Reason,* tr. Pascale-Anne Brault and Michael Naas (Stanford: Stanford University Press, 2005), the last book published during his lifetime, Derrida warned that Kant could not serve as a solution in contemporary globality.

32. Peter Sloterdijk, *In the World Interior of Capital: For a Philosophical Theory of Globalization*, tr. Wieland Hoban (Cambridge: Polity, 2013), p. 28.

Chapter 11

Sisters at the Gate: Mean Girls and Other Sibling Phenomena

Gillian Harkins

The Lot saga is a familiar one. The Lot family of Sodom and Gomorrah is visited by angels in men's form; male citizens flock to the door of the Lot home seeking to "know" the visitors. Lot offers the citizens his daughters instead, who have not yet "known" man, but ultimately the angels decide to punish the cities with fire and brimstone. Lot, along with his wife and daughters, are spared this fate so long as none turns back to look upon the cities' destruction while they leave. Lot's wife however does glance backward, and as a result turns to salt. Bereft of both human community and maternal presence, Lot's daughters seek to become mothers themselves by lying with their father (after an appropriate plying of wine to induce lethargy and forgetfulness) and reproducing the line through themselves. Daughters become mothers of their own siblings, creating a new human community from the crossing of what Juliet Mitchell calls the lateral and vertical axes of sexuality and reproduction (Mitchell 2003).

The parable of Genesis 19 has been much revisited over the centuries, lending itself to anti-homosexual scriptural interpretation as well as feminist and queer reimaginings of what lies beyond the limits of social heteropatriarchy.[1] A biblical prohibition on male sodomy has often been attributed to the tale, although both biblical and lay scholars have disputed this interpretation. Some scholars have also drawn attention to the prohibition on female knowledge exhibited in the punishment of Lot's wife, while still others examine the positive and productive role of father–daughter incest in the parable. Here a divine prohibition on male–male sexual relations seems to precede the social injunction toward father–daughter incest. Heterosexual and intergenerational incest is linked directly to social reproduction, the response to a more sovereign prohibition on a society of male homosexuality. This creates a quandary in the typical order of prohibitions and injunctions, particularly for psychoanalytic paradigms predicated on the model of Oedipus. To use Juliet Mitchell's terms from *Siblings*, a fundamental prohibition on lateral homosexual relations produces an injunction for vertical heterosexual relations leading to reproduction.

Much like the parable of Lot, *Siblings* provides an alternative account of lateral and vertical relations incipient to sexuality and reproduction. According to Mitchell, psychoanalysis has historically privileged the "vertical relationship of child-to-parent" (Mitchell 2003, x) over children's "lateral" relationships with each other.[2] The most familiar psychoanalytic model posits an Oedipus complex induced and resolved through the law of the father; a temporality at once anticipatory and retroactive induces exogamous (hetero)sexuality as a movement toward repronormativity. The perversions or wayward reproductions ensuing from alternative (or failed) resolutions of the Oedipus Complex do not undo the knot of paternal law so much as testify to its abiding function as the bedrock of psychoanalysis. For according to Mitchell it is psychoanalysis, more than the psyche, that depends upon a law of the father combining prohibition on incestuous reproduction with injunction to exogamous sexuality. It is psychoanalysis, not the psyche, that ordered all phenomena into the vertical paradigm of sexuality, regardless of the divergent material presented as primary evidence of lateral sexual relations. Clinical evidence of the lateral axis of sibling sexuality and hatred was treated as symptomatic of and subordinate to the protocols of Oedipus and his parents, until Mitchell suggests recent sociohistorical changes have separated sexuality and reproduction to such a degree that lateral formations of gender and violence have become newly legible in the clinical and case material. Psychoanalysis is now ready to encounter its forgotten siblings. By attending to such lateral relations, psychoanalysis is better able to identify and analyze distinctions between sexuality and reproduction, and thereby gender and sexual difference, in social and psychic life.

Mitchell's account shifts what is granted logical and temporal primacy in the Lot story. To return to Lot via Mitchell, the prohibition on lateral male sexual relations—the male citizens desire to "know" the angels-in-male-form—seems to precede the vertical prohibition on witnessing God's act of punishment. This secondary prohibition unites the family as a group—they are all prohibited from turning back to look upon the cities as they are punished by God—even as it separates out "Lot's wife" as its singular transgressor. Once the prohibition on seeing God's wrath is broken by the wife, the daughters assert their own position in the nexus of reproduction—its lateral and vertical coordinates—by recreating the lost human community through sex with the father. In place of a sovereign prohibition (against homosexuality) that creates a social injunction (toward reproduction), we find a lateral prohibition (against homosexuality) that creates a vertical injunction (toward reproduction). The Lot story provides an admonitory parable through the reification of Lot's wife: her effort to see sovereign power creates a crisis in the temporal and logical order of lateral and vertical regulation. As a result, she is frozen in the moment of transgression while her daughters are induced toward intergenerational and heterosexual incest to reproduce the proper order between lateral (community) and vertical (divine, generational) axes.

This treatment of the Lot parable offers additional revisions to the primary psychoanalytic model of Oedipus, supplementing the already well-developed revisionist models articulated through Electra and Antigone.[3] If as Mitchell suggests the Antigone play shows us "the three faces of the sister who both cares for and destroys: the lateral would-be murderer, the nurse and the lawgiver" (Mitchell 2003, 57), the Lot parable shows us the two faces of the sister refracted through lateral lens of sexuality and reproduction. This chapter takes the story of Lot's wife as an opening, a way into the complex problematization of "siblings" offered by Juliet Mitchell. In *Pillar of Salt: Gender, Memory, and the Perils of Looking Back*, Janice Haaken suggests that the allegory of Lot's wife admonishes against female transgression while also opening up a "disturbing void"—no one knows what she saw before her transformation—that can generate new symbolic representations of this "void" (Haaken 1998, 5). This is perhaps why Lot's wife has spoken so directly to feminist theorizations and queer revisionings of the tangled relation between gender, sexuality, and prohibition. Haaken goes on to ask how the parable might be reimagined if the female siblings told it: "And what stories might Lot's daughters have to tell?" (Haaken 1998, 267). She ponders how we might hear the stories of daughters who are sisters of one another but also sisters of their own daughters, and so on across the generations? The question implicitly asks not only what stories, but whose stories can represent the "void" between lateral and vertical sexualities without falling into its abyss?

In the readings that follow, I ask how Mitchell's treatment of the "void" at the heart of psychoanalytic theory opens up alternative approaches to lateral and vertical prohibitions and injunctions. I begin with Mitchell's own treatment of lateral relationships in *Siblings*, focused in particular on how representations of history shape her theorization of the lawgiving mother. I then turn to the cultural emergence of the "mean girls" phenomena at roughly the same moment when sibling relations can, according to Mitchell, finally be represented at the heart of psychoanalytic theory. My brief gloss of "mean girl" texts, including Halley Feiffer's *How to Make Friends and Kill Them* (2013), allows me to explore how gendered lateral relations appear as serial killing in the absence of a "lawgiving mother." I next turn to Marilynne Robinson's 1980 novel *Housekeeping* and John Cameron Mitchell's 1998 rock-opera *Hedwig and the Angry Inch* to explore how "representing" lateral gender relations might not inevitably figure them as a drive toward death. These closing readings allow me to explore the meaning of "gender" in lateral relations that move beyond the "mean girl" genre and toward alternative conditions of representational possibility.[4]

Mother's Keepers

Mitchell's *Siblings* offers a counterhistory of psychoanalytic origin figures resonant with the parable of Lot. Mitchell implies psychoanalysis is founded on a "void" very similar to the one encountered and figured by Lot's wife: "Psychoanalytic theory is a good illustration of its own thesis: only what is absent can be represented; what is present cannot be represented and hence cannot be seen" (Mitchell 2003, 30). Psychoanalysis represents the void, covering it with catachresis that does not pretend to manifest the absence as presence but rather to represent it through a vehicle that has no ground. The figures that emerge to "represent" this void are always catachrestic, of a different order than the void itself; figures such as the "law of the father," the Oedipus complex, or the "primitive mother" (Mitchell 2003, 51) are ways of representing that which has been absent. They capture a historical point of exchange, where what was present disappears and leaves in its trace a figure—such as the Father of patriarchal order—now available to "represent" the void allegedly created by an unrepresentable sovereign power (God in Lot's case). These figures appear in the wake of one system of presence, neither capturing that which was present nor that which remains absent fully in their tenor. Yet the grounds on which the family stands seem to shift.

Mitchell tracks the movement from God to father to object relations mother ("primitive mother") as part of this story of presence and absence, presentation and representation. Just as Nietzsche figures "God" as the void that appears in moralism's wake, Freud figures "patriarchy" at the site of absence just as patriarchal social relations are waning in power and authority (are less present); object relations similarly figures "matriarchy" or the "primitive mother" in the breach of its social decline. In the final decades of the twentieth century, adult centrism becomes visible just as absolute parental power is giving way to more lateral relationships of power. At this point Foucault can dethrone the king in favor of an account of power as "coming from everywhere," second wave feminisms can point beyond patriarchy to a fraternity of homosocial bonds, and psychoanalysis can finally notice the siblings always already lurking within the Oedipus Complex (Foucault 1978; Pateman 1988). Thus Mitchell suggests that a new awareness of siblings (and eventually a "lawgiving mother") is possible because of changing historical conditions: "Perhaps we can now see a distinction between sexuality (lateral) and reproduction (vertical) because, in the hegemonic white social groups of the Western world, reproduction is not the nearly inevitable consequence of sexuality, and above all because it is sharply on the decline" (Mitchell 2003, 31).[5] According to Mitchell distinctions between lateral sexuality and vertical reproduction can be represented because they are no longer "present"; what is revealed in this shift is the primacy of lateral relationships previously occluded by the representation of vertical relationships (between child and parents, for example, but also other positions in a hierarchical social order).

The seeming primacy of the vertical relationship stems from psychoanalysis' own conditions of existence, from clinical scene to theoretical principle. Mitchell uses the figure of the "lawgiving mother" to indicate how shifting conditions of existence shape relations between psychoanalytic theory and clinical practice: "There is, I suggest, no lawgiving mother in psychoanalytic theory because within the clinical setting the analyst herself or himself speaks from the position of the mother as lawgiver" (Mitchell 2003, 50). According to Mitchell, psychoanalytic theory was previously unable to see lateral relationships as primary precisely because the clinical material was presented (as presence) from within the grip of lateral relations. The presence of lateral relationships was seen to "represent" through displacement (or other figuration) those more important but unrepresentable vertical relationships governing psychic life. As historical conditions change, however, psychoanalytic theory can look back on earlier clinical material and see lateral relations that always existed, but were perhaps blocked by the very fact that the analyst in the clinical scene spoke "from the position of the mother as lawgiver." Thus only as the clinical analyst ceases to appear as lawgiving mother can they be represented—in theory—as such. Mitchell's book therefore returns to various clinical scenes and research cases to underscore the presence of lateral relations and their importance to understanding gender, sexual difference, sexuality, and reproduction.

Mitchell draws several key conclusions from her study of primary lateral or sibling relations. First, she differentiates between gender and sexual difference and assigns them to lateral and vertical relations respectively. Lateral relations are expressed in terms of gender and non-repronormative sexuality. Sexual difference proper, and its organization through the demand for reproductive intercourse, comes from the vertical axis and the Oedipus complex. This is a secondary prohibition, one that follows the regulation of lateral relations and comes to obscure the importance and proper function of laterality in general. Thus according to Mitchell "where the castration complex marks the sexual difference 'required' by sexual reproduction, gender difference marks lateral distinctions between girls and boys which include but exceed sexuality" (Mitchell 2003, 26). Mitchell implies that recent conflations of gender and sexual difference—frequently offered in the service of a more social and historical account of subjection that replaces singular sexual difference with the spectrum of gender—actually erase some of what we might consider "queer" modalities of sexuality. What Mitchell refers to as "lateral sexuality" is "anal-phallic and, at a deep level, gender indifferent" (Mitchell 2003, 41), meaning that appearance of gendering through a homo- and hetero-distinction is not significant along this axis. Gendering occurs, as we shall see in a moment, but not through the reproductive fantasies that install a model of sexual difference. Mitchell suggests we would do better to return to distinctions between gender—the effect of a lateral relation—and sexual difference—the effect of a vertical one. This would open up the potential to recognize lateral relations in modes of sexuality not organized through sexual difference.

Second, Mitchell associates lateral gendered and nonreproductive sexuality with fundamental aggression. She suggests that we learn a good deal about fundamental aggression when we shift focus to lateral relations, which allows us to see that "the task of the sibling in distinguishing between the genders is to learn that each is serially diverse and not simply a replication of the narcissistic self" (Mitchell 2003, 26). Mitchell posits a fundamental aggressivity that emerges from the crisis of "uniqueness" or singularity introduced by a sibling (or other lateral figure). If "the sibling is *par excellence* someone who threatens the subject's uniqueness" (Mitchell 2003, 10), then it is no surprise that lateral relations are marked by fundamental violence or murderousness. Lateral relations emerge in relation to an originary trauma associated with "neonatal helplessness" (Mitchell 2003, 42), which Mitchell characterizes as a "black hole, like the vortex of a whirlpool," which "attracts things to it" (Mitchell 2003, 42). Based on this fundamental condition of being "psychically obliterated by a traumatic experience, the first signs of life are fury and hatred" (Mitchell 2003, 41). In the movement from neonatal to infantile conditions, a secondary trauma comes to represent the first as the threat of being replaced by another. The encounter with the sibling (or lateral figure) draws the emerging subject toward this "black hole," threatening a return to obliteration; murderousness is "a response to the danger of annihilation" (Mitchell 2003, 43). Thus we find that the "non-reproductive nature of sibling sexual fantasy is bound up with the importance of murderousness in relation to love" (Mitchell 2003, 41).

But how does serial differentiation—articulated through gendering that is nonreproductive—stave off fundamental murderousness—articulated as the hatred of that which threatens the singularity of the subject? How might we theorize the regulation of lateral relations prior to the Oedipus prohibition and castration complex (with their inauguration of vertical sexual difference)? This brings us to the third conclusion Mitchell draws from lateral relations: that there is "a lateral sexual taboo" that is "bound up with violence" (Mitchell 2003, 27). This taboo is figured by Mitchell as a "law of the mother," that which regulates serial differentiation to resolve the problem of fundamental murderousness (Mitchell 2003, 44). Gender becomes a tool for such differentiation. Gender figures an "absence" that is the loss of "possibility of giving birth to replications of themselves—this is the "absence" that for both must be represented; it does not distinguish them from each other, but only from their mother" (Mitchell 2003, 26–27). Figuring this "absence" requires the mother, whose capacity for reproduction differentiates her from serial progeny and allows them to establish terms through which "difference" may be represented. For "both" (or all) lateral subjects must be represented. The mother becomes that against which serial representation emerges, that which governs a representational system prior to the symbolic order that figures "sexual difference" as the void/vortex. The mother's law is "a law that differentiates generationally as to who it is that can have babies and who it is that cannot. It is also a law that introduces seriality laterally among her children" (Mitchell 2003, 52).

Mitchell's account differentiates the lawgiving mother from the "primitive mother and the lawgiving *father*" (Mitchell 2003, 51) of object-relations and Freudian psychoanalytic theory respectively. Mitchell's reconsideration of gender, violence, and prohibition draws attention to the differential function of representation along lateral and vertical axes. This returns to the point with which this section opened: how psychoanalysis negotiates an alleged void, or "vortex" in Mitchell's terms, at its heart. Mitchell names the void/vortex neonatal helplessness, which "attracts things to it" into formations of violence and love that threaten to extinguish the subject unless is can find ways to represent these "things" or to represent absence as a thing. The subject's route through murderousness, serial differentiation, nonreproductive gendering, and ultimately sexual difference becomes a process of representation. At one key point along this route, "sibling sexuality and murderousness are, then, contiguous" (Mitchell 2003, 38). This contiguity must resolve through the representation of seriality. As Mitchell explains, "social groups not constructed along the apparent binary of reproduction rely on managing the violence unleashed by the trauma of threatened replication; representing seriality is crucial" (Mitchell 2003, 31). Representation precludes the eruption of violence, particularly lateral murderousness, even as it promotes gendered difference and nonreproductive modes of sexuality. And the "lawgiving mother" provides the figure for a law of serial representation, that which precedes symbolic entrance into a system of representation characterized by sexual difference.

Mean Girls

It is unclear to me whether Mitchell ultimately thinks lateral relations are fundamental and merely revealed by changes in historical condition, or whether lateral relations are themselves historically produced and therefore subject to displacement. In other words, are lateral relations an ontological a-priori or are they historically contingent and variable not only in their representation but in their presence? Is the lawgiving mother produced or revealed by the representability of sibling relations in the later twentieth century? Should we think of the lawgiving mother as akin to Lot's wife, one historical figure reified facing the void/vortex, frozen into a pillar of salt for her children? Or is she the equivalent of the sovereign authority Lot's wife was banned from seeing in action, making Lot's wife into yet another daughter in this scenario (as wife to Lot, representing a serial reproductivity that includes her own daughters)? Is the crisis in the story that Lot's wife faced the void/vortex and failed to induce serial differentiation in her children, leaving them equivalent to her in their reproductive fantasies and therefore prone to vertical incest? How might we situate Mitchell's account of sibling relations and serial representation in its historical moment and across other examples?

Mitchell provides some clues about the answer to these questions in her own reading of Freud's figuration of the "death drive." Freud arrived at his theory of the death drive only in his late writings, beginning in *Beyond the Pleasure Principle*, and Mitchell suggests that even this late account is flawed due to its suppression of "the importance of siblings" (Mitchell 2003, 35). Once we focus on "sibling murderousness," the death drive can be seen as a representation of the "psychic role of 'death'" rather than as a "drive towards annihilation" (Mitchell 2003, 35). Mitchell suggests that Freud uses "death" to represent the void/vortex she elsewhere describes as "human neo-natal helplessness"

(Mitchell 2003, 42). Where Freud sees a drive toward annihilation that he labels "death," Mitchell sees the representation of death as "inorganic" stasis (Mitchell 2003, 42) over and against representation as a process or iteration, both in its performance (the subject survives by constituting itself and others as figures of difference) and its specific figures (transfiguring hate into love, organic vulnerability into sustainable life forms). Thus "loving one's sibling *like oneself* is neither exactly narcissism nor object-love. It is narcissism transmuted by a hatred that has been overcome" (Mitchell 2003, 36). This re-reading of the death drive as a drive to represent depends upon the lawgiving mother, whose failure might be characterized as a "neglect" (Mitchell 2003, 53) that leads to "a failure of repression" (Mitchell 2003, 36) and a return of lateral violence and sexuality. This leads Mitchell to align her theory with historical observations such as "sibling abuse in the West occurs in the context of inadequate parental supervision and concern" (Mitchell 2003, 53), or that "in war, both peer-group promiscuity and the rape of same-age enemy women testify to a regression to the prevalence of sexuality between children in childhood" (Mitchell 2003, 21).

I propose we follow Mitchell's lead and take Mitchell's "lawgiving mother" as another historical figure, a catachresis before the void/vortex, in order to explore the ramifications of this figure for treating lateral relations in recent formations. While Mitchell seems to use violence and aggression as signs of the law of the mother's failure, she is very careful to say that the actual mother does not bear responsibility for resurgent violence and aggression. There is an association in her formulations between maternal absence and neglect with unregulated murderousness, but it is not necessarily the absence of the mother's law that precipitates the problem. Instead, she asks, how we might understand violence as a failure of allowing for lateral regulation on its own terms, without a lawgiving mother? How might we think about a society in which lateral regulation operated without that vertical axis? Or, as Mitchell queries, "Is this external operation of rules and regulations necessary because our cultural conditions do not allow for their internalization? Where older siblings rather than parents are the main carers of younger children, where children are left alone in their peer groups, are prohibitions accepted and internalized? Can siblings themselves be each other's lawgiver?" (Mitchell 2003, 53). I take Mitchell's questions as an opportunity to think about how the lawgiving mother becomes representable in psychoanalytic theory just as lateral relations may no longer operate in relation to this figure. Just as Mitchell suggested in relation to earlier models of vertical regulation, perhaps lateral relations are imminently self-regulating in ways that psychoanalytic theory has yet to represent.

One might say the lawgiving mother once too present in the clinical scene arrived in theory just when this role is dwindling socially. Evidence for this claim might be found in the simultaneous co-emergence of the "mean girls" phenomenon alongside the appearance of the lawgiving mother in psychoanalysis. In 2002, Rosalind Wiseman published her bestselling nonfiction book *Queen Bees and Wannabes: Helping Your Daughters Survive Cliques, Gossips, Boyfriends, and Other Realities of Adolescence.*[6] The subtitle of this volume makes maternal self-help into daughter-help. Mothers learn what might be described as daughter-directed helping tools that yet situate the mother as a peer, like a daughter within a lateral milieu. The mother assists with navigation of the lateral world (rather than regulation on a vertical axis). Here we learn terms such as "relational aggression" and other modes of peer group gendering and sexuality fundamentally linked to aggressivity. Tina Fey wrote the screenplay for the 2004 film *Mean Girls* (dir. Mark Waters) based on this book, which became part of a broader cultural phenomenon in which the phrase "mean girls" came to represent lateral gendered formations articulated through aggression and nonvertical/nonsexual-difference-based sexuality.[7]

"Mean girls" seems to represent the cultural passing of the "lawgiving mother" precisely when Mitchell can theorize it. The lawgiving mother suddenly appears in the clinical scene through its representation in theory; where she disappears is in the nonpsychoanalytic scenes of "self-help" or serial representations of mothers-turned-friends. "Mean girls" articulates a lateral relation but does so in ways that dismantle the vertical axis, such that mothers and daughters may both participate as "mean girls" (or their targets) in new fields of sexuality and aggression. While this has become a stock feature of much recent popular culture, here I will use Halley Feiffer's 2013 play *How to Make Friends and Kill Them* as a quick example of the contemporary "representation" of lateral relations among girls in the absence of a lawgiving mother. *How to Make Friends and Kill Them* focuses on the relations among three characters, Ada, Sam, and Dorrie, as their lives change (and remain the same) across three temporal settings: childhood, teenage, and young adulthood. The play begins in childhood, where sisters Ada and Sam have been "left to their own devices by their alcoholic mother," according to the play synopsis offered by Rattlesnake Theater.[8] The mother never appears on stage, although Ada comes to stand in the place of the mother as she sways drunkenly through the final young adult sequence of the play. During the opening "Childhood" sequence, the audience is introduced to Ada and Sam in a kitchen setting, where Sam repeats the phrase "you're so pretty" to Ada while she brushes her hair and asks for hugs. Ada is alternately preening and enraged at the subservient Sam, whom she calls "gay" whenever Sam expresses longing for physical contact. Eventually Dorrie enters the scene, a classmate from school whose physical and psychological abjection triangulates the aggressivity and desire otherwise tightly routed between Ada and Sam.

The play's seemingly domestic setting is belied by the heightened stylization of dialogue and performance, which earns *How to Make Friends* its description as "surrealist" or "theater of the absurd" in various reviews. The actors deliver lines with an intensity of affect far in excess of naturalist expectations, while their physical movements vacillate between the outsized and the miniaturized in a tempo not entirely tuned to the dialogue. Key phrases and gestures are repeated from childhood to teenage to young adulthood, and the characters seem to slip in and out of time as they attempt to represent their relations to themselves and each other. "It's never weird with us, is it?" one sister asks the other, while love and hate ripple across their bodies and voices. Neil Genzlinger's *New York Times* theater review situates the play directly in the "mean-girl genre," in which the characters find "ways to fill each other up and to tear each other down" (*New York Times* 2013). Ultimately the character's attempts to identify with and differentiate from each other drive toward death. Dorrie enters not as lawgiving mother, but as serial nonsibling through whom Ada and Sam will represent their difference from and desire for each other. By the time they have moved from childhood to teenage to young adulthood, murderous aggressivity will win out over lateral sexuality: Sam will kiss Ada passionately while she is semi-unconscious from alcohol; Ada will push Sam down the stairs and leave her paralyzed; and Sam will strangle Dorrie to prove that only she and Ada belong in their childhood home.

The title of the play reminds us of the drive toward death implied in lateral relations. Riffing on *How to Win Friends and Influence People* (Carnegie1936) and *How to Lose Friends and Alienate People* (Tressler 2001), the play suggests that the seeming opposites "influence" and "alienate" are resolved when mean girls kill. To sway or repulse offer two possible modes of social agency; killing is an antisocial agency that resolves tensions between love and hate by annihilating those serial others marked "friends." This is self-help meets serial killer genre. In the serial killer genre, the presence of doubles inevitably predicts violence to come. The doppelganger represents the need for serial violence in order to restore identity to the one.[9] In the play's encounter between self-help and serial killing, the childhood refusal to make "vertical" adjustments over time necessitates the representation of "mean girls." In this avant-garde production, the mean girl genre is stylized into representability in ways that reveal the void or vortex of the lawgiving mother. This representation marks the loss of lawgiving motherhood as an unrecognized presence, representing it as the absence that draws things to it until self-help becomes serial killing. Thus the play represents Mitchell's suggestion that "sibling sexuality ranges from sex with someone whom one experiences as the same, to sex with someone whose difference one wants to obliterate" (Mitchell 2003, 39). But here the mean girl genre reveals as well the specific gendering of lateral sexuality. Citing Mitchell again: "sibling relations prioritize experiences such as the fear of annihilation, a fear associated with girls, in contrast to the male fear of castration" (Mitchell 2003, 3–4). Girls become the representation of siblings as such; when sisters go unregulated, mean girls will drive onwards toward death.

The "mean girls" phenomenon provides one way to explore how the absence of a lawgiving mother leads to the presence of aggressivity and lateral sexuality. *How to Make Friends and Then Kill Them* seems to represent this logic as it unfolds across childhood, teenage, and young adulthood. But this raises additional questions about how Mitchell's own historicization works. It might be said that "mean girl" phenomena has existed far longer than its early 2000s depiction as itself a kind of regulatory principle governing the representation and circulation of lateral gender relations. Certainly North American high school relations had been depicted as riddled with enmity and aggression since the 1950s, and the specific genre now associated with "mean girls" was already articulated in its current form in 1980s teen movies such as *Pretty in Pink* (Howard Deutch 1986) or *Heathers* (Michael Lehmann 1988). Perhaps the emergence of "mean girls" as representation—as recognizable genre—fits with Mitchell's own suggestion that what is present cannot be represented, and what is represented no longer appears as presence. The phenomenon of "mean girls" may not represent the absence of the lawgiving mother so much as the presence of new mechanisms of lateral regulation. In other words, perhaps the presence of mean girls has itself become representation just as the regulatory principle of gendered cruelty and erotic violence gives way to other gendered modes and erotic mechanisms organizing lateral relationship.

Keeping House

In these final sections I would like to consider what happens if we do not presume that the absence of a lawgiving mother will reveal a fundamental aggressivity of girlhood. What if the representation of "mean girls" does indicate that some other forms of regulation are currently organizing relations between lateral and vertical axes? What kinds of traumatic vulnerability might be made visible and allowed to live, rather than be marked by death, if we read the absence of the lawgiving mother as yielding alternative arrangements of differentiation and eroticism? I will refer to two final sample texts, Marilynne Robinson's *Housekeeping* (1980) and James Cameron Mitchell's *Hedwig and the Angry Inch* (1998), to consider how the absence of the lawgiving mother might lead to something other than "mean girls" and its gendering toward death. This takes us back to Lot's wife and daughters once again, looking back upon the void whose presence can only be represented as "vortex" drawing toward itself figures of Divine sovereignty, paternal law, maternal law, and mean girls. But here I will ask how we see the daughters emerge as sisters (including of their own daughters) just as "Lot's wife" becomes a catachrestic figure of the void that lies beyond her. Lot's wife turned to a pillar of salt when she faced the void, became reified in place, while the daughters were set in vertical motion (toward incestuous reproduction). But in *Housekeeping* and *Hedwig and the Angry Inch*, the seeming absence of the mother is presented as a catachresis only in specific modes of representation. When representation leads to reification, mothers and daughters find themselves moving along pre-set paths of the lateral and vertical axis. In place of representation as reification, however, these two texts propose alternative modes that set subjects moving along alternate paths.

Housekeeping places us firmly in a world of sisters. In the opening sentences of the novel we are introduced to the first person narrator, Ruth, as she is situated in female kinship: "My name is Ruth. I grew up with my younger sister, Lucille, under the care of my grandmother, Mrs. Sylvia Foster, and when she died, of her sisters-in-law, Misses Lily and Nona Foster, and when they fled, of her daughter, Mrs. Sylvia Fisher" (Robinson 1980, 3). While the vertical axis is represented in words such as "daughter" and "grandmother," these positions will subsequently be organized along a lateral axis where all women are "sisters." In *Housekeeping* Mitchell's questions—"where older siblings rather than parents are the main carers of younger children, where children are left alone in their peer groups, are prohibitions accepted and internalized? Can siblings themselves be each other's lawgiver?"—are answered in the affirmative. *Housekeeping* is not a "mean girls" text but rather a text of lateral regulation, although like the mean girls phenomenon it transforms the lateral to include what might once have been represented as vertical relations. But in so doing it goes beyond the lateral/vertical dyad to represent alternative structures for engendering difference in the late twentieth century.

As the title suggests, the novel is concerned with the historical demands of housekeeping.[10] The walls of the house are more important boundaries than any vertical or lateral axis to be represented within it. The house in Fingerbone is first linked to a vertical, even patriarchal, narrative of descent: "Through all these generations of elders we lived in one house, my grandmother's house, built for her by her husband, Edmund Foster, an employee of the railroad, who escaped this world years before I entered it" (Robinson 1980, 3). It is the grandmother's house, her inheritance, from a marriage built through the labor of Manifest Destiny's transcontinental railroads. The "husband" who escaped "this world" labored to build it, establishing a homestead at Fingerbone where the rails took colonial westward expansion. He moved from a "house dug out of the ground" in the "Middle West" (Robinson 1980, 3), "with windows just at earth level and just at eye level, so that from without, the house was a mere mound, no more a human stronghold than a grave, and from within, the perfect horizontality of the world in that place foreshortened the view so severely that the horizon seemed to circumscribe the sod house and nothing more" (Robinson 1980, 3). This house that is part of the earth, both and neither stronghold or grave, provides a "perfect" lateral view that demonstrates the limits of a purely lateral perspective. The grandfather works on the railroad to fulfill fantasies of exotic voyage spurred by "travel literature" on the mountains of Africa, the Alps, the Andes, the Himalayas, the Rockies, and Fujiyama (Robinson 1980, 4). Serial difference here is introduced by moving from a lateral house incorporated into Mid-Western flats to a vertical movement to mountain heights.

But this patriarchal lineage of householding seems to give way rather quickly to the "primitive" and then the "lawgiving" mother. The narrator's grandfather dies in a train accident without witnesses ("no one saw it happen"), a death of the father that could be read as the first "void" as the train disappeared into a lake (Robinson 1980, 6). The lake in this reading would appear as the "primitive mother," a body whose "deeps" can be searched for signs of the lost father but which is itself "smothered and nameless and altogether black" (Robinson 1980, 9). The actual mother remains in the Fingerbone house, however, where her daughters Molly, Helen and Sylvie "pressed her and touched her as if she had just returned after an absence. Not because they were afraid she would vanish as their father had done, but because his sudden vanishing had made them aware of her" (Robinson 1980, 12). The mother becomes present to them in the wake of an absence she does not represent. As a result, she becomes a nearly perfect "lawgiving mother": "her love for them was utter and equal, her government of them generous and absolute"

(Robinson 1980, 19). She pays attention to how her daughters [or the "girls" (Robinson 1980, 10)] are differentiated by "customs and habits": "Sylvie took her coffee with two lumps of sugar, Helen liked her toast dark, and Molly took hers without butter" (Robinson 1980, 15). She represents her own difference from them on "purpose, to be what she seemed to be so that her children would never be startled or surprised, and to take on all the postures and vestments of matron, to differentiate her life from theirs, so that her children would never feel intruded upon" (Robinson 1980, 19). She represents herself as differentiated mother to allow her children to self-differentiate and move forward into "respectable" (Robinson 1980, 10) lateral and vertical relations.

And yet this perfect lawgiving differentiation yields daughters who disappear. Molly goes on missionary work in China; Helen (Ruth's mother) ultimately kills herself in the same lake that claimed her father; and Sylvie travels the continent as an itinerant. Helen and Sylvie both marry, but neither retain their husbands and Helen returns her children to Fingerbone only to end her own life. Ruth and Lucille are raised by their grandmother for five years before she dies and leaves them with her sisters-in-law Nona and Lily, who leave them in turn with their mother's sister Sylvie, who returns to Fingerbone to live with in the house with them. Despite the perfect telos of *Housekeeping's* origin story—from (colonial) patriarchal law to primitive mother to lawgiving mother—lateral sisterhood does not transition successfully into lateral heterosexual coupling and vertical mothering. Marriages are entered into and exited without significance. A seemingly new generation of female siblings are returned to their point of generational departure and reconstituted among existing female sibling relations (the various sisters). And the house remains.

At this point in the story the house becomes the central regulatory condition for relationality. "We and the house were Sylvie's" (Robinson 1980, 59), Ruth remarks. Sylvie's itinerant lifestyle quickly takes over the house, which becomes filled with dirt and debris. While "Sylvie talked a great deal about housekeeping" (Robinson 1980, 85), she "considered accumulation to be the essence of housekeeping, and because she considered the hoarding of worthless things to be proof of a particularly scrupulous thrift" (Robinson 1980, 180). Ruth comes to accept Sylvie's unique approach to bourgeois respectability, but Lucille demands more normative accumulation and "hated everything that had to do with transience" (Robinson 1980, 103). Lucille takes on the project of self-improvement as a "tense and passionate campaign to naturalize herself to" the normal world (Robinson 1980, 95), giving up on household respectability and focusing instead on creating proper lateral relations with peers. Lucille dresses them up, saying "That's *Sylvie's* house now" and "We have to *improve* ourselves!" (Robinson 1980, 123) before she ultimately gives up on Ruth and leaves to move in with "Miss Royce, the Home Economics teacher" (Robinson 1980, 140). Ultimately Lucille leaves the house behind to affirm that her "loyalties were with the other world" (Robinson 1980, 95), while Sylvie and Ruth end the novel by burning the house down and taking flight across the bridge (over the lake that claimed both grandfather and mother).

The house itself, and the demand to make it a home, becomes the "neonatal trauma" around which the novel is built. But in this instance it is a trauma of natality. Hannah Arendt (1958) uses "natality" as a figure for both birth and action, culling the nuances of labor from its conflation with commodification in the wage. Here "women's work" is the work of home making and housekeeping, including the making and keeping of kin and the management of proper vertical and lateral axes. By this measurement, the clan is a spectacular failure. But no specific law of the mother is to blame. Instead, the novel returns to "natality" as its vortex, its first trauma, and it figures the movement of serial representation from there. The conflation of labor with the wage—outside the home—is a "presence" that creates the fundamental trauma of natality. The labor of birth and work, of "creation," is what therefore must be represented in order for serial differentiation to secure possibilities for movement and change. Here *the house* represents the function Mitchell attributes to the "lawgiving mother." It is the house, its spatial relations of ceiling and floor, inside and outside, dirt and cleanliness, which inaugurates serial differentiation and its representation in gendered forms. What was demanded as "women's work" becomes a process of serial differentiation represented through various modes of making life. In place of an aggressive drive toward death, gendering lateral relations takes shape as a movement toward life.

This is made explicit when Ruth encounters a group of "children" in the woods. After Lucille leaves their home, Sylvie takes Ruth into the woods and introduces her to lateral relations very different from those coveted by Lucille. Sylvie explains that people live in the woods, "and now and then I'm sure there are children around me" (Robinson 1980, 148). Sylvie disappears for an extended period of time while a cold and hungry Ruth is left outdoors to "watch for the children" (Robinson 1980, 151). As she waits to see the children, Ruth describes the woods as follows: "Imagine a Carthage sown with salt, and all the sowers gone, and the seeds lain however long in the earth, till there rose finally in vegetable profusion leaves and trees of rime and brine" (Robinson 1980, 152). Here the woods are a "vegetable profusion" grown from seeds of salt long ago sown as the sign of imperial conquest.[11] The woods become in Ruth's mind a profusion of organic matter growing from the remains of human civilization, itself the consequence of imperial conflicts and geographies of expansion. The "rime and brine" of the present are genealogical; seeds of salt grow icy "trees" that neither signify families (vehicle) nor potential material (tenor) from which to build proper houses (ground).

It is this process of representation, the potentiality of the woods to enable Ruth to imagine "children" outside of either families or houses, that leads into her lengthy meditation on Lot's wife in the wilderness:

> If there had been snow I would have made a statue, a woman to stand along the path, among the trees. The children would have come close, to look at her. Lot's wife was salt and barren, because she was full of loss and mourning, and looked back. But here rare flowers would gleam in her hair, and on her breast, and in her hands, and there would be children all around her, to love and marvel at her for her beauty, and to laugh at her extravagant adornments, as if they had set the flowers in her hair and thrown down all the flowers at her feet, and they would forgive her, eagerly and lavishly, for turning away, though she never asked to be forgiven. Though her hands were ice and did not touch them, she would be more than mother to them, she so calm, so still, and they such wild and orphan things. (Robinson 1980, 153)

Ruth imagines her own capacity to create outside the confines of the household. "If there had been snow": a counterfactual from which is born Ruth's natal power. Ruth would have made a statue of a woman whose grief froze her looking into the past, but who now appears covered in a mantle of flowers that draw the children to her. Lot's wife would have no longer been barren, but would instead have many children around her to "love and marvel" at her. And the children in turn would imagine that it was their attention, their own natal power, which made her blossom. Lot's wife once turned to salt when she turned away from her own daughters; here the wild orphan children would forgive her "for turning away" though she does not ask it, and would welcome her still icy hands as calming, not indifferent.

Ruth imagines the statue in a place she thinks would draw children, where the "gleaming water spilled to the tips of branches" and "frost at the foot of each tree" would make them return "to see it again" (Robinson 1980, 153). This is not a death drive toward an inorganic state, but a longing to see figures that would represent an otherwise "barren" loss. The children's compulsion to repeat, as Ruth imagines it, is a desire to create life, from root to branch. So she places a statue of the lawgiving mother where there had been only loss, only a past that has turned away. This ideal figure is a calm detached mother who asks for nothing and thereby becomes "more than mother." Ruth longs to be that lawgiving mother to the wild orphan children, but she also imagines them along a lateral plane, as peers who might share her consciousness (as she once did with Lucille). Thus she imagines the "consciousness" that she senses in the woods as "persistent and teasing and ungentle, the way half-wild, lonely children are" (Robinson 1980, 154). This creates an impossible desire: "I knew that if I turned however quickly to look behind me the consciousness behind me would not still be there, and would only come closer when I turned away again" (Robinson 1980, 154). Ruth is both Lot's wife and the children she left behind. She cannot look back, to genealogy or the home, nor can she give up the desire to create figures that represent difference.

"If there had been snow," Lot's wife would have become the lawgiving mother.

But there is not snow. Instead there is salt, where Lot's wife becomes part of the growth of salty rime branches from the seeds of a Carthage past. Ruth joins the children she imagines in this alternative family tree, where the drive to represent the void constitutes a lateral natality that leads away from the neonatal trauma of the house. "For need can blossom into all the compensation it requires," we are told. "To crave and to have are as like as a thing and its shadow" (Robinson 1980, 152). Such a "blossoming" is distinct from a drive toward death, death as the representation of the void/vortex, or the house as a substitute for death. Here "blossoming" is organic growth from "need" that makes the capacity to create—to figure and materialize figuration in new grounds—into its own "compensation." Craving becomes "like" a "thing"; it figures "thing" *as if* a presence even as it makes all "having" into mere "shadow." Thus need enables the making of likenesses that masquerade as things, need "blossoms" into craving and makes "having" into the mere ghosts of things, into "shadows." The children in the woods are such "blossoms" on this salty family tree; neither thing nor shadow, they are the likenesses through which natal trauma is transfigured into a livable life.

The imaginary encounter with these children in the woods helps clarify the lateral relations among the "sisters," Sylvia, Ruth, and Lucille. Once the "we" of Lucille and Ruth was "almost as a single consciousness" (Robinson 1980, 98), but Lucille has decided they need other friends and shifted her "loyalties [to] the other world" (Robinson 1980, 95).[12] After her encounter with the children in the woods, Ruth realizes that "having a sister or a friend is like sitting at night in a lighted house.

Those outside can watch you if they want, but you need not see them" (Robinson 1980, 154). But without Lucille, she describes herself as "turned out of house" (ibid.): "Now there was neither threshold nor sill between me and these cold, solitary children who almost breathed against my neck and almost touched my hair" (ibid.). At first Ruth feels herself abandoned, but identifying with the "consciousness" of the serial children who are not bothered by being cast out, she decides, "it is better to have nothing" (Robinson 1980, 159). Having "nothing" is however having Sylvie: Sylvie says Ruth is "like another sister to me" (Robinson 1980, 182); Ruth thinks "Sylvie and I (I think that night we were almost a single person)" (Robinson 1980, 209). To crave is to make likeness into things, to have likeness as the shadow that is oneself.

The police and neighbors worry about this blurring of the lateral and vertical axes, concerned that Sylvie is "making a transient" of Ruth by riding a freight car (Robinson 1980, 177). "When did I become so unlike other people?" (Robinson 1980, 214), Ruth wonders after the two burn down the house and walk across the bridge to leave town. She lists the trauma of natality—her conception and desertion by her mother— as normal trauma that should in fact make her *like* other people. Birth and abandonment by the mother are normal traumas that make people into serial replicas of familiar difference. Instead Ruth opines, "I believe it was the crossing of the bridge that changed me finally" (Robinson 1980, 215). In the novel gender differentiation ultimately takes place through stasis and movement; there are those who keep house, and those who move through open space. Ruth and Sylvie become unlike others by being "cast out to wander, and there was an end to house-keeping" (Robinson 1980, 209). But the novel also situates this gendering as historically and socially specific. It is not gendering as such, but late twentieth-century gendering for whiteness as a social formation attached to the novel's colonial genealogy of "manifest domesticity" (Kaplan 2005). The capacity to use imagination to create difference, to usurp the role of the lawgiving mother and constitute new formations of likeness, emerges from the particular natal trauma of householding on the Western front.

All Sewn Up

Hedwig and the Angry Inch completes this meditation with the creative destruction of "rock-n-roll" as gender performance.[13] The show opens with Yitzhak, one of Hedwig's doubles/nemeses who is also her husband, shouting to the audience: "Ladies and Gentlemen, whether you like it or not...Hedwig!"[14] In the opening line of the rock opera, Yitzhak invokes one of the most famous hailings of sexual difference to introduce the star of the show-within-a-show, the transgender performer Hedwig. But here Lacan's children are not riding a train that promised to arrive at its sexually differentiated destinations, "Ladies" and "Gentlemen," but rather are departing from those stations to find their way toward a new lateral platform (Lacan 1957, 146–178). Hedwig's performance of celebrity is a constant insistence on singularity, even as the show itself is constituted on the principle of doublings that are one. From "The Origins of Love," a retelling of Plato's tale of how humans were driven into three types by Zeus, to the doubling of Yitzhak and Hedwig (crossing and prohibiting genders and denying room enough for two on the stage), to the erotic entanglement of Hedwig and Tommy Gnosis, both played by a single actor on stage but by two different actors in the film adaptation.[15] The stage show unfolds as an on-stage monologue delivered by Hedwig, who is playing a show in a minor venue while Tommy Gnosis, her former lover and now wildly successful protégé, performs in a major venue nearby. In the stage production the same actor, as Hedwig, performs all the roles save that of Yitzhak and the on-stage band members. In the film production, one actor performs adult Hansel/Hedwig while all other existing roles, and new additional roles, are embodied in separate actors. Thus the seriality performed in and as "Hedwig" in the stage version is displaced literally onto the screen, as a representation of serial embodied difference.

This process of representing seriality—as one on stage, as multiple on screen—problematizes the dynamics of absence/presence embedded in accounts of the lawgiving mother and "neonatal trauma" thus far. The allegedly physical borders of sexual difference are here reconstituted as the spatial imaginaries of serial representability. Early on in the show Hedwig tells the story of her youth in East Berlin, when she was a young "girlyboy" called "Hansel" who loved to listen to rock music on the radio ("Midnight Radio"). When the young adult Hansel is mistaken for a young girl by US soldier Luther Robinson, whose offer of candy as seduction implies a vertical relation, Hansel's mother inaugurates a new lateral relationship between them by providing Hansel with her own identity: Hedwig. The mother provides a name, passport, and "sex" by arranging the operation to make Hansel Hedwig. This will enable Luther and Hansel to flee East Berlin through marriage once Hansel "becomes" Hedwig/a woman/the mother. In the film production, this plays out as a visual transformation in which many characters have a role. Hansel/ Hedwig and Hedwig are two, with a passport and operation promising to make them like one. In the stage production, however, only one performer in one costume performs these characters on stage, creating a physical catachresis at the site of the mother: "Hedwig" the mother is performed—at a distance, as mimicry—by "Hedwig" the performer, who also performs "Hansel" admitting to once wearing "my mother's camisole" as an example of putting on "women's clothes" before the sex change ("Sugar Daddy"). The mother not only does not lay down the law of difference—from herself, from serial others—but becomes the spectacular site of indifference and identification where vertical and lateral axes meet.

After a "botched" sex change, Hedwig is born with an "angry inch" and identification not with the mother, but with the Berlin Wall ("Tear Me Down"). Hedwig moves to Junction City, Kansas with Luther, but is abandoned by him on the very day the Berlin Wall comes down. Within the show, the Berlin Wall figures the "neonatal trauma" of Hedwig's birth, a void/vortex that sets in motion the seeming collapse of vertical/lateral relations ("Sugar Daddy"), gendering processes of agency (migration and movement as entrapment rather than feminist liberation), and fall into gendered low-wage labor that demands specific gender performances (expressed in "Wig in a Box"). If a 1980 white feminist imaginary located the home as neonatal trauma, here the Wall of geopolitics is written into the body as "natality." As Hedwig shouts to her audience in "Tear Me Down": "Don't you know me Kansas City? I'm the new Berlin Wall; try and tear me down." The song's interlude features a lengthy speech by Yitzhak, who intones: "We thought the wall would stand forever. And now that it's gone, we don't know who we are anymore. Ladies and Gentlemen, Hedwig is like that wall, standing before you in the divide." Yet "Tear Me Down" also reminds its audience that "there ain't much of a difference between a bridge and a wall." As bridge, Hedwig builds lateral connections among people who "don't know who they are anymore." But as *This Bridge Called My Back* and other women of color feminisms have argued, the labor of being the connection is different from the labor of building connections (or that of crossing over them once they exist, as do the escapees of *Housekeeping*) (Moraga and Andzaldua 1984). The neonatal trauma of the Wall is in other words linked to a broader international, racial, and gendered division of humanity and labor than that treated in *Housekeeping*. Hedwig's bridge connects vertical sexual difference with intersectional gendered "differences" that expand the visible domain of lateral or serial relations.

And so we go to Hedwig and Tommy Speck/Gnosis' love duet "Wicked Little Town," performed first by Hedwig to Tommy (although seemingly addressing herself in a small bar in the Midwest) and second as "Reprise," sung now by Tommy to Hedwig (although seemingly addressing her through a large audience from the position of celebrity). In the stage performance the characters sing "together" to the degree that they are performed by the same actor, potentially two sides of the same character (from "The Origins of Love"). The reference to Lot's wife comes in the first iteration of the song, performed during the period when Hedwig still works as teenager Tommy Speck's babysitter: "The fates are vicious and they're cruel. You learn too late you've used two wishes like a fool; and then you're someone you are not, and Junction City ain't the spot, remember Mrs. Lot and when she turned around." In an ironic resignifying of the patriarchal possessive, "Mrs. Lot" figures a void in the middle of a song about discovering you find you are "someone you are not" in a place that is "not the spot." Finding oneself in this nonbeing nonplace, the "wicked little town" of "Junction City," demands that one recall "Mrs. Lot," but not necessarily why or to what end.

What then is "Mrs. Lot" doing here? Why does she stand at the crossroads where identity and location are negated? How does the potential conflation of vertical and lateral relations between Hedwig and Tommy tempt "fate"? If "the fates are vicious and they're cruel," does Lot's wife need to be recalled as the lawgiving mother who would give order back through serial differentiation? Or does she represent the danger of fighting fate, yet another lateral figure that fails to obey the law and therefore is reified in one spot, forever? In her discussion of Lot's wife, Janice Haaken suggests that "the contemporary challenges to patriarchal authority brought about by the women's movement require complex readings of the legendary past and alternative ways of looking back" (Haaken 1998, 7). Here I ask how "the women's movement" relates to a feminism that cares for genders not merely beyond (or before) sexual difference, but also genders not serialized in relation to feminine violence and aggressivity. While Haaken's book implicitly cautions against "the perils of looking back," John Cameron Mitchell's "Wicked Little Town" enjoins its addressee to "remember Mrs. Lot and when she turned around" when confronted with a void in the lateral and vertical axes of identity and sexuality.

Hedwig's ironic modernization of "Lot's wife" into "Mrs. Lot" emerges from the post-1970s successes of feminist kinship reform; the effort to liberate women from the patronymic and patriarchal system of kinship through the universal "Ms." makes "Mrs." into a sardonic remainder of legal coverture in linguistic sexism. To recall "Lot's wife" as "Mrs. Lot" renders her simultaneously archaic, residual, and dominant, in Raymond Williams's famous schema (Williams 1985). She represents the archaic remnant of "traditional" marital arrangements, the residual form of female self-making still actively chosen by many women, and a dominant option among kinship terms freely "chosen" by women across a range of liberal feminist positions. Thus in this context the call to "remember Mrs. Lot and when she turned around" might not refer primarily to women turned pillar of salt or men smote (smitten?) in Sodom and Gomorrah. Instead, it might refer more pointedly to the ways in which post-1970s feminisms remember when constrained by the limited "choices" in the present. When feminisms face the past, what do they see? How do the "choices" of liberal feminism in particular, of feminism as "choice," constrain what appears as gender difference and sexuality in various contexts? As "Wicked Little Town" continues, "and when you've got no other choice, you know you can follow my voice along the dark turns and noise of this wicked little town." It might be that having "no other choice" is what it means to remember "Mrs. Lot."

But perhaps "Wicked Little Town," sung twice by two characters who may be one, across genders as well as the line of sexual difference, might move us slightly farther away from the vortex of neonatal trauma and its archaic, residual and dominant representations. The stage reprise features the actor playing Hedwig stripped down to a bare chested torso, marked with Tommy Gnosis's trademark ash cross, transforming into Gnosis (or knowledge, Hedwig's own sovereign act of naming Tommy's transition from "boy" into singularity/celebrity) or perhaps revealing the sameness of the two in the body of the one (the film presents two actors who become mirror images in an alternate or unreal space). The reprise lyrics tell us of a "boy" who encounters serial difference beyond sexual difference yet also beyond the paradigms of "gender" articulated through the mean girl genre: "Forgive me, For I did not know. 'cause I was just a boy and you were so much more; than any god could ever plan, more than a woman or a man." If remembering Mrs. Lot in the first song becomes a call to "follow my voice" when "choice" seems limited (remembering "Mrs. Lot" as a feminist choice, indeed), the reprise suggests that perhaps there is no Sovereign lurking to create either violence or love: "maybe there's nothing up in the sky but air." In place of the Zeus myth of "The Origins of Love," or the injunction to remember Sodom and Gomorrah, the romantic ballads sung by and between the same person/two people—a "boy" and "so much more"—suggest that in the right hands the void/house/wall/bridge might become "something beautiful and new." As Tommy Gnosis/Hedwig sings: "and now I understand how much I took from you: That, when everything starts breaking down, you take the pieces off the ground and show this wicked town something beautiful and new."

Notes

1. On the story's relation to twentieth-century spectatorship, see Martin Harries, *Forgetting Lot's Wife: On Destructive Spectatorship*, New York: Fordham University Press, 2007.
2. *Siblings* builds upon Mitchell's earlier study of hysteria and siblings, *Mad Men and Medusas: Reclaiming Hysteria and the Effects of Sibling Relations on the Human Condition*, New York: Basic Books, 2000.
3. See for example Judith Butler, *Antigone's Claim: Kinship between Life and Death*, New York: Columbia University Press, 2002.
4. A note on my own method: While it troubles me to touch on each of these texts only in passing, I find myself compelled to offer serial observations rather than a single sustained reading of one sample text in order to situate Mitchell's psychoanalytic theory in relation to historically specific moments of sibling representation.
5. Mitchell's account of the social conditions of psychic life is beyond the scope of this chapter; "social changes take generations to affect the psychology of the unconscious ego and superego but nevertheless they do have a place there in the end" (49).
6. On the mean girls phenomena see Jessica Ringrose, "A New Universal Mean Girl: Examining the Discursive Construction and Social Regulation of a New Feminine Pathology" *Feminism & Psychology*, 16.4 (2006): 405–424 and Emily Ryalls, "Demonizing 'Mean Girls' in the News: Was Pheobe Prince 'Bullied to Death'?" *Communication, Culture & Critique*, 5.3 (September 2012): 463–481.
7. Mark Water, Dir. Script Tina Fey. *Mean Girls* (2004). See also Margert Talbot, "Girls Just Want to Be Mean" *The New York Times* (February 22, 2002).
8. Rattlestick Playwrights Theater website: http://www.rattlestick.org /how-to-make-friends-and-then-kill-them/.
9. The adult genre figures homoerotic desire and the impulse to annihilate and replace as childlike in fixation and frequently seeking Oedipal triangulation with an erotic other (in which they displace the doppleganger for themselves); see Lisa Duggan, *Sapphic Slashers: Sex, Violence and American Modernity*, Durham: Duke University Press, 2001; Mark Seltzer, *Serial Killers: Death and Life in America's Wound Culture*, New York: Routledge, 1998.
10. A review of criticism on *Housekeeping* exceeds the scope of this essay; relevant articles include W. Burke, "Border Crossings in Marilynne Robinson's *Housekeeping*" *MFS: Modern Fiction Studies* 37.4 (Winter 1991): 716–724; Christine Caver, "Nothing Left to Lose: *Housekeeping's* Strange Freedoms" *American Literature* 68.1 (1996): 111–137; G. Handley, "The Metaphysics of Ecology in Marilynne Robinson's *Housekeeping*" *MFS: Modern Fiction Studies* 55.3 (Fall 2009): 496–521; T. Hedrick, "'The Perimeters of Our Wandering Are Nowhere': Breaching the Domestic in *Housekeeping*" *Critique: Studies*

in Contemporary Fiction 40.2 (Winter 1999): 137–151; S. Lin "Loss and Desire: Mother–Daughter Relations in Marilynne Robinson's *Housekeeping*" *Studies in Language And Literature* 9 (June 2000): 203–226; T. Magagna, "Erased by Space, Ignored by History: Place and Gender in Marilynne Robinson's West" *Western American Literature* 43.4 (Winter 2009): 345–371; J. Smyth, "Sheltered Vagrancy in Marilynne Robinson's *Housekeeping*" *Critique: Studies In Contemporary Fiction* 40.3 (Spring 1999): 281–291.

11. On the reference to Carthage see Marilynne Robinson, "My Western Roots" *Old West–New West: Centennial Essays,* ed. Barbara Howard Meldrum, Moscow: University of Idaho Press, 1993.

12. Meanwhile Lucille seeks to return to the lateral view of the grandfather's Mid-West origins and colonial dreams; "Lucille had begun to regard other people with the calm, horizontal look of settled purpose with which, from a slowly sinking boat, she might have regarded a not-too-distant shore" (92).

13. Relevant criticism on *Hedwig and the Angry Inch* includes Steve Feffer, "'Despite all the amputations, you could dance to the rock and roll station': Staging Authenticity in *Hedwig and the Angry Inch*" *Journal of Popular Music Studies* 19.3 (September 2007): 239–258; Holly M. Sypniewski, "The Pursuit of Eros in Plato's Symposium and *Hedwig and the Angry Inch*" *International Journal of the Classical Tradition*, 15.4 (2008): 558–586; Cowan, Sharon. "'We Walk Among You': Trans Identity Politics Goes to the Movies" *Canadian Journal of Women and the Law*, 21.1 (2009): 91–117.

14. The stage production of *Hedwig and the Angry Inch* features music and lyrics by Steven Trask and book by John Cameron Mitchell, who also played the title role. It was originally produced in 1998 off-Broadway at the Jane Street Theater and won Obie and Outer Circle Critics Awards.

15. The film was written and directed by John Cameron Mitchell, music and lyrics by Stephen Trask (2001). The cast included John Cameron Mitchell as Hansel/Hedwig, Ben Mayer-Goodman as young Hansel, Miriam Shor as Yitzak, and Micheal Pitt as Tommy Speck/Gnosis. Trask performed the lead vocals of Speck/Gnosis.

References

Arendt, Hannah. 1998. *The Human Condition* (1958) Chicago: University of Chicago Press.

Carnegie, Dale. 1998. *How to Win Friends and Influence People* (1936), New York: Pocket Books.

Feiffer, Halley. 2013. *How to Make Friends and Then Kill Them*. Directed by Kip Fagan. Rattlestick Playwrights Theater.

Foucault, Michel. *The History of Sexuality, Volume I: An Introduction*, Trans. Robert Hurley, New York: Vintage, 1978.

Haaken, Janice. 1998. *Pillar of Salt: Gender, Memory, and the Perils of Looking Back,* New Brunswick, NJ: Rutgers UP.

Kaplan, Amy. 2005. *The Anarchy of Empire in the Making of U.S. Culture,* Cambridge: Harvard University Press.

Lacan, Jacques. [1957] 1977. "The Agency of the Letter in the Unconscious, or Reason Since Freud." *Écrits: a Selection.* Trans. Alan Sheridan. London: Tavistock, 146–178.

Mitchell, John Cameron. 1998. *Hedwig and the Angry Inch.* Jane Street Theater. Film adaptation 2001, Director John Cameron Mitchell.

Mitchell, Juliet. 2003. *Siblings: Sex and Violence,* Cambridge, UK: Polity Press.

Morgaga, Cherrie and Anzaldua, Gloria, eds. 1984. *This Bridge Called My Back: Writings by Radical Women of Color,* New York: Kitchen Table Press.

Pateman, Carole. 1988. *The Sexual Contract,* Stanford: Stanford University Press.

Robinson, Marilynne. 1980. *Housekeeping,* New York: Picador.

Tressler, Irving Dart. 2011. *How to Lose Friends and Alienate People* (1937). CreateSpace Independent Publishing Platform.

Williams, Raymond. 1985. *Keywords: A Vocabulary of Culture and Society,* New York: Oxford University Press.

Wiseman, Rosalind. 2002. *Queen Bees and Wannabes: Helping Your Daughters Survive Cliques, Gossips, Boyfriends, and Other Realities of Adolescence,* New York: Crown.

Chapter 12

How Can We Live Ourselves?
An Interview with Juliet Mitchell

Preti Taneja

When sibling theory started to take shape in your mind, how far then, did you sense the implications it could have?

That's quite a difficult question to answer. It was such a revelation, it didn't really occur to me to wonder about its implications as a first response to that revelation. I was just completely stunned—why is nobody talking about this? First of all I thought siblings were nowhere. Then that they are absolutely everywhere. I had re-read all the clinical material and the historical material and anthropological material and they were at every turn. A little while later I went to a conference on siblings, in the European University in Florence with some historians who had been working on cousins and affinal kinship, including siblings. Everyone was excellent—Lee Davidoff, David Sabean. They were very welcoming but dismissive of my naivety, my sense of revelation. Naturally, as they rightly stressed, they had known about this all along. In a way, indeed they had, but they hadn't seen how staggering it was. They had been writing about siblings and aunts and uncles and the cousinage and all of the rest of it, the lateral was of course part of the field that they were looking at. However, my amazement wasn't diminished by their dismissing it. It still seemed to me quite staggering. For them, as for most clinicians, of course siblings were there. For me it was the size of the presence of the sibling dimension and the size of the absence of this dimension in our overarching thinking that staggering. So it was a revelation on the spot of the present time, rather than the future looking how big the implications were. It was already there, huge—why wasn't anybody making anything of the fact that it was so huge?

I want to jump forwards in time to today, and ask you how you have seen that theory manifest itself in the popular and in the public domain rather than in psychoanalysis itself for example, books that make a splash in popular culture, films and film theory. For example, Andrew Solomon, who was your Ph.D. student used the structure of the intersecting vertical and horizontal to frame his highly acclaimed book *Far from the Tree*.

Yes, Andrew does brilliant interviews. There is also some very interesting and important work that has used siblings to change the field. If I say names I am bound to forget the most important. But the type of work I have in mind—Denis Flannery, Lee Davidoff, Ruth Perry, and already there in my field of psychoanalysis, René Kaës. But also many others have joined those earlier pioneers who took siblings for granted. So some are using siblings to change their field, and others in the present are doing something similar to what the people I met in Florence did in the past—which is to say, it is as though they have always known about them. By showing they have always known about siblings they are revealing that they *never* have known about the implications in a way.

In psychoanalysis, siblings have always been portrayed in all the clinical work. Robbie Duschinsky's chapter on the Rat Man is a case in point. Freud's material is all about the Rat Man's sisters and brothers, his case history is about the father and the fiancé. Freud does link the fiancé to a sister but that does not enter into the explanation that is entirely Oedipal. In one sense this should not surprise us: Freud is demonstrating the importance of Oedipus and nothing else is of interest. There is plenty of material for his perspective. But once you wonder about the absence in the theory and the presence in the practice, then the material somersaults into view in a different way.

What is staggering again, then is the combined presence of siblings and also the absence of the implications. That's why I turned to the question: 'What is it that's making people miss the implications of this at the same time as working with it?' It's as though they still haven't quite seen the size of it, or the surprise of it—it becomes a question: Why have we missed it? I know there have been times when (a) we haven't missed it and (b) where people like me have been astounded by it. But each time people noticed it they were like me, saying, "Good Heavens, why have we missed this?" And that's been true in anthropology as well as psychoanalysis.

In the chapter on "Siblings and Infantile Sexuality," Daru Huppert suggests that even though sibling studies do appear, they have little impact on psychoanalysis as a discipline. Or that the importance of siblings is noted and carefully described, only to be comprehended on Oedipal terms. So that is the question really: Why is this—is it

because of phallocentric nature of society? (i.e., the "brotherhood of men" still holds such a firm grip?)

Daru was my Ph.D. student and gave my sibling lectures wonderfully when I was on sabbatical in Cambridge. He has now trained and become a psychoanalyst. He is absolutely right. They don't make it the Law of the Mother. At the same time, the Law of the Mother has got a hearing elsewhere but not been developed with siblings.

What I am actually saying is that there is a Law of the Mother that is as important as the Law of the Father. We have missed it on two counts. In the field of psychoanalysis the analyst has enacted the position of the mother giving laws, and one does not see what one enacts; but we have also missed it because we don't think mothers can have laws. Someone pointed out to me that Lacan used the phrase "Law of the Mother" very early on – a fascinating little reference which I didn't know, but actually what Lacan means is that it still comes under the Law of the Father, whereas I think it is a separate law. Not what the mother says about her relationship to the child or the child's to her, which I emphasized in *Mad Men and Medusas*, (2000)—that is there: but the key is her particular legislation between her children, so it is on the horizontal axis. And her threat is the threat of separation, just as in the Oedipal story the threat is the threat of castration if one goes on having incest in one's mind with the mother. So there is a different threat in the Law of the Mother, which is effective (more or less!): the threat of separation. I won't love you if you kill this baby. Winnicott noticed this threat of separation but didn't relate it to the baby, to the siblings. He calls it a "trauma of separation," but he does not link it to what is so deadly that is in his clinical material: the mother is legislating *between children*. Her own children. In addition I think there is an anti-woman thing in it—the mother simply isn't that important—she is always making reference to the Father's Law —but her threat of a separation from her is her own law. This has huge implications because it's pre-Oedipal, and it sets up as an aspect of social life that is based on a repudiation of the family.

Which is deeply subversive...

...Yes deeply subversive...Both giving the mother a new status and the children a new task.

...subversive of society's understanding of women and women in the family, which is what you talked about in *Psychoanalysis and Feminism*.

That's right yes, and before that in *Women, the Longest Revolution* (1966). But I was doing something different in *Psychoanalysis and Feminism*,

I was looking at this question of why, despite all the social changes that we do effect, equal pay, the vote etcetera still there is this extraordinary inequality. Even when it seems that the economy, the democracy, communism, socialism when, we should be getting closer to equality, we are often two steps forward and one step backwards, or one step forwards and two steps backwards—there is always that backwards drift, a sort of entropy within sexual difference, and that's what I was looking at 40 years ago, but on the vertical axis. I wasn't looking at the horizontal. However, when I went back because it's the 40th anniversary of *Psychoanalysis and Feminism* and Judith Butler refers to the last chapter, I was amazed to find how much there is on siblings in my conclusion.

In the general situation of sexism, men dominate over women. In the specific culture of patriarchy, fathers dominate over brothers. So there is a suppression of women and an oversight of siblings. There is the dominance of the vertical. Even someone whose work is quite exceptional, and who includes siblings and a "sibling complex" like René Kaës makes them only Oedipal. I go back to a very successful book by Carole Pateman— *The Sexual Contract*, (1988) in which she argues very effectively about the importance of the lateral sexual contract between brothers. As indeed does Freud in *Totem and Taboo*. But for both of them it is still in terms of patriarchy, instead of seeing it in terms of fratriarchy. There is an essay by Cynthia Cockburn saying we don't use andrarchy and fratriarchy; if we do they don't have staying power. Well why don't they have staying power? So people are observing it all again, but not picking up on the peculiarity of it, as a question. I mean the peculiarity of the simultaneous overwhelming presence of siblings in our observations, and their overwhelming absence in theory. I would now go further and ask—*why* don't we have them in the theory? That is a question in itself.

That is actually my next question. Let's get to the silt at the bottom of the river and disturb it a little bit, and ask *why* that is the case.

I don't know that I have gone there yet. I think that it is probably part of the "undertow," the entropy. Primarily, the undertow belongs to sexual difference, which is only a marker but one that falls over reproduction. Reproduction is the vertical axis where we reproduce, like our mothers and fathers before us. It is inter-generational, and we have to take over from them in that they have to die and we have to take over and be life, as it were, and give life. And I think that's where the undertow on the position of women and men is really experienced. Whereas I see gender as a lateral relationship; siblings are the starting point of the horizontal axis. The gendered sibling toddler must become a big girl or boy in the social group it forms and finds. It is still gendered, but there is a gender distinction between the sexes that is more flexible. So I can understand Judith Butler's argument that things will change—they probably will change for gender in economically privileged circumstances, but they are not changing somewhere for the sexual difference. And of course we are also all both. If we don't have children it doesn't mean we are not sexually differentiated in terms of how we live in the world. That question of how we live in the world is to do with both—a muddle of gender and sexual difference. It's how we separate them analytically, and there you find this stasis of conservatism as I spelled it out in *Psychoanalysis and Feminism*, gender is maybe more as Butler is wanting it to be—that it will change in time—for sure! Gender is more flexible because we are all always bisexual. But something is nagging me here. Gender also is not egalitarian between sisters and brothers. Far from it.

But really the idea that we are all bisexual, that gender can be this much more flexible formation of kinship and formation of families and different kinds of ways of thinking about social groups and in time things will change—in its own way that is as frightening and radical as the idea of what you call "the rock in the stream," that is always stopping us from progressing, this entropy pulling us back—F. Scott Fitzgerald describes us as beating on, boats against the current, borne back ceaselessly into the past. Gender and sexual difference are two radical and scary ideas for contemporary society.

Exactly. I found it scary because I remembered the conclusion to *Women the Longest Revolution.* (I generally try to end my book on an up note that gets missed because the tenor of the books is so dismal that the fact that I look for a way out gets missed!) It's exactly that sense of liberation, or liberality that ends the 1966 article (the first thing on this question I published.) In the mid-1960s with the sexual revolution sexuality seemed the weakest link, where change would come. I looked at my 1966 hopes in 2000 and thought, well wait a minute, this is exactly where everything has gone pear-shaped in a terrible way—for example, the sexual exploitation of women is now paramount.

Women the Longest Revolution uses the weakest link to look for the possibility of change. That was just before, or on the cusp of the Women's Movement. *Psychoanalysis and Feminism*, which was written at the height of second-wave feminism, argues that we have to address what is intractable, what is important, is what is most intractable—as Jacqueline Rose points out in her reply to Butler. But you're asking a question more about something scarier in the contemplation of the fluidity of gender.

…I think that people who look forward to that, they are looking forward to a nongendered family. There have been all sorts of probably

small-scale utopian attempts at that and they probably worked in a way.
So is it frightening?

If you look at the way in which marriage has been made legal for homosexual couples in some places, and yet in other parts of the world, it is illegal, you would be killed—we have this move forwards and the move backwards, and sexual difference seems to underpin that fear.

Yes in the same way we can celebrate all these new reproductive technologies that liberate sexual reproduction among the rich. Also rich nations and individuals are moving towards nonreproductive populations, and having the poor to care for children if they have them, and the poor are still having children in the old way. So a big divide will be rich and poor around reproduction. You may get nongendered in the two-career family as it used to be called, but you will still get a gender-division in the people looking after those children. We can't entirely escape other people in the world—so even if the rich don't reproduce, or marginally reproduce, and are nongendered, they are going to be surrounded by the rest of the world that is gendered and in a divisive way, and reproductive in a sexually differentiated way, and above all, highly sexually exploitative.

You have been challenged on your use of the word "trauma" in sibling theory. Why do you think that resistance to the idea of it being trauma exists?

Yes, it has been very well challenged in an extremely interesting article by Claudia Lament; it is very good to have it raised with such intelligence and sensibility to the whole problem. It was a question I started with early on because another very good book by psychoanalysts preceded my own on siblings—Vamik D. Volkan and Gabriele Ast's *Siblings in the Unconscious and Psychopathology* (1997). Sometimes they call the new baby a "difficulty" and sometimes they call it a "trauma" for the older child. Then I found Winnicott referring to a "separation trauma" from the mother but not a sibling trauma, when I was already calling it a sibling trauma. That seemed to legitimate calling this a trauma. The clinical work indicated that it is traumatic. A pathological outcome will be traced back to the pre-Oedipal experience but only a footnote will mention that this was a time of the birth of the new baby.

It first occurred to me as a trauma because I was studying male hysteria. The hysteric *always* produces a trauma. But it's as though they have misplaced the trauma, or it got lost. The traumatic experience is indicated by a crazy fear or phobia. The trauma is always something else to what it could possibly be. The trauma in male hysteria, goes back to

Charcot and others in the nineteenth century—where there had been an accident at work, a fight in the street, for men. Psychoanalysis discovered the accident concealed an earlier trauma that is subsequently linked to the Oedipal castration complex. But the present trauma, the accident or whatever, is always stressed in male hysteria, or when male hysteria was being mooted. Then there is something violent as well as sexual in the present-day trigger and this suggests something violent as well as sexual with the intrinsically earlier, actual traumatic experience. The fear of his father for Little Hans hides the fear of his mother falling pregnant, hides the birth of his sister Hannah. In *Mad Men and Medusas* (2000), I spend some time on Eisler's tram-man that Lacan reinterpreted—behind a road accident is a traumatic abortion, and behind that is a sibling birth. Separation from the mother threatens to leave one as helpless as when one was a baby. Because one has been replaced by the new baby, this would signify death. Death may be represented by castration, but it is experienced as annihilation under the Sibling Trauma and the Law of the Mother that follows.

Male hysteria is the origins of psychoanalysis because it makes the pathology generic. So I came to sibling trauma and then had to think—am I right—is it just a difficulty or is it a trauma? And I wrote a not entirely successful article about that, but it was my question in 2006.

Now why does it matter that it is a trauma? If it is a difficulty you can *really* get over it—it has no structural effect on the psyche. If it is a trauma it comes back every time you have another trauma. There are the two aspects of the sibling trauma: you lose your place, your position in the world, because another person is the baby you were yesterday—that's the trauma that underlies the wish that you want to get rid of them, this person is the same as you and you want to get rid of them: you also love them because they are yourself. The narcissism could have an incestuous outcome. It's a double whammy sort of trauma.

Developmentally there has to be a degree of separation from the walking, talking child from mother who is no longer completely preoccupied with the toddler as she was when it was a baby. But Winnicott with his enormous clinical experience with children recognized that this necessary stage was traumatic. My work was to add the two traumas together and propose that the mother also threatens a traumatic separation if the toddler harms the baby. This, joking with a dead Lacan, I call the Law of the Mother.

In fact, my joke is serious—I think this law stands to the horizontal axis as the Oedipus does to the vertical axis. It is not subservient to that law under patriarchy. I don't know—I would think it would depend on the social context.

I think it's a *law* of the mother, it's a real prohibition: "you will lose me, I will separate from you if you do this," and nobody wants to lose their mother. I mean what do people cry for on the battlefield? They need their mother, always. They can criticize their mother till the cows come home; nobody else must do so because it is a real threat, a real danger. There's an earthquake—and you want your mother. But that is not the mother of patriarchy, that's a mother who threatened to separate because you might have murdered, or had incest with your sibling. After all, she did, in a sense separate, by having a sibling, who took over your role as the baby. So it's a threat with a possible meaning to it, just as castration is a threat with a possible meaning to it, because women are perceived as "already castrated" because the mother doesn't have a penis. Those are threats—you look at reality, and think "Oh My God, that could happen." This is all necessary trauma—to grow up we have to know deep down that there are people other in the world as important as us. As with the Oedipus complex, that can come back with any other trauma.

Yes it's true that on an empirical level the idea of losing one's mother is the great schism, in a way—it contains within it the idea of losing oneself in the world. I'm not denigrating the idea of losing the father, because of course that's awful, but the idea of losing a mother, and the betrayal that comes with that—

Yes, I think if we look at it Oedipally, the loss of father is probably also that for the boy, and the loss of mother stays that for the girl. But if we look just at separation from the mother in terms of the Law of the Mother, then I think for the girl and boy it's really terrifying to lose your mother.

Without breaking any psychoanalytic code, would you be able to illustrate that with any examples from your practice, or more archetypal examples even?

Why do we obliterate what happens on the lateral relations? One reason is psychiatry makes us see the mother ultimately as subordinate to the father. From the small child's perspective, the mother is huge. We are not seeing the mother on an equal plane—a mother whom we could have lost without anything to do with the father. I am saying that there is a mother who we could have lost irrespective of the father, and we're again submerging that and assuming in the literature, for example, in *Twelfth Night*, all is subordinated to the father. But actually we know empirically that when people are crying for their mother they are not always referring to their father. What you want is a case history—well—we are all that case history!

So the resistance to the idea of trauma perhaps exists because to think about it as trauma is perhaps too traumatic.

Yes, no one wants there to be two traumas. But it is also a rather large claim that there is one on the vertical Oedipal, and one on the lateral horizontal. One invokes the Law of the Father, the other produces the Law of the Mother. So whoops wait a minute, we have two *foundational* trauma—trauma that produce psychological defences. More accurately— the laws and the threatened punishment—separation and castration, produce psychological defences. I am then going on to say these defences are different psychological defences in the Oedipal vertical castration complex and the lateral sibling Mother's Law. What I am arguing has major implications, that the vertical gives us repression, in the deep unconscious, things are repressed; and we don't *know* that we ever wanted our mother sexually, we don't *know* penis envy and the castration complex and the dread of castration, and the mark of neurosis in all of us; they come up in an analysis. The psychological defences we use against the threat of the Law of the Mother are different: the desires that she is prohibiting are ones that are to do with narcissism and psychosis rather than neurosis. The defences such as splitting, denial, foreclosure, repudiation, dissociation, and they are why, when we look at social relationships, social groups formed by peers, and by friends and foe, all the heirs to sibling relations, the social group that is founded on that repudiation of the family when the separation from the mother occurs; this social group, a peer group converts the psychotic into the normative. That's why these groups so easily descend into violence and craziness. Everybody has always asked the question and theorized about why individuals are sane and groups of the same individuals able to be crazy. I am saying: turn the question on its head: the same individual if they are a sibling, is able to be crazy, because still, somewhere, they are the crazy two-year-old.

This book covers a range of subjects yet it overall refrains from investigating the wider implications of sibling theory that you have articulated in articles such as "The Law of the Mother: Sibling Trauma and the Brotherhood of War." Could you outline that thinking here?

I think that because we have seen the family largely as developing into society, or society grown up out of the family, we haven't seen this other aspect of society—the repudiation of the family after the threat of separation from the mother, where she pushes the child out of the family and into the social group. In a way this is a very positive thing, I think the latency child is a very interesting child, a very creative child and those childhood relationships are marvelous. I heard J. K. Rowling criticized on a radio program for putting Harry Potter in such an elitist situation as a boarding school and she said, you know, children are only interesting at that age when they are on their own, and it was a good device to get them away from the family. She's absolutely right: children are fascinating when they are first in those groups, very loving, very creative. But they also have those first experiences of best friends and enemies, bullying.

Sibling theory effects how we look at war, and how we look at gendering, as dividing between gendered girls who are not warlike, and gendered males who are boys who have to become warlike. And of course because there is fluidity—men can be pacifists and take a feminine position, and women can equally be warlike, and commit sexual abuse and throw bombs etc.—because there is more flexibility—but actually as a definition, these lateral boys become warriors and these lateral girls become nurses.

We need to think differently about society in relation to war and war in relation to society. Put simply we always think of it as society creates war, whereas reading through siblings and gender it is war that creates society. It isn't just the family and kinship, or class or race or anything whatever that constructs society: war itself constructs society, as much but differently from kinship. So you have kinship marriages and kinship alliances but you also have absolutely built in a situation of war because that is what society has been created for; war creates it.

Can you give a phenomenology of this?

You've got a toddler—it thinks it's the family's baby—it loses its position in the family, so it wants to destroy the new baby; but it also loves that baby, because it thinks it is its baby self. So those two emotions amount to the desire to murder and commit incest. The mother prohibits them, and says—effectively, or the effect of the prohibition is—if you do that to your baby sister or brother, I won't love you anymore. At the same time she wants to look after the new baby, who has to be looked after, so she says to the toddler you are the big boy now, the big girl, go and play with your friends. And the toddler does. It gets angry with the mother for deserting it, and walks away from the family and toddles off, and forms a social group as a move from siblings to friends. At the same time as the love that would have led to incest if it hadn't been forbidden, there is the hate that would have led to murder if it hadn't been forbidden. So if the love goes into friendship and into marriage and its equivalents as a positive relationship, where does the bad part go? It goes to creating a foe. You have best friends and you have enemies. So in that juncture you are making a friend/foe division, which as a division will pertain forever more. The child plays competitive games to moderate it, but the underside of it is that it's war. So at the same time as you are forming the positive social group, the candidates for war are also a precondition for that social group. There has to be a social group that is disowned or attacked, that's where the murderousness goes. Then we bring in a gender perspective and say, well, this means that gender female goes into the "life" or positive side of the social group and become future exchange objects in a kinship group; wives, partners etc. What happens to the boy? He becomes the soldier.

Can sibling theory be applied to nation-states and how their power relationships operate—blocks of power that can be seen as siblings or cousins in a way, and then that has to be worked out against the "other" that has been decided on—if that's the case, then what happens to the Law of the Mother? Does it only work at the baby toddler level?

No not at all. It is always there. The aim of the Law of the Mother was to stop the murder and incest between equals. An effect might be to produce enemies, but the mother didn't say—go off and fight, she said—go off and play. I think you find this as a sort of current or red-thread in the writing of someone like Virginia Woolf, where she notoriously said, we have to think back through our mothers. This has always been taken only on the vertical, and as always, about presence—a line of mothers. Woolf was abused by an older half-brother; sibling relationships are central to her work: you think of *The Waves, Between the Acts, The Years*—particularly *The Years*, fantastic novels about siblings and lateral relations. Woolf's mother died when she was 13, so I think she was probably also thinking back through the mother she had lost, that she was separated from. This could be a factor in why Woolf won't support war in *The Three Guineas* for instance.

The Law of the Mother *can* be used as a reinforcement of the Law of the Father, and to endorse boys becoming soldiers, warriors—but the mother's law actually says "don't kill." One could find some place where you could put a wedge into it there, and say well OK let's think about the Mother's Law in terms of promoting a sort of a play—it's a bit idyllic, and I'm being idealistic, but I think it's a place to look and I think somewhere like the work of Woolf is a good place to look. She had the biography to support thinking about siblings and mothers, and the creative intelligence with which to pioneer these issues.

This may be at a tangent—but why am I thinking suddenly about the exchange between Einstein and Freud about "Why War?"—and Freud explained his theory of the death drive as explaining war when he added something I find very interesting. He suggested that the question we can address is why some people don't want war, not why most people do.

If we see war as a way of establishing society, then thinking about peace has to be something we have to work for against our norms. This could be the through the positive use of the Law of the Mother, which I think is buried in Woolf's reference. Freud also had a very interesting idea that war had to do with aesthetics rather than ethics. There is even the aesthetic of military castles, or unfortunately drones that can be beautiful. Why can beauty be that deadly? Because they are so close together, and that is where the Law of the Mother could be taken. So it isn't saying women are more peaceful, it is saying the position could be a wedge on the side of peace.

Daru Huppert, in *Siblings and Sexuality*, also talks about that irritability which is very interesting, and somehow because the sibling is so close to oneself, a sort of mimesis almost...

Yes, that is very important for what I am interested in now, in my work on intersubjectivity; that sort of mirroring of the self, as with Viola in *Twelfth Night*, that you pointed out to me recently—she just *is* Sebastian so who else is she, if he's dead, where is she? It's that mirroring which is different from the Lacanian mirroring where the ego is constructed in alienation. And that's what irritability is, it is something on your skin so to speak. It is about the minimal difference that exists between siblings: too close is irritation.

War is always with us, so on the horizontal axis and on gender distinctions, we have to struggle for peace. Because of the possibility of gender flexibility there could be a struggle for peace. War and its gendering brotherhoods can be horrific but it is not the same as the "undertow" I wrote about with sexual difference in *Psychoanalysis and Feminism*.

Is there note of hope—that war in itself is not inevitable?

I always have two aspects to hope, in addition to a base sense of the voluntarism of optimism that one has anyway. One strand to hope is that if we can get the analysis better, we can think better about something—that is hope to me in itself. For instance, Claudia Lament's disagreement with me that what the toddler goes through is a difficulty, not a trauma. It is very well argued and it forces me to think further. I have almost a physical sense of a move forward and upward. That is far more satisfying than squabbling or even saying "Hurrah for you." If something is taken creatively forward in thinking, that is always hopeful in itself. Then the second stage of hope is a more voluntaristic thing that I want to think there is some way out of this. So I will try and find a way, even if it is going to be 90 per cent wrong, there might be 10 per cent that is right.

Returning to Freud's point about aesthetics, and your own early scholarly work (you began as a lecturer in English Literature). Do you think that creative writers have always known about siblings and how they organize society, how sibling relationships construct how we are in the world much longer than perhaps any other discipline? Can you say something about the relationship between creativity and understanding how we live in the world?

Well we can go straight to Shakespeare, can't we? We can go straight to Shakespeare and siblings, which is the book I am working on now, and say "My God, he knew." Quite what he knew we still have to discover— but he certainly knew. It's like Freud saying—"Gosh, Sophocles knew," Freud found the Oedipus complex in his patients and in himself, but could only give it a formula, a name, through Sophocles.

What is it about creativity that allows us access to that?

The unconscious. Creativity is a shorter path to the unconscious. As Louise Bourgeois said, it's such a privilege to have this quicker access, to be down there working with the unconscious. Louise Bourgeois knew all about siblings as I wrote in 2011. Mignon Nixon introduced me to the work of the artist and as she shows in her chapter "Minimal Difference: On Siblings, Sex and Violence," art got there first.

Art also lets the creator off in a way, because imagination comes into play, and to fictionalize or to create sculpture, you don't have to show your workings

Absolutely, you just show the final result and you leave it to the other person to make what they can of it as well. You can't really direct the reception, if you are trying too hard to direct the reception, you are trying too much in the conscious field. It is also to do with—how terrible it was when we bombed the libraries and museums in Baghdad: there was something if possible—an excess, a supplement to the terrible violence, a madness beyond the mad. If it is: shall we save this museum or save this school, of course, you save the school. But there is actually something horrific about the destructiveness of the good things of civilization. Of course if someone gave me that choice I would save the children, *obviously*, but what a horrendous choice, because you are going to the *heart* of something that is the best about humanity. So that even if you know it's a drone that has been put in a museum, it has been put there for its aesthetic quality, not for its destructive quality.

There is something really exciting about this theory as well as it being so shocking and dangerous to the status quo. In his chapter

"Hysteria between Big Brother and Patriarchy," Paul Verhaeghe states that patriarchal society is shifting towards a society of siblings, where the horizontal level is far more important than the vertical one, and your theory might prove even more revolutionary than you yourself thought. What can you say to this? Can sibling theory be on a par with or even transcend the Oedipal model?

I don't think I thought my theory was revolutionary—it opened some revolutionary doors—it's a different thing from somebody having a revolutionary theory like Einstein or Darwin or Marx—it's not a revolutionary theory—it's an observation with revolutionary implications. But it opens doors to look at things in a very radical way, and so in a sense my amazement at it was exactly about that. The implications of the presence and absence of it felt huge. We are not of course, talking about having or not having sisters and brothers, we are talking about looking at the world differently.

So what about the second part of the question? If society shifts towards different kinds of family models and we become more—especially in Western cultures more accepting of others and more integrated with others, through intermarriage, homosexuality, bisexuality, and all these different structures of family, is that going to cause a sea change, an impact on the ways psychoanalysts think and allow the sibling theory to come into its own?

There are big social changes connected with the economy of late capitalism that have to do with the horizontal as opposed to the vertical, no question about it. That is a fundamental reason why there is such an interest in siblings I think, and why people like me think about them—we are of our time. But then you need to think further about them to understand what the forces were that made you think about them. You need the theory then to understand why you saw this thing in the first place. And what you saw isn't completely unique, there have been other societies with very different socioeconomic dimensions that have probably privileged siblings over parents. We now have this extraordinary longevity for example, well what about societies with very short longevity? I mean your sister or brother is the longest relationship you have in your life, or you may not have siblings, but you have substitutes for those siblings if you don't—you always in a sense have something that is a lateral relationship of that sort.

But is seems absolutely crucial that psychoanalysts do recognize the complementarity of the sibling and Oedipal theories—

Terri Apter, author of *The Sister Knot* (2007), was a discussant when I gave one of the sibling talks here in Cambridge and she took it as a triumphant repudiation of Freud's theory of the castration complex and it isn't that at all, not at all. People always see things as either/or when really it is both/and.

Thinking about it laterally (!), or creatively, the either/or is the sexual difference and the both/and is the gender. With that in mind, I want to ask a couple of questions to do with the application of the theory in contemporary society and contemporary life. What do you think feminism should be doing to grasp and combat fixed notions of sexual difference and do you think these ideas can translate to global contexts?

My personal mantra has always been that feminism puts politics in command of what is going on. So if there is social change towards the lateral and the horizontal, then feminism needs to be at the forefront of thinking of that in relation to gender, but that it doesn't mean you discount sexual difference. We need to be thinking about demographic change, and thinking about that in terms of wealth and poverty and all the rest of it...by putting politics in command feminism needs to think ahead of what is going on too.

The global communications revolution is lateral and the hegemonic social classes and nation-states of the world with their huge demographic changes and new reproduction technologies are embedded in the vast territories of the world where the question is: who would be a woman? Which is about sexual difference. So we don't want to just look at ourselves, we want to contextualize ourselves, and look at what's happening where sexual difference is absolutely dominant. And everywhere where gender distinction prevails as a primary marker falling over war and peace.

Questions of theory are very important but so much of your work is about how the reality on the ground can be changed using theory. Formulate the theory, get it working, and then see how it can be applied.

I think they have to happen together. What is on the ground is the material for thinking the theory.

Where next for the theory and for psychoanalysis' relevance to the conditions of our times—there is greater hysteria in patriarchy, trauma from war, ongoing gender violence...?

Well just take the concept of a war on terror. It's a new concept of war. There have always been terrorists but no one before has gone to war with the world. "War on terror" could tell you more about sibling theory, and sibling theory could tell you more about the war on terror. That seems to me to be a matter of urgency.

Who should be doing that thinking? And how should it be applied?
All of us, all of us.

So that does suggest to me that there is something so groundbreak-ing about articulating siblings into our consciousness in society—when you look back over this book, and think about the next stage, where are you going in your own thinking now? Where can we follow you next?
I think everybody in a way has to work where they are. So if I was a novelist I would be working one way, and as I am a psychoanalyst I am working in another way because that's what I have to work with. Although I see my work as interdisciplinary, some of my disciplines are subsidiary to others. So part of me is working to say look: psychoanalysis has been very useful for feminist theory generally; understanding the unconscious has been incredibly important, and still is, and therefore I do think psychoanalytic theory is very important no matter how small a minority of people in the world think so. I think the unconscious is part of the human condition and that's why it is important to understand it. So I am interested in working to introduce sibling theory into psycho-analysis, and in relation to that, using my original discipline of literature. I do still think through literature, in fact when I started training as a psychoanalyst many years ago I realized how much literature was part of my bloodstream. My free associations were very literary. So I see working on Shakespeare and siblings as contributing something to psychoanalysis from Shakespeare, and asking Shakespeare what he can tell us. It isn't one way—I am not psychoanalyzing Shakespeare's plays, not at all. I am a psychoanalyst looking at Shakespeare, but I am looking at what he can teach me.

Yes the exciting thing about this project is that even though psycho-analysis might only apply to one-fifth of the world or whatever, for good or for ill, because of colonialism, Shakespeare does [apply to the world].
Yes, I hadn't thought of that, quite right. Many people think Freud is totally irrelevant, but actually what he is looking at is not irrelevant, and his way of looking at is isn't totally irrelevant either. I just want to make that as a statement. And Freud stays relevant as Darwin stays rel-evant, even though people say well, this and this wrong, Einstein stays relevant—even Marx. Freud is of that ilk—I mean he made a majorly important discovery and found a way of understanding it.

The other task is always the oppression of women—the longest revolution. I wanted to see: if we can understand more about siblings and lateral relations, we can also understand more about gender inequity. After all it was feminism that created sisterhood with all its difficulties. Anne Oakley and I wrote in the preface to one of the books we edited how difficult sisterhood was. I mean it felt marvelous as a women's movement but my God it wasn't easy. We really don't know much about sisterhood where we know much more about brotherhood. There are a number of good books but we haven't really brought them together, and said, let's take this understanding of sisterhood into the politics of feminism.

Can you and I both thank Susan and Robbie for their inspiration and very hard work in creating this book as an intellectual and political contribution to our tasks.

JCWM

March 31, 2014

Bibliography

Allegaert, P. and Brokken, A., eds. 2012. *Nerveuze vrouwen. Twee eeuwen vrouwen en hun psychiaters.* (Trans.: *Two Centuries of Women and Their Psychiatrists*). Museum Dr. Guislain, Gent: Lannoo.

Althusser, L. [1962] 2005. "Contradiction and Overdetermination." In *For Marx.* Translated by Ben Brewster, 87–128. New York: Verso.

Anzieu, D. 1986. *Freud's Self-Analysis.* New York: International Universities Press.

Apollodorus. 1976. *Gods and Heroes of the Greeks.* Translated by Michael Simpson. Amherst, MA: University of Massachusetts Press.

Arendt, H. [1958] 1998. *The Human Condition.* Chicago: University of Chicago Press.

Armstrong, R. H. 2005. *Freud and the Ancient World,* New York: Cornell University Press.

Athenaeus. 1930. *Deipnosophistae.* Translated by Loeb Classical Library. London: William Heinemann.

Balint, E. 1998. *Before I Was I.* Edited by Michael Parsons and Juliet Mitchell. New York: Other Press.

Bane, S. 1980. *Democracy's Body: Judson Dance Theatre 1962–1964.* Ann Arbor, MI: UMI Research Press.

Bauman, Z. and Lyon, D. 2013. *Liquid Surveillance.* Cambridge: Polity Press.

Beigler, J. S. 1975. "A Commentary on Freud's Treatment of the Rat Man." *Annual of Psychoanalysis* 3: 271–285.

Blackburn, R. 1972. *Ideology in Social Science.* London: Fontana/Collins.

Bryan-Wilson, J. 2009. *Art Workers: Radical Practice in the Vietnam War Era.* Berkeley: University of California.

Butler, J. 1990. *Gender Trouble: Feminism and the Subversion of Identity.* New York: Routledge.

Butler, J. "Ideologies of the Superego." Presented at the Centre for Gender Studies, Cambridge University, May 2009.

Butler, J. 2013. "Rethinking Sexual Difference and Kinship in Mitchell's Psychoanalysis and Feminism." *differences* 23(2): 1–19.

Callinicos, A. 2013. "Is Leninism Finished?" *Socialist Review,* January 13, 2013.

Carnegie, D. 1936. *How to Win Friends and Influence People.* Cedar.

Central Committee of the Socialist Workers Party 2013. "The SWP and Women's Oppression." http://socialistunity.com/wp-content/uploads/2013/03/SWP -internal-bulletin-special-conference-march2013.pdf

Chiland, C. 2004. "Gender and Sexual Difference." In *Dialogues on Sexuality, Gender, and Psychoanalysis*. Edited by Iréne Matthis, 79–91. London: Karnac.

Colonna, A. and Newman L. 1983. "The Psychoanalytic Literature on Siblings." *Psychoanalytic Study of the Child* 83: 285–309.

Communist Party of Great Britain 2013a. "Transcript of the Disputes Committee Report to Conference." http://www.cpgb.org.uk/home/weekly-worker/online -only/report-of-swps-disputes-committee-and-conference-debate

Communist Party of Great Britain 2013b. "Callinicos Threatens 'Lynch Mobs.'" http://www.cpgb.org.uk/home/weekly-worker/online-only/callinicos -threatens-lynch-mobs

Connell, R. 2012. "The Books that Inspired." http://blogs.lse.ac.uk/lsereview ofbooks/2012/04/22/academic-inspiration-raewyn-connell/

Crick, B. 1984. *Socialist Values and Time, Fabian Tract 495*. London: The Fabian Society.

Crockatt, P. 2013. "A View of 'The Rat Man.'" Unpublished manuscript.

De Georges, P. 2009. "A Thought that Burdens the Soul," *Psychoanalytic Notebooks* 18: 55–65.

Deutsch, H. 1932. "Obsessional Ceremonial and Obsessional Acts." In *Psycho-Analysis of the Neuroses*. Translated by W. D. Robson-Scott, 175–197. London: Hogarth Press.

D'Huy, J. 2012. "Aquitaine on the Road of Oedipus? The Sphinx as a Prehistoric Story." *Société d'études et de recherches préhistoriques des Eyzies* 61: 15–21.

De Wachter, D. 2012. *Borderline Times*. Gent: Lannoo.

Feiffer, H. 2013. *How to Make Friends and Then Kill Them*. Directed by Kip Fagan. Rattlestick Playwrights Theater.

Ferenczi, S. [1925] 1908. "Analytic Conception of Psycho-Neuroses." In *Further Contributions to the Theory and Technique of Psycho-analysis*. London: Karnac.

Ferro, A. 1999. *The Bi-Personal Field*. Routledge: London.

Feuerbach, L. A. [1843] 1986. *Principals of the Philosophy of the Future*. Translated by Manfred Vogel. New York: Hackett & Co.

Fisher, M. 2009. *Capitalist Realism: Is There No Alternative?* Winchester & Washington: Zero Books.

Flax, J. 1992. "Juliet Mitchell." In *The Routledge Dictionary of Twentieth-Century Political Thinkers*. Edited by Robert Benewick and Philip Green, 228–229. London: Routledge.

Foley, M. 2010. *The Age of Absurdity. Why Modern Life Makes It Hard to be Happy*. London: Simon & Schuster.

Fornari, F. 1975. *The Psychoanalysis of War*. Bloomington, IN: Indiana University Press.

Foucault, M. [1963] 1997. *The Birth of the Clinic. An Archaeology of Medical Perception*. Translated by A. Sheridan. London: Routledge.

Foucault, M. 1972. *Histoire de la folie à l'âge classique*. Paris: Gallimard.

Foucault, M. [1975] 1977. *Discipline and Punish*. Translated by Alan Sheridan. London: Penguin.

Foucault, M. [1976] 1978. *The History of Sexuality, Volume I: An Introduction*. Translated by Robert Hurley. New York: Vintage.

Freud, A. and Dann, S. 1951. "An Experiment in Group Upbringing." *Psychoanalytic Study of the Child* 6: 127–168.

Freud, A. 1966. "Obsessional Neurosis: A Summary of Psycho-Analytic Views as Presented at the Congress." *International Journal of Psycho-analysis* 47: 116–122.

Freud, S. and Breuer, J. [1893] 1991. "On the Psychical Mechanism of Hysterical Phenomena: Preliminary Communication." In *Studies in Hysteria Penguin Freud Library Vol. 3*. London. Penguin.

Freud, S. [1893] 2001. "Charcot." In *The Standard Edition of the Complete Psychological Works of Sigmund Freud Vol. 3*. Translated by James Strachey, 11–23. London: Hogarth Press (*SE3*).

Freud, S. [1894] 2001. "The Neuropsychoses of Defence." *SE3* 41–61.

Freud, S. [1895] 2001. "Project for a Scientific Psychology." *SE1* 283–397.

Freud, S. [1896] 2001. "Heredity and the Neuroses." *SE3* 151–156.

Freud, S. [1896] 2001. "Further Remarks on the Psychoneuroses of Defence." *SE3* 162–185.

Freud, S. [1897a] 1998. "Letter from Freud to Fliess, January 3rd 1897." *The Complete Letters of Sigmund Freud to Wilhelm Fliess, 1887–1904*. Edited by Jeffrey Masson, 219–221. Cambridge, MA: Harvard University Press.

Freud, S. [1897b] 1986. "Letter from Freud to Fliess, October 3rd 1897." *The Complete Letters of Sigmund Freud to Wilhelm Fliess, 1887–1904*. Edited by Jeffrey Masson, 267–270. Cambridge, MA: Harvard University Press.

Freud, S. [1898] 2001. "The Psychical Mechanism of Forgetfulness." *SE3* 287–303.

Freud, S. [1899] 2001. "Screen Memories." *SE3* 303–322.

Freud, S. [1901] 2001. "Fragments of an Analysis of a Case of Hysteria." *SE7*, 1–122.

Freud, S. [1905] 2001. "Three Essays on the Theory of Sexuality." *SE7* 123–246.

Freud, S. [1907] 1976. "Letter from Freud to Jung, April 14th 1907." In *The Freud/Jung Letters*. Edited by William McGuire, 33–4. New York: Picador.

Freud, S. [1907] 2001. "Obsessive Actions and Religious Practices." *SE 9* 115–128.

Freud, S. [1909a] 2001. "Notes upon a Case of Obsessional Neurosis." *SE 10* 153–318.

Freud, S. [1909b] 1976. "149F: Letter from Freud to Jung, 30th June 1909." In *The Freud/Jung Letters*. edited by William McGuire, 116–7. New York: Picador.

Freud, S. [1909] 2001. "Analysis of a Phobia in a Five Year Old Boy." *SE10* 5–148.

Freud, S. [1910] 2001. "Five Lectures of Psychoanalysis." *SE11* 1–56.

Freud, S. [1914] 2001. "On Narcissism: An Introduction." *SE 14* 67–102.

Freud, S. [1915] 2001. "Instincts and Their Vicissitudes." *SE 14* 109–140.

Freud, S. [1915b] 2001. "The Unconscious." *SE14* 159–215.

Freud, S. [1915c] 2001. "Thoughts for the Times on War and Death." *SE14* 273–300.

Freud, S. [1916] 2001. "Introductory Lectures." *SE 15–16* 1–463.

Freud, S. [1917] 2001. "On Transformations of Instinct as Exemplified in Anal Eroticism." *SE17* 127–133.

Freud, S. [1917] 2001. "The Development of the Libido and the Sexual Organisations." *SE16* 329–338.

Freud, S. [1918] 2001. "The Taboo on Virginity." *SE11* 191–208.

Freud, S. [1919] 2001. "A Child is Being Beaten." *SE17* 179–204.

Freud, S. [1920] 2001. "Beyond the Pleasure Principle." *SE18* 1–64.

Freud, S. [1923] 2001. "The Ego and the Id." *SE19* 12–68.

Freud, S. [1924] 2001. "The Dissolution of the Oedipus Complex." *SE19* 171–180.

Freud, S. [1924] 2005. "The Dissolution of the Oedipus Complex." In *The Essentials of Psychoanalysis*, 395–401.

Freud, S. [1924] 2001. "An Autobiographical Study." *SE20* 7–76.

Freud, S. [1925] 2001. "Inhibitions, Symptoms and Anxiety." *SE20* 87–178.

Freud, S. [1925b] 2001. "A Note Upon the 'Mystic Writing-Pad." *SE19* 225–232.

Freud, S. [1925] 2005. "Some Psychical Consequences of the Anatomical Distinction between the Sexes." In *The Essentials of Psychoanalysis*, 402–411. Vintage: London.

Freud, S. [1926] 2001. "The Question of Lay Analysis." *SE20* 177–258.

Freud, S. [1927] 2001. "Fetischismus." *SE21* 149–158.

Freud, S. [1930] 2001. "The Future of an Illusion and Other Works." *SE21* 1–56.

Freud, S. [1933] 2001. "New Introductory Lectures." *SE 22* 1–182.

Freud, S. [1933] 2001. "On Femininity." *SE22*, 112–135.

Freud, S. [1938] 2001. "Findings, Ideas, Problems." *SE23* 299–300.

Freud, S. [1955]. 2005. *The Essentials of Psychoanalysis*. Translated by J. Strachey. Vintage London.

Gilmore, K. 2013. "Theory of Sibling Trauma and Lateral Dimension." *Psychoanalytical Study of the Child* 67: 53–65.

Glover, E. 1947. "Basic Mental Concepts—Their Clinical and Theoretical Value." *Psychoanalytic Quarterly* 16: 482–506.

Green, A. 1995. "Has Sexuality Anything to Do with Psychoanalysis?" *The International Journal of Psychoanalysis* 75: 871–883.

Green, A. 1999. *The Work of the Negative*. Translated by Andrew Weller, New York: Free Association Books.

Green, A. 2000. *Chains of Eros*. London: Karnac.

Green, A. 2001. *Life Narcissism and Death Narcissism*. London: Karnac.

Green, A. 2005. "The Illusion of a Common Ground and Mythical Pluralism." *International Journal of Psychoanalysis* 86: 627–632.

Goldstein, P. 2000. "Orwell as a (Neo)conservative: The Reception of 1984." *Journal of the Midwest Modern Language Association* 33(1): 44–57.

Grosz, E. 1990. *Jacques Lacan: A Feminist Introduction*. London: Routledge.

Guntrip, H. 1975. "My Experience of Analysis with Fairbairn and Winnicott." *International Review of Psychoanalysis* 2: 145–156.

Haaken, J. 1998. *Pillar of Salt: Gender, Memory, and the Perils of Looking Back.* New Brunswick, NJ: Rutgers UP.

Hegel, G.W.F. [1807] 1977. *Phenomenology of Spirit*. Translated by A. V. Miller, Oxford: Oxford University Press.

Hegel, G.W.F. [1832] 2010. *The Science of Logic*. Translated by George Di Giovanni. Cambridge: Cambridge University Press.

Heyman, I., Fombonne, E., Simmons, H., Ford, T., Meltzer, H., and Goodman, R. 2001. "Prevalence of Obsessive–Compulsive Disorder in the British Nationwide Survey of Child Mental Health." *The British Journal of Psychiatry* 179: 324–329.

Hoare, Q. 1967. "Discussion on 'Women: The Longest Revolution.'" *New Left Review* 41: 78–81.

Holland, N. 1975. "An Identity for the Rat-Man." *International Review of Psycho-Analysis* 2: 157–169.

Honneth, A. 1996. *The Struggle for Recognition*. Cambridge: Polity.

Huppert, D. 2014. "Die Eigenschaften des Unbewussten." In *Sigmund Freud Vorlesungen 2014*. Vienna: Mandelbaum.

Ingle, S. 1993. *George Orwell: A Political Life*. Manchester: Manchester University Press.

Israël, L. 1984. *Hysterie, sekse en de geneesheer*. Leuven/Amersfoort: Acco

Jameson, F. 2010. *Valences of the Dialectics*. New York: Verso.

Jones, E. 1955. *The Life and Work of Sigmund Freud*. New York: Basic Books.

Kaplan, A. 2005. *The Anarchy of Empire in the Making of U.S. Culture*. Cambridge: Harvard University Press.

Kelly, M, 1983. "Preface." *Post-Partum Document*, xv. London: Routledge.

Klein, M. [1928] 1998. "Early Stages of the Oedipus Complex." In *Love, Guilt And Reparation, Writings of Melanie Klein 1921–1945*, 186–198. London: Vintage.

Klein, M. [1930] 1975. "The Importance of Symbol-Formation in the Development of the Ego." In *Love, Guilt And Reparation, Writings of Melanie Klein 1921–1945*, 219–232. London: Vintage.

Klein, M. 1932. *The Psychoanalysis of Children*. London: Hogarth Press.

Krauss, R. 1976. *Passages in Modern Sculpture*. Cambridge, MA: MIT Press.

Künstlicher, R. 1998. "Horror at Pleasure of His Own of which He Himself is Not Aware: The Case of the Rat Man." In *On Freud's Couch*, edited by. I. Matthis and I. Szecsödy, 127–162. Northvale, NJ: Jason Aronson.

Lacan, J. [1953] 1977. "Function and Field of Speech and Language." In *Écrits: A Selection*, translated by Alan Sheridan, 30–113. New York: Norton.

Lacan, J. [1956] 1991. *The Seminar of Jacques Lacan: The Psychoses 1955–56, Book III*. Edited by John Forrester. New York: Norton.

Lacan, J. [1957] 1977. "The Agency of the Letter in the Unconscious, or Reason Since Freud." In *Écrits: a Selection*. translated by Alan Sheridan. London: Tavistock.

Lacan, J. [1958] 2002. *The Seminar of Jacques Lacan V: The Formations of the Unconscious*. Translated by Cormac Gallagher. London: Karnac.

Lacan, J. [1966] 2006. *Ecrits*. New York: Norton.

Lacan, J. 1966. "Le Stade du miroir comme formateur de la fonction du Je." In *Ecrits*, pp. 93–100. Paris: Seuil.

Lacan, J. 1966. "Position de l'inconscient." In *Ecrits*, 829–850. Paris: Seuil.

Lacan, J. [1969–70] 1991. *Le Séminaire, livre XVII, L'Envers de la psychanalyse*. Edited by J. A. Miller. Paris: Seuil.

Lacan, J. [1972–73] 1975. *Le Séminaire, livre XX: Encore*. Edited by J.-A. Miller. Paris: Seuil.

Lacan, J. [1974]. 1990 *Television: A Challenge to the Psychoanalytic Establishment*. Translated by D. Hollier. New York: Norton.

Lacan, J. 2004 [1962–63]. *Le Séminaire, livre X, L'angoisse*. Edited by J.-A. Miller. Paris: Seuil.

Lambert-Beatty, C. 2008. *Being Watched: Yvonne Rainer and the 1960s*. Cambridge, MA: MIT Press/October Books.

Lament, C. 2013. "An Introduction." *Psychoanalytical Study of the Child*. 67: 1–13.

Laplanche, J. 1976. *Life and Death in Psychoanalysis*. Baltimore, MD: John Hopkins.

Lear, J. 1990. *Love and Its Place in Nature*. London: Faber.

Limentani, A. 1984. "To the Limits of Male Heterosexuality: The Vagina Man." In *Between Freud and Klein: the Psychoanalytic Quest for Knowledge and Truth*. London: Free Association Books.

Loewald, H. 2000. "The Waning of the Oedipus Complex." *Journal of Psychotherapy Practice and Research* 9: 239–249.

Lovell, T. 1996. "Feminist Social Theory." In *The Blackwell Companion to Social Theory*. Edited by Bryan Turner. Oxford: Blackwell.

Mahoney, P. 1986. *Freud and the Rat Man*, New Haven, CT: Yale University Press.

Mahoney, P. 2007. "Reading the Notes on the Rat Man Case." *Canadian Journal of Psychoanalysis* 15(1): 93–117.

Marx, K. [1844] 1977. "Critique of Hegel's Dialectic and General Philosophy." In *Karl Marx: Selected Writings*. Edited by David McLellan. Oxford: Oxford University Press.

Marx, K. [1846] 1994. "The German Ideology." In *Karl Marx: Early Political Writings*. Edited by Joseph O'Malley. Cambridge: Cambridge University Press.

Marx, K. [1867] 2011. *Capital, Volume 1*. Translated by Samuel Moore and Edward Aveling. New York: Dover.

Matte-Blanco, I. 1975. *The Unconscious as Infinite Sets*. London: Duckworth.

Matthews, W. 2002. "The Poverty of Strategy: EP Thompson, Perry Anderson, and the Transition to Socialism." *Labour/Le Travail*, 50: 217–241.

McNay, L. 2007. *Against Recognition*. Cambridge: Polity.

Merleau-Ponty, M. [1949–1952] 2010. *Child Psychology and Pedagogy*. Translated by Talia Welsh. Evanston, IL: Northwestern University Press.

Mieville, C. 2013. "The Stakes." http://www.leninology.com/2013/01/the-stakes .html

Milner, M. 1969. *The Hands of the Living God: An Account of a Psycho-analytic Treatment*. London: Hogarth Press.

Mitchell, J. [1964] 1984. "Wuthering Heights: Romanticism and Rationality." In *Women: The Longest Revolution*, 127–144. London: Virago.

Mitchell, J. 1966. "Women: The Longest Revolution." *New Left Review* 40: 11–37.

Mitchell, J. 1967. "Reply to Q. Hoare." *New Left Review* 41: 81–83.

Mitchell, J. 1973. "Female Sexuality." *Journal of Biosocial Science* 5(1): 123–136.

Mitchell, J. 1974a. "Aspects of Feminism." In *Women: The Longest Revolution*, 77–126. London: Virago.

Mitchell, J. 1974b. *Psychoanalysis and Feminism*. 1st edition, New York: Basic Books.

Mitchell, J. [1974c] 1984. "On Freud and The Distinction Between the Sexes." In *Women: The Longest Revolution*, 221–232. London: Virago.

Mitchell, J. [1974d] 1984. "Femininity, Narrative and Psychoanalysis." In *Women: The Longest Revolution*, 287–294. London: Virago.

Mitchell, J. 1983. "Psychoanalysis and Child Development." *New Left Review*, 140: 92–96.

Mitchell, J. 1986. "Reflections on Twenty Years of Feminism." In *What is Feminism*, 34–48. Oxford: Blackwell.

Mitchell, J. 1988. "Angela McRobbie: An Interview with Juliet Mitchell." *New Left Review*, 170: 80–91.

Mitchell, J. 1999a. "'Introduction, 1999." In *Psychoanalysis and Feminism*. New York: Basic Books.

Mitchell, J. 1999b. "Feminism and Psychoanalysis at the Millennium." *Women: A Cultural Review*, 10(2): 186–191.

Mitchell, J. 2000. *Psychoanalysis and Feminism*. 2nd edition, New York: Basic Books.

Mitchell, J. 2000. *Madmen and Medusa: Reclaiming the Effects of Sibling Relations on the Human Condition*. London: Penguin.

Mitchell, J. 2002. "Reply to Lynne Segal's Commentary." *Studies in Gender and Sexuality*, 3(2): 217–228.

Mitchell, J. 2003. *Siblings: Sex and Violence*. Cambridge, UK: Polity.

Mitchell, J. and Spigel, S. 2003. "The Power of Feelings." *Psychodynamic Practice*, 9(1): 87–89.

Mitchell, J. 2006a. "From Infant to Child: The Sibling Trauma, the Rite de Passage, and the Construction of the 'Other' in the Social Group." *Fort Da* 12: 35–49.

Mitchell, J. 2007. "On Asking Again: What Does a Woman Want?" In *The Claims of Literature: The Shoshana Felman Reader*. Edited by Emily Sun, Eyal Peretz, and Ulrich Baer, 201–209. New York: Fordham University Press.

Mitchell, J. 2008. "What Do We Mean by Gender Studies?" Paper presented at the Multidisciplinary Workshop at the University of Cambridge Centre for Gender Studies, January 22, 2008.

Mitchell, J. 2011. "Emancipation in the Heart of Darkness: An Interview with Juliet Mitchell." *Platypus Review* 38: 1–6.

Mitchell, J. 2013. "Siblings: Thinking Theory." *Psychoanalytical Study of the Child* 67: 14–34.

Mitchell, J. and Oakley, A. 1976a. "Introduction" to *The Rights And Wrongs of Women*, 7–16. London: Penguin.

Mitchell, J. and Oakley, A. 1976b. "Women and Equality." In *The Rights And Wrongs of Women*, 379–399. London: Penguin.

Mitchell, J. and Rey, L. 1975. "Comment on 'The Freudian Slip.'" *New Left Review* 94: 79–80.

Morgaga, C. and Anzaldua, G, eds. 1984. *This Bridge Called My Back: Writings by Radical Women of Color*. New York: Kitchen Table Press.

Myerson, P. G. 1966. "Comment on Dr Zetzel's Paper." *International Journal of Psycho-analysis* 47: 139–142.

Nixon, M. 2008. "Book of Tongues." In Nancy Spero: *Dissidances*, 30. Barcelona and Madrid: Museu d'Art Contemporani de Barcelona and Museo Nacional Centro de Art Reina Sofia.

Nixon, M. 2014. "Louise Lawler: No Drones." *October* 147 (Winter 2014).

Nunberg, H. and Federn, E., eds. 1962. *Minutes of the Vienna Psychanalytic Society*, Volume 1. New York: International Universities Press.

Oliver, K. 2009. *Animal Lessons*. New York: Columbia University Press.

Orwell, G. [1937] 2001. *The Road to Wigan Pier*. London: Penguin.

Orwell, G. [1946] 2002. "What is Socialism?" *In Essays*. New York: Everyman.

Orwell, G. 1949. *Nineteen Eighty-Four*. London: Penguin.

Owens, C. 1983. "The Discourse of Others: Feminists and Postmodernism." In *Beyond Recognition: Representation, Power, and Culture*. Berkeley: University of California Press.

Pateman, C. 1988. *The Sexual Contract*. Stanford: Stanford University Press.

Penny, L. 2013. "The SWP and Rape: Why I Care about This Marxist-Leninist Implosion." *Guardian*, March 12, 2013.

Phillips, A. 1988. *Winnicott*. London: Fontana Press.

Rainer, Y. 1966. "A Quasi Survey of Some 'Minimalist' Tendencies in the Quantitatively Minimal Dance Activity Midst the Plethora, or an Analysis of Trio A." In Yvonne Rainer. 1974. *Work 1961–73*. Halifax: Press of the Nova Scotia College of Art and Design.

Robinson, M. 1908. *Housekeeping*. New York: Picado.

Ross, C. 2012. *The Leaderless Revolution: How Ordinary People Will Take Power and Change Politics in the Twenty-First Century*. New York: Blue Rider Press.

Rubin, G. 1975. "The Traffic in Women." In *Toward an Anthropology of Women*, edited by R. Reiter, 157–210. New York: Mon Rev.

Rubin, G. and Butler, J. 1994. "Sexual Traffic." *differences* 6(2+3): 62–99.

Segal, L. 2001. "Psychoanalysis and politics: Juliet Mitchell, Then and Now." *Studies in Gender & Sexuality* 2: 327–343.

Solono-Suarez, E. 2009. "Learning to Read Obsessional Neurosis." *Psychoanalytic Notebooks*, 18: 29–42.

Spillius, E. 1989. *Melanie Klein Today*. London: Karnac.

Stoller, R. 1968. *Sex and Gender*. New York: Science House.

Stoller, R. 1973. *Splitting*. New Haven, CT: Yale University Press.

Stroeken, H. P. 2007. "Note on the Extraordinary Similarity between the Worlds of Freud and of the Ratman." *International Forum of Psychoanalysis* 16: 100–102.

Swindells, J. and Jardine, L. 1990. *What's Left? Women in Culture and the Labour Movement*. London: Routledge.

Talbot, M. 2002. "Girls Just Want to Be Mean." *The New York Times* (February 22, 2002).

Tasca, C., Rapetti, M., Carta, M. G., and Fadda, B. 2012. "Women and Hysteria in the History of Mental Health." *Clinical Practice & Epidemiology Mental Health* 8: 110–119. Published online October 19, 2012.

Tressler, I. 1937. *How to Lose Friends and Alienate People*. Palmera Publishing.

Turnheim, M. 2007. "Über die innere Spaltung der Freudschen Geste und die Frage der Rückkehr." In *Freudlose Psychoanalyse?* Vienna: Turia und Kant.

Vanheule, S. 2011. *The Subject of Psychosis: A Lacanian Perspective*. London and New York: Palgrave Macmillan.

Verhaeghe, P. 1995. "From Impossibility to Inability: Lacan's Theory of the Four Discourses." *The Letter* 3: 76–100. (Digital version on http://www .psychoanalysis.ugent.be).

Verhaeghe, P. 1999 [1987). *Does the Woman Exist? From Freud's Hysteric to Lacan's Feminine*. New York: The Other Press.

Verhaeghe, P. 2001. *Beyond Gender*. New York: Other Press.

Verhaeghe, P. 2001. "Mind your Body & Lacan's Answer to a Classical Deadlock." In *Beyond Gender. From Subject to Drive*. Edited by P. Verhaeghe, 99–132, New York: Other Press.

Verhaeghe, P. 2004. *On Being Normal and Other Disorders*. London: Karnac.

Verhaeghe, P. 2004. "Phallacies of Binary Reasoning: Drive beyond Gender." In *Dialogues on Sexuality, Gender and Psychoanalysis*. Edited by I. Matthis, 53–66. London: Karnac. http://www.psychoanalysis.ugent.be

Verhaeghe, P. 2009. *New Studies of Old Villains. A Radical Reconsideration of the Oedipus Complex*. (Foreword by Juliet Mitchell). New York: Other Press.

Verhaeghe, P. 2014a. *What about Me?* Brunswick: Scribe Publications.

Verhaeghe, P. 2014b "Today's Madness Does Not Make Sense." In *Lacan on Madness: Madness, Yes You Can't*. Edited by P. Gherovici and M. Steinkoler London: Routledge, Taylor & Francis Group.

Veszy-Wagner, L. 1967. "Zwangsneurose und latent Homosexualitat." *Psyche* 21: 295–615.

Volkan, V. and Ast, G. 2000. *Siblings in the Unconscious and Psychopathology*. Madison: International University Press.

Walker, T. 2013. "Why I am Resigning." http://www.cpgb.org.uk/home /weekly-worker/944/swp-why-i-am-resigning

Walkerdine, V. 1997. *Daddy's Girl*. Cambridge, MA: Harvard University Press.

Wandschneider, D. 2010. "Dialectic as the 'Self-Fulfilment' of Logic." In *The Dimensions of Hegel's Dialectic*. Edited by Nectarious G. Limnatis. New York: Continuum.

Williams, B. 1993. *Shame and Necessity*. Berkeley: University of California Press.

Williams, R. 1973. "Base and Superstructure in Marxist Cultural Theory." *New Left Review* 82: 3–16.

Williams, R. 1980. *Problems in Materialism and Culture*. New York: Verso.

Williams, R. 1982. "George Orwell." *Culture and Society*, 285–294. London: Hograth Press.

Williams, R. 1985. *Keywords: A Vocabulary of Culture and Society*, New York: Oxford University Press.

Winnicott, D. [1953] 1965. "Psycho-Analysis and the Sense of Guilt." In *The Maturational Processes and the Facilitating Environment: Studies in the Theory of Emotional Development*, London: Tavistock.

Winnicott, D. 1971. *Playing and Reality*. London: Tavistock Publications.
Wittgenstein, L. 1984. "Philosophische Untersuchungen." In *Werkausgabe Band 1*. Frankfurt: Suhrkamp.
Wiseman, R. 2002. *Queen Bees and Wannabes: Helping Your Daughters Survive Cliques, Gossips, Boyfriends, and Other Realities of Adolescence*. New York: Crown.
Zeh, J., 2012. *The Method*. London: Harvill Secker.
Zetzel, E. R. 1966. "1965: Additional Notes Upon a Case of Obsessional Neurosis: Freud 1909." *International Journal of Psycho-analysis* 47: 123–129.

Contributors

Judith Butler is Maxine Elliot Professor in the Department Comparative Literature and the founding director of the Program of Critical Theory at the University of California, Berkeley. She is the author of influential texts including *Gender Trouble: Feminism and the Subversion of Identity* (Routledge, 1990), *Bodies That Matter: On the Discursive Limits of "Sex"* (Routledge, 1993), *Excitable Speech* (Routledge, 1997), *Antigone's Claim: Kinship between Life and Death* (Columbia University Press, 2000), *Precarious Life: Powers of Violence and Mourning* (2004); *Undoing Gender* (2004), *Frames of War: When Is Life Grievable?* (2009). More recently, she coauthored *Is Critique Secular?* (2009) and *The Power of Religion in Public Life* (2011).

Robbie Duschinsky is Reader in Psychology and Society at Northumbria University. He is currently the recipient of a Wellcome Trust New Investigator Award, for research on the role of psychology in clinical and social welfare interventions. With Leon Rocha, he edited *Foucault, The Family and Politics* (Palgrave 2012) and has published in journals such as the *Sociological Review*, the *Journal of Social Policy*, and the *European Journal of Social Work*.

Gillian Harkins is Associate Professor of English and Adjunct Associate Professor of Gender, Women and Sexuality Studies at the University of Washington, Seattle. Harkins is the author of *Everybody's Family Romance: Reading Incest in Neoliberal America* (University of Minnesota Press, 2009) and coeditor of Special Issues of *Social Text* on "Genres of Neoliberalism" with Jane Elliott (Summer 2013) and *Radical Teacher* on "Teaching Inside Carceral Institutions" with Kate Drabinski (Winter 2012). She has also published articles on twentieth and twenty-first century literature, film and visual culture, higher education and the prison industrial complex, and feminist, queer, and critical race studies. Her new book-in-progress, *Screening Pedophilia: Virtuality and Other*

Crimes Against Nature, examines the emergence of the "pedophile" as virtual image in twentieth and twenty-first century literature, forensics, and film.

Daru Huppert is a candidate at the Viennese Psychoanalytical Society. He was head psychologist at a large care in the community centre in Vienna. His Ph.D. on psychic traumatization of child survivors of Nazi persecution was supervised by Juliet Mitchell. His research interests are on Freudian psychoanalysis and the unconscious. He has taught at Cambridge University and the Sigmund Freud University in Vienna.

Rachel Leigh teaches at the Cambridge Lehrhaus Centre for Jewish Thought. Her research interests have focused on human psychology and identity.

Mignon Nixon is Professor of History of Art at the Courtauld Institute of Art, University of London, and an editor of October magazine (New York). She has published widely on intersections of art, feminism, and psychoanalysis. Her current book project is *Sperm Bomb: Art, Feminism, and the American War in Vietnam*. In 2011–12, she and Juliet Mitchell co-taught a seminar on art and psychoanalysis at the Courtauld.

Jacqueline Rose is Professor of English at Queen Mary University, London. Her research focuses on modern subjectivity at the interface of literature, psychoanalysis, and politics, as well as on the history and culture of South Africa and of Israel–Palestine. Her most recent publications include *Proust among the Nations* (Chicago University Press, 2012); *The Last Resistance* (Verso, 2007) and *Conversations with Jacqueline Rose* (Seagull Press, 2010).

Gayatri Chakravorty Spivak is University Professor at Columbia University. She is the author of several books including *Other Asias* (2005) and *An Aesthetic Education in An Era of Globalization* (2012); a new work, *Readings*, was published in October 2014 by Seagull Books. In 2012, Spivak was the Kyoto laureate in Art and Philosophy, and in 2013 she was awarded the Padma Bhushan. She is also a Member of the Council on Values of the World Economic Forum. She is an activist in rural education and ecological social movements, and is involved in training teachers and guiding ecological agriculture in the western Birbum district in West Bengal, India. Additionally, some of her current projects include consortial initiatives in continental Africa, Himalayan Studies initiatives in Kathmandu-Kolkata-Kunming, and thinking globality together in French India and Senegambia. As well as these activities, she is presently re-translating Derrida's *Of Grammatology*, and finishing a book on W. E. B. Du Bois. Daughter of a feminist mother and gender-neutral father, Spivak is deeply involved in feminism across the spectrum.

Preti Taneja is Leverhulme Postdoctoral Research Associate to Professor Juliet Mitchell, working on siblings, Shakespeare, and psychoanalysis. She is Visiting Lecturer in English Literature, at Royal Holloway, University of London, UK and Jesus College Cambridge, UK. Prior to academia, she worked for over a decade as a human rights filmmaker, researcher, and writer specializing in minority rights. She has published extensively on the plight of religious, ethnic and linguistic minorities in Iraq since 2003, and on arts and rights in *The Guardian*, *Open Democracy*, and Reuters Alertnet.

Eline Trenson has a Masters in Clinical Pyschology and works as an assistant at the Department for Psychoanalysis and Counselling Psychology. She also coordinates and organizes the training in psychoanalytical therapy.

Paul Verhaeghe is Senior Professor at Ghent University and holds the chair of the Department for Psychoanalysis and Counselling Psychology. He teaches clinical psychodiagnostics, psychoanalytic therapy, and gender studies. He has published eight books and more than 200 papers. His two most recent books present a critique of contemporary psychotherapy, and address the link between contemporary society and new forms of mental disorder. His personal website contains material available to download: http://paulverhaeghe.psychoanalysis.be/

Susan Walker is a Senior Lecturer in Sexual Health, in the Faculty of Health, Social Care and Education at Anglia Ruskin University, UK. She originally trained and worked as a GP during which time she developed an interest in the gendered social and psychological factors underlying health related behavior. She pursued her interests in gender and psychoanalytical theory by undertaking a Ph.D. in the University of Cambridge. Her thesis addressed the effects of gendered body image upon contraceptive outcomes, using psychoanalytical theory, and was supervised by Professor Juliet Mitchell. Her present research interests focus on the intersection of gender, sociology, and medicine. She is a co-recipient of an ESRC Research seminar grant, on the topic of Understanding the Young Sexual Body.

Index

Lightning Source UK Ltd.
Milton Keynes UK
UKHW021304011221
394872UK00010B/3025